TRANSFORMED

How to Make the Decisions
That Change Your Life

BILL HARLEY & JEAN HARLEY

Minneapolis, Minnesota

Minneapolis

SECOND EDITION DECEMBER 2022

TRANSFORMED: How to Make the Decisions That Change Your Life.
Copyright © 2017 by William B. Harley & Jean K. Harley.
All rights reserved.

No part of this book may be used or reproduced in any manner whatsoever without written permission except in the case of brief quotations used in critical articles and reviews. For information, write to Calumet Editions, 6800 France Avenue South, Suite 370, Edina, MN 55435.

10 9 8 7 6 5 4 3 2
Cover and interior design: Gary Lindberg
ISBN: 978-1-959770-72-5

For Erin and Laura, Rich and Teddy, Sofia, Daniel and Kira

Table of Contents

Foreword 1

PART 1: UNDERSTANDING COMPASSIONATE CONSULTATION 3

Chapter 1: Two Keys to Navigating Change, Spiritual Growth & Social Advancement 5

Chapter 2: Our Decision-Making Legacy and the Emergence of Compassionate Consultation 8

Chapter 3: Achieving Transformative Understanding & Spiritual Growth through Compassionate Consultation .25

PART II: CREATING A COMPASSIONATE ATMOSPHERE & CULTURE FOR CONSULTATION 33

Chapter 4: Understanding the Transformative Power of Compassion 35

Chapter 5: Cultivating Compassion 49

Chapter 6: Putting Compassion into Action 68

Chapter 7: Creating the Compassionate Consultation Atmosphere 93

Chapter 8: Creating the Compassionate Consultation Culture 120

Chapter 9: Accessing the True Self & Quieting the Lower Nature . . .148

PART III: MAKING COMPASSIONATE CONSULTATION DECISIONS 167

Introduction to PART III 168

Chapter 10: Using the Steps of Compassionate Consultation 169

Chapter 11: Harnessing the Power of Questions 192

Chapter 12: Seeing Decision-Making Patterns in
Compassionate Consultation 209

Chapter 13: Making Transformative Decisions within
the Individual 221

Chapter 14: Making Transformative Decisions with Twos 248

Chapter 15: Making Transformative Decisions with Families 281

Chapter 16: Making Transformative Decisions with Groups 311

Postscript (and details about free PDF with additional content) 333

About the Authors 335

Bibliography 337

Endnotes. 341

Acknowledgements

We wish to acknowledge the encouragement and support of our many friends and clients over several years as we worked on this book. In particular we wish to thank Marie Scheffer, Kimberly Kleis, Judy Milston, Martha Schweitz and Elizabeth Williams who either read the manuscript and gave us valuable feedback or encouraged us in other ways that made a major difference. In addition, we want to thank our publisher, Gary Lindberg, who read our large tome of a book and helped us see that two separate books needed to be extracted from the one—this being the second of the two books.

Most of all, we want to thank our daughters, Erin Harley and Laura Harley, who championed this work, repeatedly read and critiqued evolving manuscripts, and never lost faith in our ability to finish it. Finally, we want to thank each other for unwavering, reciprocal support, patience, encouragement and effort without which this book would not have been completed.

"The heaven of divine wisdom is illumined with the two luminaries of consultation and compassion."

Bahá'u'lláh, Tablets of Bahá'u'lláh, p. 168

Also by Bill Harley & Jean Harley

Now That I'm Here, What Should I Be Doing? (Discover Life's Purpose)

Transformed

How to Make the Decisions That Change Your Life

Bill Harley & Jean Harley

Foreword

This is a book about a transformative decision-making process designed to address the conditions and complexities of modern life for individuals, pairs, families, neighborhoods, villages, cities, organizations, states, nations, and the world community. This process not only fosters wise, just, and practical decisions, but spiritual and social advancement for both the people using it and those impacted by the decisions. Our previous book[1] — about the purposes of life; the spiritual, intellectual, and social growth patterns designed into life by an all-loving Creator; and how to take action in alignment with these purposes and patterns—described this decision process briefly and promised an in-depth exploration in our next book. The book you are now reading is our attempt to fulfill that promise.

    This remarkable problem-solving and decision-making process came to our attention in 1968, and we began trying to use it in all areas of our lives. Like millions of others around the world, this decision process has helped us navigate our personal development, cultivate a lasting marriage, raise enlightened children, guide and nurture our grandchildren, assist our aged parents, deal with chronic illnesses, find and practice professions that allow us to be of meaningful service to others, and build responsible, spiritually-centered communities that are the hallmark of an emerging global civilization.

    Over the past thirty years, working respectively as a professional coach and organization development consultant and as a psychotherapist, we have also applied this problem-solving and decision-making methodology with our individual, group, and organizational clients. Whether working with a depressed and anxious individual, a married couple on the verge of divorce, an individual seeking a more meaningful life path, a work group in the midst of conflict, an organization seeking to design its future, or a community trying to take responsibility for its own social, material, and spiritual development, this methodology has provided the guidance needed to make transformative decisions that foster healing, deepened understanding, spiritual growth, social advancement, and unity.

Certainly humanity is at a very early stage in learning to apply this decision-making process in all areas of life. This book is an attempt to share learning generated by our own application efforts. Let's get started.

PART I:
Understanding Compassionate Consultation

Chapter 1

Two Keys to Navigating Change, Spiritual Growth and Social Advancement

In addition to learning from our personal struggles in life, our professional lives have given us the privilege of intimately and repeatedly witnessing the challenges individuals and groups experience as they struggle to cope with changing circumstances and grow. Over the years we have noticed two key characteristics which appear in individuals and groups that most successfully navigate change, spiritual growth, and social advancement. The first is the use of the transformative decision-making process referred to in the foreword; the second is an orientation toward life we referred to as a Wall-Seeking perspective in our previous book, *Now That I'm Here, What Should I Be Doing? Discover Life's Purpose.* When these two distinguishing characteristics are present, transformation occurs; that is, positive change, spiritual growth, and social advancement accelerate. When they are absent, the individual or group remains relatively static.

The first of the two distinguishing characteristics, then, relates to the **decision-making methods** the individuals and groups employ. In His Writings, Bahá'u'lláh,[2] the prophet-founder of the Bahá'í Faith, introduces a method for individual and group decision-making, problem solving, and deepened understanding which He calls Consultation. He also couples Consultation with the attribute of compassion. As we used Consultation over the years and consciously combined it with the use of compassion, we created the term "Compassionate Consultation" to describe the mindful combination of these two elements in decision-making. (We will capitalize references to Consultation and Compassionate Consultation as a decision-making process except when the terms appear in quotations to distinguish them from more traditional applications of the term "consultation.")

We have striven to use Compassionate Consultation extensively in our personal and professional lives; and the models and methods of Consultation we share in this book, all inspired by Bahá'u'lláh's teachings, have been used successfully with individuals, marriages, families, work groups, and communities. However, we have also learned that using Compassionate Consultation to make decisions is a spiritually demanding discipline. While we are all pre-wired, so to speak, to *use* Compassionate Consultation, the *successful practice* of it requires us to bring forth latent spiritual, intellectual, social, and emotional capacities. These latent capacities are delineated in the Bahá'í Writings and will be explored in the chapters ahead.

Readers of our previous book will recall that we supported the life purpose and spiritual growth principles we discussed with quotations from the scriptures of all the major world religions—humanity's common faith heritage. Readers of the present book will notice that we continue to do so with many of the principles we discuss here, but that we support the Compassionate Consultation principles we discuss with quotations almost exclusively from the scriptures of the Bahá'í Faith, the most recent of the world's revealed religions. This is because that is where the source information is. There are no other scriptural sources on the subject of Consultation.

The second of the two distinguishing characteristics of those who most successfully navigate change, spiritual growth, and social advancement relates to the **perspective they hold on life**. Our previous book surveyed the scriptures of the world's religions and identified three ultimate purposes of life: to know and love God; to acquire spiritual attributes (e.g., patience, love, forgiveness, detachment, humility, a sense of justice, etc.); and to carry forward an ever-advancing civilization. Understanding and acting from these three life purposes is part of the distinguishing perspective we refer to here.

The other part of the distinguishing perspective is the recognition that an all-loving Creator has designed life as a testing ground and spiritual growth lab tailored uniquely for each of us so that we experience tests, difficulties, and "walls" that we need to scale—often with great difficulty—in order to progress spiritually, intellectually, and socially. By seeking and welcoming these walls rather than avoiding them, we accelerate our growth and become wall-seekers rather than wall-avoiders. Readers of our previous book will recall the story of the lover seeking the beloved and encountering watchmen who block his path while mystically guiding him to a wall he must decide to scale in order to grow and find the beloved. In this book, we will substitute the terms "resistance," "obstacles," and "triggers" for the term "watchmen" to describe the forces that bring our attention to opportunities for growth and prompt us to scale and go over walls that separate us from deeper awareness. And we will substitute the term "growth-seeker" for the term "wall-seeker" to describe a person who proactively accepts these tailored life challenges in the context of using Compassionate Consultation to make transformative decisions.

Holding this distinguishing, two-dimensional perspective on life creates readiness and capacity for accelerated change, spiritual growth, and social advancement on the part of individuals and groups. It also contributes mightily to the effective practice of Compassionate Consultation.

Chapter 2

Our Decision-Making Legacy and the Emergence of Compassionate Consultation

We have proposed that optimally managing change and fostering spiritual growth and social progress requires not only a spiritual perspective but the ability to make transformative decisions from this spiritual perspective. Without these two ingredients, we are left with the world of today, a world with tantalizing possibilities and seemingly intractable problems.

The Decision-Making Crisis

Decisions, large and small, determine the course and quality of life—for an individual, a couple, a family, a community, an institution, an organization, a country, and the world.

Today, at both the macro and micro levels, the world is experiencing a decision-making crisis. Whether one looks at the relationships between nations or the relationships within nations at all levels of society, it is apparent that fragmentation, adversarial behavior, and human suffering are outpacing our decision-making resources. Today, it seems more common for decision-making to further divide people than to unify them, to create the perception of injustice rather than justice, and to increase ineffectiveness rather than reduce it. What is more, decision paralysis is increasingly the response to complex problems on the part of leaders and governmental bodies.

At the same time, problems, dilemmas, and even opportunities are becoming so complex and multi-dimensional in the modern world that traditional decision-making methods—even when well-practiced—are proving inadequate to the task of achieving wise, just, robust, and unifying outcomes. Speaking of the era in which we live, the Bahá'í Writings say:

> ...the people are encircled with pain and calamities and are environed with hardships and trouble. Every trial doth attack man and every dire adversity doth assail him like unto the assault of a serpent.[3]

What is more, emerging problems loom on the global horizon in the health, political, environmental, food, water, energy, educational, religious, and economic spheres that will devastate humanity unless dramatically improved deliberation and decision-making processes are brought to bear on them. The collective price to humanity of continuing to make sub-optimal decisions is growing exponentially. Humanity is in dire need of more effective ways to take counsel together.

Traditional Decision-Making Methods

Let us briefly consider the four traditional methods of decision-making that are in general use in the world today. The current condition of the world reflects both the benefits and limitations of these four decision-making methods.

Command Decision-Making

In command decision-making, the person with the authority or responsibility unilaterally decides. This type of decision is potentially the fastest kind of decision that can be made; but decision quality can easily suffer in complex situations because no single person is knowledgeable, experienced, fair, or creative enough to make decisions as well as an effective group. In addition, command decisions typically generate resentment, distrust, disunity, and low commitment to the resulting plan of action in the other people affected by them.

Advisory Decision-Making

In advisory decision-making, the authorized or responsible individual first confers with others (sequentially or as a group) for input and advice while making it clear that he or she still reserves the right to decide unilaterally. Ideally, the decision-maker then reports back to those with whom she or he conferred to explain the rationale for her or his decision. While this decision type has the strength of bringing more diverse perspectives to bear on an issue, it still relies heavily on the listening skills, open-mindedness, and judgment of just a single person. Advisory decisions also typically generate resentment, distrust, disunity, and low commitment to the resulting plan of action in the other people affected by them.

Majority Rule Decision-Making

In majority rule decision-making, the responsible individual convenes a group to decide and, after a fuller discussion than usually occurs with the previous two decision types, allows the vote of the majority to determine the outcome. A significant strength of majority rule decisions is that a diverse array of perspectives may be generated to potentially edify the group's thinking. We say "potentially edify" because if participants are driven by ideology, special interest, or prejudice, they may be unwilling to fully consider the edifying perspectives of others.

These dynamics point us to the most significant limitation of majority rule decision-making: while the majority wins, the minority loses, and the minority often walks away feeling antagonism toward the decision, low commitment to the resulting plan of action, and an inclination to undermine the decision while girding for battle in preparation for the next round of decision-making. Because of the win/lose framework of majority rule decisions, an adversarial system is established in which skill in argument and richness in power resources often carry the day, and the truth of the matter often remains hidden. We see this type of system play out in many of our political, economic, and legal systems, and it tends to foster what scholar Michael Karlberg has accurately described as a culture of contest and protest.[4]

Consensus Decision-Making

In consensus decision-making, the responsible individual convenes a group to decide, and after full discussion, the group members agree on the best decision that everyone will support. This approach has the strengths of generating a greater exchange of diverse perspectives, better decision quality, and better commitment to the resulting plan of action than the other three decision types. However, it also has the limitation that, despite everyone being willing to support the decision, the level of commitment to the resulting plan of action is typically variable in the participants. And this can lead to poor follow-through, recriminations, and disunity. In addition, the absence of prayer for divine guidance and any formal reference to spiritual principles and values in the decision-making process (these shortcomings are relevant to all four decision types) mean that sophisticated decisions can be reached that are detrimental to the individual, society, and culture. As an example, a group of bank robbers could reach a very sophisticated consensus decision on how to rob a bank, but the outcome would damage rather than advance the quality of civilization and the spiritual condition of the decision-makers.

A New Decision-Making Method

Bahá'u'lláh has provided a superior decision-making system—what we are calling Compassionate Consultation—that retains the strengths of the traditional decision-making types, eliminates their weaknesses, and delivers additional strengths as well.

Compassionate Consultation Decision-Making

While there is certainly still a useful place for all four of the traditional decision-making methods described above (and surely there is not adequate time in the day for all decisions to be made by groups), Bahá'u'lláh offers the process He calls Consultation as an optimum way for human beings to reason, take counsel, and decide together on the most important and difficult issues of life. In our personal lives and in our work with both individual and organizational clients over the last thirty plus years, we have seen how powerfully the use of Consultation—or even just elements of Consultation—can enhance decision quality, deepen understanding, create unity of purpose, and propel people forward socially, materially, and spiritually.

In his book, *Consultation: A Universal Lamp of Guidance*, John Kolstoe defines Consultation as "a process for producing a change in order to accomplish some definite purpose," and it "involves a sharing and interaction of thoughts and feelings in a spirit of love and harmony."[5] Given this definition, it is evident that Consultation is a human interaction process that can be used for many purposes including to make a decision, solve a problem, address an issue, deepen understanding, assess a situation, gain new insights or knowledge, probe for deeper meanings, examine other points of view, identify and take advantage of an opportunity, discover the facts, strengthen convictions, create a vision of the future, identify a problem, identify barriers, identify strategies, identify objectives and goals, plan a course of action, generate inspiration, assess priorities, clarify purposes, and reflect on a situation or experience. While our primary focus in this book will be on using Consultation to solve problems and make decisions, it is important to keep in mind Consultation's broad applications.

The Origin of Consultation

Bahá'u'lláh introduces Consultation in His Writings as an optimal way for groups to deliberate, make decisions, solve problems, take advantage of opportunities, and explore issues. He envisions that Consultation will enable people at all levels of a highly diverse global civilization to make highly effective, spiritually-illumined, and unifying decisions. He makes clear that Consultation will be needed to both build and live in this spiritually-centered global civilization. Bahá'u'lláh states:

> Take ye counsel together in all matters, inasmuch as consultation is the lamp of guidance which leadeth the way, and is the bestower of understanding.[6]

And:

> No welfare and no well-being can be attained except through Consultation.[7]

These weighty statements make it clear that the use of Consultation is a powerful way to enhance wisdom, deepen understanding, and promote the welfare of humanity. These benefits alone make it critically important for everyone to better understand and practice the process of Consultation.

For Whom is Consultation Intended?

In His Writings, Bahá'u'lláh describes the history of humanity on this planet as a record of the progressive movement of humankind through its collective infancy, childhood, and adolescence toward its adulthood—all under the tutelage of the Manifestations or Messengers of God [8] Who have come to humanity through the centuries.[9] And now, with the world having shrunk to a neighborhood as a result of advances in science and technology, and the family of humankind interacting increasingly in all its diversity racially, ethnically, religiously, economically, legally, and politically, we are moving into our collective adulthood.

While the problem-solving and decision-making methods of the past are still useful to us, they are inadequate to the complex tasks of dealing effectively with and unifying the modern world. Just as a good educator would not limit his/her students to the use of arithmetic when they are ready to learn more sophisticated branches of mathematics, so Bahá'u'lláh has introduced Consultation to humanity at this stage in our evolution because we now have the capacity to use it, are ready for the transformation it can affect in us individually and collectively, and will be unable to move forward successfully without it. Referring to the era in which we live, Bahá'u'lláh says:

> **Great and blessed is this Day—the Day in which all that lay latent in man hath been and will be made manifest.**[10]

Because achieving our collective adulthood on this planet will require that we "manifest" skill in the use of Consultation, one of our intents in this book is to make the process of Consultation more accessible to individuals and groups by describing attitudes, requisites, behavioral standards, models, tools, and examples that can help foster its effective use.

What Does Consultation Entail?

Consultation is a process for dramatically enhancing wisdom and understanding around any issue and, if desired, reaching a decision that leads to action. 'Abdu'l-Bahá,[11] one of only two authorized interpreters of Bahá'u'lláh's Writings, says:

> **…true consultation is spiritual conference in the attitude and atmosphere of love.**[12]

Consultation, then, involves two pivotal components: a *procedure* ("spiritual conference") and an *atmosphere* ("the attitude and atmosphere of love").

The Consultation Procedure

While the Writings of Bahá'u'lláh, 'Abdu'l-Bahá, and Shoghi Effendi[13] (the second of the two authorized interpreters of Bahá'u'lláh's Writings) are strictly prescriptive regarding the *atmosphere* required for Consultation to occur, they are more loosely descriptive regarding the *procedure*. One implication from the preceding quotation from 'Abdu'l-Bahá describing Consultation may be that when the *atmosphere* is right, Consultation can occur almost regardless of *procedure*.

However, for learning about Consultation and optimizing individual and group functioning during Consultation, getting clear about procedure is helpful. A specific procedural structure or systematic methodology can help us learn new skills, and once these skills have been established, we can be more free and flexible with procedure. In this way, we can honor both developmental needs and what Shoghi Effendi called:

> ...the whole spirit of Bahá'u'lláh's system: rigid conformity to great essential laws, elasticity, and even a certain necessary element of diversity, in secondary matters.[14]

Accordingly, in this chapter we will introduce two possible Consultation procedures that were created based on the Writings of 'Abdu'l-Bahá. Becoming oriented to these procedures may initially feel mechanical and academic. However, in later chapters we will give examples to show how these and other Consultation procedures can be used to dramatically improve decision-making for individuals, couples, families, and other groups.

The 3-Step Model of Consultation

Kolstoe infers three basic procedural steps for Consultation[15] based on the following quote from 'Abdu'l-Bahá:

> They must in every matter search out the truth and not insist upon their own opinion, for stubbornness and persistence in one's views will lead ultimately to discord and wrangling and the truth will remain hidden. The honoured members must with all freedom express their own thoughts, and it is in no wise permissible for one to belittle the thought of another, nay, he must with

moderation set forth the truth, and should differences of opinion arise a majority of voices must prevail, and all must obey and submit to the majority.[16]

The three *procedural* steps Kolstoe identifies from the quote are contained in what we will call the 3-Step Model of Consultation shown in Figure 2.1. The 3-Step Model would be preceded by prayers for assistance on the part of the Consulting members. This model will be addressed more fully in Chapter 10, but it is introduced now as one potential procedure for Consultation.

THE 3-STEP MODEL OF CONSULTATION

1. Understanding the situation
2. Deciding what to do
3. Executing or carrying out the decision

Figure 2.1

The 6-Step Model of Consultation

When 'Abdu'l-Bahá describes the coming together of the disciples of Jesus Christ after His crucifixion in order to decide what to do, a more comprehensive Consultation procedure is suggested. It is through this Consultative decision-making process that the disciples realize the implications of Jesus Christ's mission and their consequent responsibilities.[17] 'Abdu'l-Bahá says:

> The most memorable instance of spiritual consultation was the meeting of the disciples of Jesus Christ upon the mount after His ascension. They said 'His Holiness Jesus Christ has been crucified and we have no longer association and intercourse with Him in His physical body; therefore we must be loyal and faithful to Him, we must be grateful and appreciate Him, for He has raised us from the dead, He made us wise, He has given us eternal life. What shall we do to be faithful to Him?' And so they held council. One of them said 'We must detach ourselves from the chains and fetters of the world; oth-

erwise we cannot be faithful.' The others replied 'That is so.' Another said 'Either we must be married and faithful to our wives and children or serve our Lord free from these ties. We cannot be occupied with the care and provision for families and at the same time herald the kingdom in the wilderness. Therefore let those who are unmarried remain so, and those who have married provide means of sustenance and comfort for their families and then go forth to spread the message of glad-tidings.' There were no dissenting voices; all agreed, saying 'That is right.' A third disciple said 'To perform worthy deeds in the kingdom we must be further self-sacrificing. From now on we should forgo ease and bodily comfort, accept every difficulty, forget self and teach the Cause of God.' This found acceptance and approval by all the others. Finally a fourth disciple said 'There is still another aspect to our faith and unity. For Jesus' sake we shall be beaten, imprisoned and exiled. They may kill us. Let us receive this lesson now. Let us realize and resolve that though we are beaten, banished, cursed, spat upon and led forth to be killed we shall accept all this joyfully, loving those who hate and wound us.' All the disciples replied 'Surely we will—it is agreed; this is right.' Then they descended from the summit of the mountain and each went forth in a different direction upon his divine mission.[18]

This remarkable example[19] is at first confusing to consider as the basis for a model of Consultation procedure because of the absence of disagreement expressed by the Consulting members. However, it must be remembered that 'Abdu'l-Bahá is providing an example of *superior* Consultation ("the most memorable instance of spiritual consultation") and it can be seen to represent a certain pattern of Consultation in which the members' hearts and minds rapidly move together as one body to a decision. This decision-making pattern will be further described in Chapter 12 (see Pattern 1).

From this example, we can identify a 6-Step Model of Consultation, shown in Figure 2.2, that is compatible with, but more detailed than, the

3-Step Model. This model has proven robustly effective with a large range of difficult issues addressed in our group facilitation practice over the past thirty years. Let us examine how the example of the disciples provides a foundation for the 6-Step Consultation Model.

THE 6-STEP MODEL OF CONSULTATION

1. Convening by Praying for Divine Guidance
2. Identifying & Agreeing on the Facts
3. Identifying & Agreeing on the Issue
4. Identifying & Agreeing on the Spiritual Principles
5. Identifying & Agreeing on the Solutions
6. Identifying & Agreeing on Implementation Steps

Figure 2.2

Step 1: Convening by Praying for Divine Guidance

From the setting described by 'Abdu'l-Bahá we can infer a first step involving the disciples convening as a group at the spot where their Lord had been crucified and establishing an atmosphere of reverence ("The most memorable instance of spiritual consultation was the meeting of the disciples of Jesus Christ upon the mount after His ascension"). It is likely that the group members acknowledged themselves as the remaining disciples of Jesus Christ and then prayed for guidance and assistance in the manner Jesus had taught them. Regardless of our inferences from the setting, 'Abdu'l-Bahá has specified elsewhere that one of the essential requirements for Consultation to take place is that "They must when coming together turn their faces to the Kingdom on High and ask aid from the Realm of Glory."[20]

So, Step 1 of the 6-Step Consultation Model is: Convening by Praying for Divine Guidance. **Note**: In organizational or other group settings where formal prayers for guidance are currently deemed inappropriate, we typically substitute a period of meditation for Step 1 in which we ask each member to take a few moments in silence and call upon outer or inner strength for guidance and assistance with the issue the group is addressing. In settings where even this is deemed inappropriate, we substitute a review of some of the Behavioral Standards for Compassionate Consultation for Step 1 (see Chapters 7 and 8). However, either of these substitutions for the true purpose of Step 1 will weaken the potential power of the deliberation process.

Step 2: Identifying & Agreeing on the Facts

Next, the disciples appear to identify and agree upon the facts of their situation. Notice that some of the "facts" are in the form of *scientifically verifiable data* ("...Jesus Christ has been crucified, and we have no longer association and intercourse with Him in His physical body"), some are in the form of *feelings* ("...we must be grateful and appreciate Him..."), and some are in the form of *beliefs* or *intuitions* ("...He has raised us from the dead, He made us wise, He has given us eternal life."). Facts during Consultation include all these forms of data, and they appear to allow the disciples to clarify and agree upon their circumstances. Step 2 of the 6-Step Consultation Model, then, is: Identifying & Agreeing on the Facts.

Step 3: Identifying & Agreeing on the Issue

Having convened by praying for Divine guidance, and having agreed upon the facts, the disciples are ready to go to the next step. They now appear to identify and agree on the problem or issue that is challenging them by posing the open-ended question, "What shall we do to be faithful to Him?" It seems clear that the disciples agree on this question as the issue since the narrative continues, "And so they held council." The articulation of the issue question provides the benefits of focusing the attention of the disciples as a group on the subject to be addressed and preparing them to go to the next step. Consequently, Step 3 of the 6-Step Consultation Model is: Identifying & Agreeing on the Issue.

Step 4: Identifying & Agreeing on the Spiritual Principles and
Step 5: Identifying & Agreeing on the Solutions

With the issue agreed upon, the disciples now turn to the heart of their "spiritual consultation," which 'Abdu'l-Bahá conveys with the statement, "And so they held council." In the narrative, the holding of council seems to take a specific procedural form. The procedure from this point forward appears to follow a repetitive pattern of identifying and unanimously agreeing on a spiritual principle and then identifying and unanimously agreeing on a solution that aligns with the spiritual principle. The procedural form and sequence (with parenthetical explanations added) is as follows:

Spiritual Principle:

We must detach ourselves from the chains and fetters of the world.

Solution:

Otherwise (unless we detach ourselves from the world) we cannot be faithful (the solution, to be faithful, requires that we detach ourselves from the world).

Unanimous Agreement:

That is so.

Spiritual Principle:

Either we must be married and faithful to our wives and children or serve our Lord free from these ties.

Solution:

We cannot be occupied with the care and provision for families and at the same time herald the kingdom in the wilderness. Therefore, let those who are unmarried remain so, and those who have married provide means of sustenance and comfort for their families and then go forth to spread the message of glad-tidings.

Unanimous Agreement:

That is right.

Spiritual Principle:

To perform worthy deeds in the kingdom we must be further self-sacrificing.

Solution:

From now on we should forgo ease and bodily comfort, accept every difficulty, forget self, and teach the Cause of God.

Unanimous Agreement:

This found acceptance and approval by all the others.

Spiritual Principle:

There is still another aspect to our faith and unity. For Jesus' sake we shall be beaten, imprisoned, and exiled. They may kill us.

Solution:

Let us receive this lesson now. Let us realize and resolve that though we are beaten, banished, cursed, spat upon, and led forth to be killed we shall accept all this joyfully, loving those who hate and wound us.

Unanimous Agreement:

Surely we will—it is agreed; this is right.

In summary, this segment of the disciples' "spiritual consultation" seems to identify the next steps of the 6-Step Model as follows:

4. Identifying & Agreeing on the Spiritual Principles; and
5. Identifying & Agreeing on the Solutions.

Step 6: Identifying & Agreeing on Implementation Steps

With both the relevant spiritual principles and the solutions agreed upon, the disciples turn to the last step of their "spiritual consultation." This step is implicit in the last sentence of 'Abdu'l-Bahá's narrative: "Then they descended from the summit of the mountain and each went forth in a different direction upon his divine mission." The sixth step involves identifying and agreeing upon who will do what by when and then taking action. While 'Abdu'l-Bahá's narrative does not provide the details of this implementation step, the implication that the details have been handled is conveyed by the fact that "…each went forth in a different direction upon his divine mission." Consequently, Step 6 of the 6-Step Consultation Model is: Identifying & Agreeing on Implementation Steps.

More will be said about the 6-Step Model later in Chapter 10 and in Appendices I and II of the free PDF available at **billandjeanharley.com/actionplan**. Our purpose at this point is simply to introduce the 6-Step Model as a second potential procedure for Consultation.

The Consultation Atmosphere

While additional models will be introduced in Chapter 10 as possible *procedures* for Consultation, consideration of the 3-Step and 6-Step decision-making models begins to clarify the picture regarding what the Consultation steps can look like. However, the procedural steps are only part of the picture. What are the *atmospheric* requirements for true Consultation to occur?

Two Essential Requirements

'Abdu'l-Bahá identifies two essential requirements that together create the atmospheric cornerstone for true Consultation. He says:

> The first condition is absolute love and harmony amongst the members of the assembly. They must be wholly free from estrangement and must manifest in themselves the unity of God....They must when coming together turn their faces to the kingdom on High and ask aid from the Realm of Glory.[21]

This first requirement calling upon the Consulting participants to manifest "absolute love and harmony" toward each other is echoed by a related cause and effect relationship referred to by 'Abdu'l-Bahá when he introduces his narrative about the disciples of Jesus Christ:

> Therefore true consultation is spiritual conference in the attitude and atmosphere of love. Members must love each other in the spirit of fellowship <u>in order that</u> good results may be forthcoming. Love and fellowship are the foundation.[22] (Emphasis added)

It is the Consulting members' ability to "love each other in the spirit of fellowship" that makes possible that "…good results may be forthcoming." Elsewhere, 'Abdu'l-Bahá says:

> Love is the source of all the bestowals of God. Until love takes possession of the heart, no other divine bounty can be revealed in it.[23]

Since love must possess the heart before any "other divine bounty can be revealed in it," and receiving divine assistance and guidance during Consultation is a "divine bounty" and "bestowal," it seems clear that our ability to receive divine assistance will be impeded during Consultation if something other than love is possessing the members' hearts.

The second requirement for creating a proper Consultative atmosphere is that the participants must invite God's participation and assistance in an attitude of worshipful supplication. As previously referenced, 'Abdu'l-Bahá says:

> They must when coming together turn their faces to the Kingdom on High and ask aid from the Realm of Glory.[24]

As in a quotation from the *Book of Isaiah*, "Come now, and let us reason together, saith the Lord,"[25] we see that God wants to be an invited contributor to our deliberations and the atmosphere we create.

Taken together, these two essential requirements establish the atmospheric cornerstone which allows Consultation to manifest its powers. And since one of these requirements is described in the fifth preceding quotation as a "condition" and the other in the second preceding quotation as a "must" by 'Abdu'l-Bahá, the assumption would be that without them, true Consultation cannot occur.

An Atmosphere of Compassion

Bahá'u'lláh helps us understand the atmosphere required for Consultation even further when He says:

> The heaven of divine wisdom is illumined with the two luminaries of consultation and compassion.[26]

Here "the attitude and atmosphere of love" is embodied in the word "compassion." Compassion manifests itself as a loving, sympathetic consciousness of the distress another person is experiencing *and* being moved to alleviate it.

Having compassion requires developing an understanding of another person's perspective, which means we must disengage from our preconceptions and judgments.

With compassion comes the ability to be fully present with, and focused on, other people, to recognize that they are human beings struggling through life just as we are, and to see their lives as making sense based on their unique experiences. Compassion involves an ability to "feel with" others by acknowledging our similarities and connection to them and being moved to reduce their distress.

When we are having a very bad day, we may find ourselves feeling angry, impatient, and *disconnected* from ourselves and everyone around us. But, in the midst of these negative feelings, if we think of those we love, our hearts may soften and dilate. This is because when we think of ourselves in *connection* with others, and when we think of those to whom we feel connected, we will usually feel compassion for ourselves and for them. When this change of heart occurs, the atmosphere within and around us changes to one of compassion.

It follows then that the more widely we are able to acknowledge our connection with others, the more we are able to access compassion. In this way, compassion is like a muscle that each of us can develop further. When we find ourselves able to acknowledge our connection to all the other players in the spiritual drama of our lives and feel compassion for them—that is, feel both empathy toward them and a desire to *alleviate* their suffering—we are able to create the Consultative atmosphere with them.

The Twin Decision-Making Luminaries

Bahá'u'lláh tells us that when both Consultation and compassion are present (the "two luminaries"), they illuminate "the heaven of divine wisdom." While it is true to assume that Consultation in *concept* always includes compassion, it is also true that in *practice* people often try to use Consultation without compassion—seeing Consultation purely as a *procedure* which is separable from the required *atmosphere*.

But the implication of Bahá'u'lláh's words is that Consultation alone as a *procedure* and compassion alone as an *atmosphere* are not sufficient to gain access to "divine wisdom." One could say that the light generated by only one of the two luminaries is inadequate to illuminate "the heaven of divine wisdom." Like a room that is illuminated by only one point of light, much remains hidden in shadow. But when two separate points of light—both Consultation and compassion—are present, we get an intellectually robust deliberative procedure combined with a loving and spiritual atmosphere that together fully illuminate the room. As a result, darkness is eliminated, things can be seen as they truly are, and we have access to divine wisdom and understanding.

A Vision of Combining *Procedure* & *Atmosphere* for a Better Way to Decide

'Abdu'l-Bahá's example of Jesus Christ's disciples deliberating after the crucifixion (included earlier in this chapter) provides an elevated vision of both the *procedure* and *atmosphere* of Consultation combining to achieve transformative results. The smooth, graceful movement of the group's

Consultation, the openness and intense listening to each other's ideas, and the naturally emerging unanimous decisions all suggest an atmosphere of love, fellowship, and compassion. The disciples seem to be mindful of the divine guidance available to them, and they confer out of a sense of reverent devotion. They move freely through the various steps of Consultation as the spirit moves them. The atmosphere is unified and focused. Everything seems to spring from spiritual principle. Despite the great diversity of human types represented in Jesus Christ's disciples, and despite the tremendously complex crisis in which the disciples find themselves, they reach a set of inspired, critically important, and unanimous decisions—and they do it rapidly. In the aftermath of the decisions they are able to move immediately into separate actions with complete unity of purpose. And as is typically the case with this transformative process, their combining of Consultation with compassion results in decisions and actions that help them achieve the ultimate purposes of life: bringing them closer to God, developing their spiritual attributes, and carrying forward an ever-advancing civilization. Indeed, at the end of His narrative, 'Abdu'l-Bahá says:

> **This was true consultation. This was spiritual consultation and not the mere voicing of personal views in parliamentary opposition and debate.**[27]

Compassionate Consultation

Throughout this book we will refer to the combination of compassion with Consultation as *Compassionate Consultation* to remind us that *both* "luminaries" need to be present; and we will capitalize the term to distinguish it as a unique deliberation and decision-making method. The dual-word term is also a reminder that the decision-making procedure, atmosphere, and resulting decisions take into account both the spiritual and material aspects of any given situation and draw upon both divine assistance and the human powers of heart and mind.

Chapter 3

Achieving Transformative Understanding & Spiritual Growth through Compassionate Consultation

Bahá'u'lláh says:

> Consultation bestoweth greater awareness and transmuteth conjecture into certitude. It is a shining light which, in a dark world, leadeth the way and guideth. For everything there is and will continue to be a station of perfection and maturity. The maturity of the gift of understanding is made manifest through consultation.[28]

The outcomes resulting from prayerful Consultation described above are synonymous with spiritual growth: the increase in awareness; the movement from conjecture to certitude; learning to be led and guided by a Higher Power; perfecting our attributes; and achieving a maturity of understanding to guide us toward more enlightened action in alignment with spiritual principles. Those committed to practicing Consultation expect challenging issues to arise in life and see these issues as things that need to be proactively addressed and resolved in order to yield the increased understanding and spiritual growth latent within them. By doing so, we progress in our achievement of the three ultimate purposes of life: to know and love God, to acquire spiritual attributes, and to contribute to an ever-advancing civilization. This is the measure of our spiritual condition, our spiritual reality, and our spiritual growth at any given moment.

Because Compassionate Consultation is a vehicle for both deciding *and* for fostering spiritual growth and social advancement, it will be useful early in our exploration to consider some models of growth and development that help us understand what is happening inside ourselves as we strive to transform ourselves and our circumstances. These models of change and growth will also be reflected in some of the Consultation procedural models discussed later in this book.

Individual & Group Change & Spiritual Growth

Spiritual growth requires change, and change requires effort. Change that leads to spiritual growth involves a process of replacing one learned response to a situation with a better, newly learned response to the same situation that more fully honors the three purposes of life or other spiritual laws and principles. The change could be aimed at the *doing* level, the *being* level, or both. It could also be at the *individual* level, the *group* level, or both.

Three Models of Change & Spiritual Growth

To change and grow spiritually we need to make *different* decisions and choices. The following three models give us insight into the internal mechanics involved when we make such decisions and choices. For now, we want to just clarify the three models. Later, in Parts II and III of the book, we will provide examples of how to apply the models using Compassionate Consultation.

The Basic Change & Spiritual Growth Model

A basic model of change and growth, which emphasizes the conscious effort required to successfully change and grow, is illustrated in Figure 3.1. This model was described in detail in our first book, *Now That I Am Here, What Should I Be Doing?*

In **Step 1** of Figure 3.1, the **Current State**, we are responding to a given stimulus with **an old habit pattern** that is no longer serving us. Nevertheless, the current state is characterized by *stable conditions* (our habit pattern produces stable and consistent responses), *predictability* (we know what to expect), and *certainty* (we exercise our habitual response with *no deliberate thought* and can rely on the usual results). *Minimal learning, change, and growth are taking place.*

The Basic Change & Spiritual Growth Model

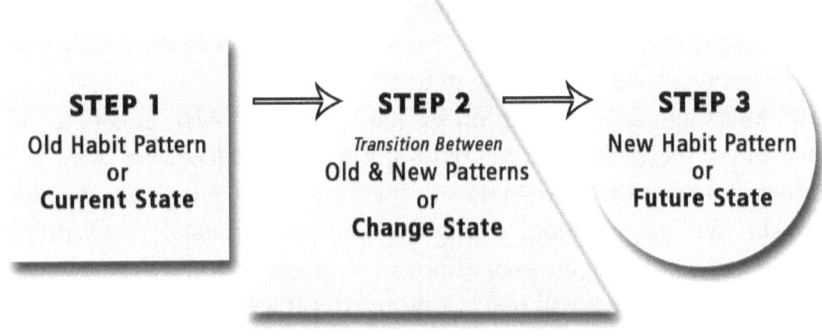

Figure 3.1

In **Step 2**, the *Change State*, we begin reacting to the same stimulus with a ***new response***. The change state is characterized by *unstable conditions* (our new response produces unstable and inconsistent reactions), *unpredictability and variability* (we don't know what to expect), and *uncertainty* (we exercise our new response using *very deliberate thought* and get uncertain results). *Extensive learning, change, and growth are taking place.*

In **Step 3**, the *Future State*, we are responding to the given stimulus with ***the new habit pattern*** that is serving us more effectively. The future state is characterized by *stable conditions* (our new habit pattern produces stable and consistent reactions), *predictability* (we know what to expect), and *certainty* (we exercise our new habit with *no deliberate thought* and can rely on improved results). *Once again, little learning, change, and growth are taking place.* **However, the Future State becomes the Current State for the next round of change and spiritual growth.**

The Swamp of Change & Spiritual Growth— A Universal Dynamic

The foregoing description makes the change process sound simple and inevitable. The fact is that *huge amounts of effort* must be expended to navigate through Step 2; and change efforts are usually accompanied by a great deal of struggle, stretching, regression, recommitment, failure, and ultimately success. Step 2 (the change state), the transition between the old and new habit pattern, is the place where our dissatisfaction and frustration with the old habit pattern (the current state) has led us to struggle to make a change and grow beyond it. During Step 2, the new habit pattern (the future state) is not yet in place—we are struggling between two worlds, the "what was" and the "what will be."

Years ago one of our professional colleagues, Alan Scheffer,[29] likened this in-between state to crossing a swamp. Indeed, we often refer to Step 2—the in-between state—as the *Swamp of Change and Spiritual Growth*. Without question, you will get wet and muddy. You will slip, stumble, and fall. Despite your efforts to be graceful, you will be awkward and clumsy. Your feet will feel heavy, and to get across the swamp to Step 3 (the new habit pattern or future state) you will have to continue despite fatigue, frustration, and sometimes despair.

It is important to keep in mind that the "swamp of change" dynamics apply to individual, group, organizational, community, and global change. It is equally important to remember that these dynamics are occurring in the Consulting members individually and sometimes collectively during the Compassionate Consultation decision-making process. Regardless of context, transformation is very hard work.

The K + V + A Model of Change & Spiritual Growth

A second model of change and spiritual growth is described by 'Abdu'l-Bahá:

> The attainment of any object is conditioned upon knowledge, volition and action. Unless these three conditions are forthcoming there is no execution or accomplishment.[30]

The equation implied by 'Abdu'l-Bahá's words is shown in Figure 3.2. Let us examine the elements of this model. 'Abdu'l-Bahá's words suggest that for any kind of lasting change and spiritual growth to occur in individuals, groups, or organizations, the following three steps must occur:

$$K + V + A = AT$$

Knowledge + Volition + Action = Attainment

Figure 3.2

1. Knowledge

The first step in making change is to gain adequate knowledge, awareness, and understanding of the circumstances in and around the context where change and growth are being considered. This knowledge may include knowledge of ourselves, of others, and of other data or factual information. The knowledge, awareness, and understanding must accumulate to the point where they are adequate to propel us to the next step: volition.

For example, imagine you are getting feedback from your family and friends that you are always distracted with your smartphone. You take this feedback to heart and realize that you are damaging your relationships. You consider making a change and begin by deepening your knowledge. You begin noticing how often you reflexively check your phone, what thoughts and feelings are going through you when you do so, what payoffs you are getting from doing so, and what it is costing your relationships to continue in this way. You also start to notice how others around you are using their electronic devices. You realize that you feel unimportant when another person you are with continually checks his or her phone; you experience how it can feel rude, disrespectful, and hurtful. Your knowledge accumulates to the point that you experience some volition to change.

2. Volition

Knowledge must somehow engage our volition, our capacity to will or desire something. In other words, there must be motivation. We are motivated when something is important to us, when we have feelings and emotions about it. Psychologist John Bradshaw separates the word emotion into "e" and "motion" to make the point that it is the energy (e) that comes from emotions that puts us in motion.[31] Emotion gives us the energy to act. Enough emotion must accumulate to create a critical mass of volition before action can occur. Regardless of how much knowledge we gain regarding the change and growth we are considering, the potential will remain untapped unless and until we generate adequate volition. Bahá'u'lláh says:

> Unto each one hath been prescribed a pre-ordained measure, as decreed in God's mighty and greatest Tablets. All that ye potentially possess can, however, be manifested only as a result of your own volition.[32]

Volition can manifest itself as the desire to move away from what is not serving us; or it can manifest itself as a desire to move toward what we believe would be better—and ideally both. Ultimately, the volition must accumulate to the point where it is adequate to lead us to the next step: action.

Continuing the example, imagine that you are startled to realize how much of each day you are spending on your smartphone. You notice that the people in your life who are best at relationships commit their energies to being fully present with their family, friends, and associates, and you start desiring the kind of close relationships they have. You begin imagining yourself going through your days like they do—where *they have* a smartphone, but it does not *have them*. This vision becomes increasingly attractive and preferable to you. You resolve to take new action.

3. Action

If knowledge and volition are present, but there is no action, no change or spiritual growth will occur. Knowledge and volition must accumulate to the point that they fuel action. Put another way, action is the manifestation of knowledge and volition in *deeds*.

The actions that take one in the direction of new behavior may initially be clumsy, but through practice they become more graceful and established as a pattern. Clearly, the action must be congruent with the knowledge and volition for effective change and spiritual growth to occur. When this congruence is present, it contributes to the establishment of a pattern of self-disciplined action and success on the part of an individual, group, organization, or community that brings with it a sense of increased self-worth and confidence in the ability to navigate the next round of change and growth.

Continuing the example, imagine that you start putting your smartphone in your briefcase when you come home to your family in the evening and leave it in the car when you meet with friends and colleagues. You force yourself to focus on the other person, and rather than just listening reactively, you start using curiosity to ask questions that engage the other person. Over time, you gradually get more graceful at this and find yourself enjoying the strengthening of your relationships.

A significant benefit of taking action is that it accelerates the generation of more knowledge and volition. If we are reading a book to increase our knowledge and volition about learning to swim, taking action by jumping into the pool dramatically accelerates learning. It helps us separate what we *thought* we knew from what we *actually* know about swimming; and this ideally generates more volition, which then informs new action. A cycle of attainment is thus created that can become self-sustaining.

It is important to keep in mind that Knowledge, Volition, and Action dynamics are at play whenever an individual or group uses Compassionate Consultation to decide.

The D x V x F Model of Change and Growth

A third model of change and growth, originally developed by David Gleicher and referred to with refinements by Robert Jacobs,[33] is shown in Figure 3.3.

$$D \times V \times F > R$$

Dissatisfaction x Vision x First Steps > Resistance To Change

Figure 3.3

In this model, the concept is that *Dissatisfaction* times *Vision* times *First Steps* must be greater than the *Resistance To Change* that exists in the individual, group, or organization for the change and growth to be successful and lasting. The **D** refers to dissatisfaction with the current situation, the **V** to a positive vision or picture of a preferred future that is deemed possible, the **F** to carefully designed, realistic, and achievable first steps that can be taken to move toward the vision **V**, and the **R** to resistance to crossing the swamp of change, which is supported by the gravitational pull of existing habits that keeps the present situation in place.

The point of this model is that if **D**, **V**, or **F** is equal to or near zero, there will be little or no change and growth because **R** will not be overcome. For example, if the **D**issatisfaction with the present state and a **V**ision of the preferred future state are both strong, but no **F**irst Steps are taken, little or no change and growth will occur. Similarly, if **D**issatisfaction and **F**irst Steps are strong, but there is no galvanizing **V**ision of the future state to motivate us, little or no change and growth will occur. And finally, if **V**ision and **F**irst Steps are strong, but there is no **D**issatisfaction with the present state, little or no change and growth will occur. In essence, *there must be a critical mass of energy in each of these three elements if lasting change and growth are to occur.*

It is important to remember that Dissatisfaction, Vision, and First Step dynamics are present in many Compassionate Consultation decision-making sessions.

The Three Models as Patterns for Advancement and Consultation

The foregoing three models identify advancement patterns for practitioners of Compassionate Consultation and for growth-seekers. Solving problems, making decisions, and scaling walls to growth in our lives involve the movement from the Current State through the Change State to the Future State, the progression from Knowledge to Volition to Action, and/or advancing from Dissatisfaction to Vision to First Steps. If these patterns and evolutionary steps are completed in alignment with the three purposes of life or other spiritual principles, they represent steps forward on the paths of spiritual growth and social advancement. As we will see, all three of these change and growth models align with one or more of the Compassionate Consultation Models described in this book.

To further deepen our understanding of how "the twin luminaries of consultation and compassion" can foster extraordinary results requires that we give both luminaries closer scrutiny. In the pages that follow in Part II, we will deepen our investigation of the attribute of compassion, explore the twelve requisites and behavioral standards that create both the atmosphere and culture which allow Compassionate Consultation to flourish, and examine how to engage our true selves, or higher nature, in the Consultative process.

PART II: CREATING A COMPASSIONATE ATMOSPHERE & CULTURE FOR CONSULTATION

Chapter 4

Understanding the Transformative Power of Compassion

Because the development and use of compassion is of such *enormous* importance for anyone who aspires to practice Consultation, we are devoting the next several chapters to different facets of compassion. While the number of published books and articles about Consultation has been quite limited to date, still less has been written about the role of compassion in conjunction with Consultation.

What Is Compassion?

The *Oxford English Dictionary* defines compassion as: "The feeling or emotion, when a person is moved by the suffering or distress of another, and by the desire to relieve it; pity that inclines one to spare or to succor."[34] In terms of Consultation with others, compassion may move us to come to the aid of another, to help another identify a wall to growth that he or she needs to scale, to sensitively understand another person's perspective in a disagreement, or to open-mindedly and open-heartedly see other points of view when trying to solve a problem or take advantage of an opportunity. In the context of Consultation within the individual, compassion may move us to come to our own aid and help ourselves scale a wall the Creator has provided to stimulate our growth. In all these cases, compassion is more than mere empathy—*it moves us to take action to relieve the stress and distress of others or ourselves*. In this sense, Compassion is an extremely powerful motivator.

Compassion is deeply respectful because it comes from the belief that people have understandable reasons for their thoughts, feelings, and perspectives. That I do not understand another's perspective does not mean that I am right and they are wrong, or that I am smart and they are not. It means that we have different ways of seeing things. Having compassion does not necessarily mean that I agree to think, feel, or behave the way the other person does, but that I commit to trying to understand their thoughts, feelings, and perspectives. It is compassion that enables us to dilate our hearts and minds to truly see others or ourselves in an open, non-judgmental, empathetic way. Compassion is the motivating force that allows us to be interested and willing enough to step into a another person's reality, to see it as they see it, and to understand it as they understand it with a desire to relieve that person's anxiety, frustration, discomfort, or distress.

Take a moment to think about a person in your life with whom you are able to express your honest thoughts, feelings, beliefs, concerns, needs, and wants. What qualities does this person have? Most likely, compassion ranks high on the list. One of the primary needs human beings have when dealing with an issue is to feel *truly* understood; in fact, this is usually more important to a person than getting others to agree with him or her. This means that, whether in a work, family, or community decision-making situation, if I think that I was able to express my perspective and was compassionately understood, even if the decision or solution reached was different from my own opinion, I am still likely to feel good about myself and the others involved. I am also likely to convey compassion to others because compassion is contagious. Additionally, I will be more likely to actively participate in the implementation of the decision or solution, and I will have positive feelings about the deliberation and decision-making process and be inclined to use it again. *Feeling truly understood can only occur in the presence of compassion.*

The Seat of Compassion is the Human Heart

Compassion is defined by *Merriam-Webster's 11th Collegiate Dictionary* as "sympathetic consciousness of others' distress together with a desire to alleviate it."[35] Because Compassionate Consultation is typically used to address issues, solve problems, take advantage of opportunities, and create plans for change, it is usually accompanied by distress in the Consulting members. The compassion that desires to alleviate that distress in others and in ourselves arises from our hearts and is an indispensable component in the search for truth, resolution, and understanding.

During Compassionate Consultation, a person's *head* may be occupied with Consultation, but her or his *heart* needs to be occupied with compassion. While the process of Consultation is generating *thought* leading to understanding, the presence of compassion is generating *feeling* leading to understanding. The mind by itself is not entirely trustworthy when searching out the truth as it relates to the world or ourselves. In the *Bhagavad Gita* it is written:

> The mind is restless, Krishna, impetuous, self-willed, hard to train: to master the mind seems as difficult as to master the mighty winds.[36]

The mind can easily produce rationales to explain our behaviors and support our points of view while failing to recognize that our rationales are based on bias, self-interest, or misinformation. If our mental activity is accompanied by hard-heartedness and a lack of compassion, the truths we seek will remain hidden.

Couples' relationships in particular can test compassion resources. While partners may have committed to using Consultation to solve problems and make major decisions in their married life, it is not uncommon for them to get bogged down in contention, blame, and stonewalling. The missing ingredient is compassion. A discussion can become a battle of wills rather than an opportunity to learn where the other is coming from and to understand what is behind the other person's thinking, feeling, and distress. An open, compassionate heart seeks to understand these. However, a heart that is constricted from a lack of compassion will not admit the merits of an opposing view. 'Abdu'l-Bahá tells us:

> They must in every matter search out the truth and not insist upon their own opinion, for stubbornness and persistence in one's views will lead ultimately to discord and wrangling and the truth will remain hidden.[37]

The seat of compassion is the human heart, and compassion is the vehicle through which one's inner spiritual eye and truest spiritual self-manifest themselves and discover reality. Saint Augustine said:

> Our whole business therefore in this life is to restore to health the eye of the heart whereby God may be seen.[38]

Bahá'u'lláh says:

O MAN OF TWO VISIONS!

Close one eye and open the other. Close one to the world and all that is therein, and open the other to the hallowed beauty of the Beloved.[39]

Let's look at an example to see what a difference adding compassion, or the heart element, to a disagreement can make.

The Example of Dane and Ellen—Adding Compassion Changes the Picture

Thirty-year-old Dane and twenty-nine-year-old Ellen are married with two small children. Dane works full time as a car mechanic, and Ellen is a part-time waitress. They make ends meet but have only a small amount of money left over each month. Ellen wants a dining room set. Dane says they do not have the money, and the dining room set is not important enough to warrant taking out a loan. He thinks Ellen does not appreciate how hard he works, that she is resentful toward him because they do not have more money, and that she keeps bringing up the dining room set out of hostility. Ellen is upset. She has been cutting out sale ads on dining room sets since they moved into their house two years ago. She is angry at Dane, believes he does not care if she is happy, and only thinks of himself (she notes that he does spend money to bowl in a league once a week). The marriage has become strained. Each partner feels resentment.

Now, let's add compassion. When Ellen's heart dilates with compassion, she sincerely wants to understand the reasons why Dane will not agree to purchase a dining room set, and she asks him questions which do not carry a judgmental tone. He says his father always told him that the man's main responsibility is to provide security for his family, and he needs to have a certain amount of savings in the bank as a reserve in order to live up to that responsibility. Dane says he worries that if there is an emergency or he gets laid off, the current amount of their savings would be inadequate to carry them through.

Then it is Dane's turn to call up compassion. He dilates his heart and reminds himself that Ellen must feel very strongly since she has been pushing for a dining room set for so long. He sincerely wants to understand her reasons for such strong feelings and his questions reflect his sincerity. Ellen tells Dane that when she was growing up, the dining room of her parents' home was the gathering place for the extended family. Mom always had the coffee going, and every day someone stopped by. That was how the family stayed connected. The dining room table was the place where connection occurred—it was the hub of the entire family. The dining room felt warm and welcoming, and that's how Ellen wants her home to be. The dining room set is the center of her dream for a family that enjoys closeness and well-being.

While the names have been changed (as they have been in all the non-personal examples used in this book), this is an example from real life. Compassion on the part of the listener enabled the speaker to go deeper into the core beliefs that were driving the feelings and behaviors that were causing problems. Each partner was enabled to see and understand the "good reasons" for the other's perspective. Because each partner felt understood by the other, negative emotions were quieted and positive emotions amplified. The presence of compassion also motivated both of them to try to alleviate the distress of the other. Consequently, they were able to find a solution to their dispute that was highly satisfying to both of them. Their Compassionate Consultation process also improved their relationship because the resentments both were feeling had been constructively dealt with. Their compassion transformed their usual deliberation pattern.

This example demonstrates how the presence of compassion assures that the Consultative process will occur in a context where relationships and individual dignity are protected, where the issue at hand will be seen in the context of a larger spiritual drama (Ellen's valuing of family connection and unity and Dane's valuing of his roles as provider and protector of the family), and where the movement toward understanding will not be blocked by resentment. The open-ended questioning method that Ellen and Dane used to access compassion and deepen their understanding together is explained in more detail in Chapter 14 (see section title, "The Example of Dane & Ellen Revisited").

Compassion Creates an Understanding Heart

Most of us are drawn to someone with an "understanding heart," and we commonly associate this quality with wisdom. It is also a dimension of compassion. Many historians agree that the wisest of all sovereigns was King Solomon. The Old Testament records how, shortly after Solomon became king, he had a dream in which God asked him what he wanted from his Creator. After thanking God for His mercy and kindness in the past, Solomon says:

> And now, O LORD my God, thou hast made thy servant king instead of David my father: and I am but a little child: I know not how to go out or come in.
>
> And thy servant is in the midst of thy people which thou hast chosen, a great people, that cannot be numbered nor counted for multitude.
>
> Give therefore thy servant an *understanding heart* to judge thy people, that I may discern between good and bad: for who is able to judge this thy so great a people? And the speech pleased the LORD, that Solomon had asked this thing.
>
> And God said unto him, Because thou hast asked this thing, and hast not asked for thyself long life; neither hast asked riches for thyself, nor hast asked the life of thine enemies; but hast asked for thyself understanding to discern judgment; Behold, I have done according to thy words: lo, I have given thee a wise and an *understanding heart*; so that there was none like thee before thee, neither after thee shall any arise like unto thee.[40] (Emphasis added)

To have an understanding heart is to have compassion, and these qualities are fundamental to making discerning judgments and wise decisions—whether one is leading a government, consoling a friend, or conferring with others in a group. In all three roles, one must have empathy for others and a desire to justly relieve the distress of others for good results to be obtained.

In the modern era, Bahá'u'lláh renews this mandate by calling on all of humanity to possess an understanding and compassionate heart. His first counsel in *The Hidden Words* is:

O SON OF SPIRIT!

My first counsel is this: Possess a pure, kindly and radiant heart, that thine may be a sovereignty ancient, imperishable and everlasting.[41]

"A pure, kindly and radiant heart" is an excellent description of a compassionate and understanding heart, and its radiance dramatically affects the atmosphere and spirit of Consultation.

Seeing a Situation from Multiple Perspectives

Compassion enables us to see and understand an experience or situation from multiple perspectives. Without compassion, our thinking can become stuck so that we see only our own self-centered or habitual perspective. Although most of us would probably describe ourselves as compassionate people, it seems that most problems and conflicts in the world are caused by people's apparent inability to see a situation or experience from any perspective other than their own. It is apparent that compassion is in very short supply. Compassion's counterpart, Consultation, is also in very short supply. What a changed world it would be if compassion and Consultation replaced contention and adversarial debate opening the way to wise and just decisions, deeper understanding, and harmonious unity of purpose.

Compassion Is a Master Key

Compassion acts as a master key to unlock a host of related compassionate characteristics including cooperation, caring, support, respect, trust, forgiveness, charity, gentleness, understanding, love, responsibility, non-violence, courage, tolerance, faithfulness, generosity, kindness, humility, curiosity, resourcefulness, encouragement, honesty, loyalty, and patience. The presence of compassion *flips a switch* that moves human beings into a range and flow of spiritual attitudes and behaviors that are essential for the creation of the Consultative atmosphere and group culture that foster Compassionate Consultation (see Chapters 7 and 8). When one is emotionally flooded and contending stubbornly with a colleague or family member, this switch can be very difficult to flip. The abilities to **recognize the choice point** *where compassion needs to be generated* and to **flip the internal switch** *that allows us to apply it* are two key skills of those who excel at Compassionate Consultation (and growth-seeking). Together, these two key skills make up the "compassion muscle" which must be coordinated with the "Consultation muscle" for true Compassionate Consultation to emerge.

Compassion Is a Change Agent

One of the ways compassion fosters change during Consultation is that it creates an atmosphere in which people feel free to voice and explore their ideas, feelings, and perspectives and thereby deepen and share their awareness. The compassionate atmosphere also fosters sensitive and empathic listening, which can be particularly powerful in fostering change and growth. Psychologist Carl Rogers said that if he as the therapist can *listen* to a person closely enough that he can truly understand how something seems and feels to that person, potent forces of change will be released in that person.[42] Everyone has a need to feel truly understood, and compassionate listening means that not only are our words heard and understood, but the emotion attached to the thought is also recognized and understood. This is a basic premise of all successful counseling, psychotherapy, and coaching sessions. It is also a basic premise of all successful Compassionate Consultation sessions.

Compassion Enhances the Reflecting-Back Technique

Because understanding the perspective of another person is imperative in Consultation, reflecting-back is a technique that can be used to enhance understanding. After a speaker has spoken, the listener repeats back what the speaker has said. The original speaker then tells the listener whether he or she has heard correctly, and, if not, the speaker must repeat the part that has not been heard correctly and the listener reflects it back again. This continues until the speaker acknowledges that she or he has been truly heard. Then the original speaker becomes the listener, the original listener becomes the speaker, and the procedure is repeated. The potential weakness of this technique is that it is often used in a way that merely reports thought content as when a listener mechanically reports back, "I hear you saying that our checking account was overdrawn so you couldn't pay for the groceries."

This technique can be significantly enhanced if the parties consciously address the *feeling component* in addition to the *thought content component*. This is where compassion comes into play. The feeling component addresses questions such as: *What emotion is the speaker feeling? How strongly does the speaker appear to be experiencing the feeling? What is behind this feeling? How can I relieve the person's distress?* The feeling component can be successfully addressed using the reflecting-back technique *only* when compassion is present. The presence of compassion might enable the listener described at the end of the last paragraph to report back, "I hear you saying that our checking account was overdrawn so you couldn't pay for the groceries and that you were both humiliated in front of the cashier and intensely angry with me for failing to make the deposit I had promised to make. I am so sorry."

Having compassion enables us to listen with awareness that is free of judgment. We are not only trying to truly understand what another person is thinking, but what he or she is feeling as well. Understanding does not necessarily mean we agree with those thoughts and feelings, but it does mean that we comprehend and respect the perspective and want to alleviate the other's distress. When compassion is present in these ways, it tends to subdue anger and resentment and cleanse the emotional field.

Compassion Determines the Quality of Results

The way a decision, a solution, or deeper understanding is reached using Consultation truly determines the quality of the results. This is partly because *process*, or how things are done, is usually more important to human beings than *content*, or what gets done. How things get done relates to the presence or absence of compassion. In addition, the presence of compassion enables human beings to gain access to the full value contained in their thoughts, feelings, hearts, and spirits because they feel safe to expose what lies deep within. Often, the truth of a matter is revealed in this way.

In a decision-making environment that lacks compassion, participants will feel judged; and when we feel judged, we protect ourselves by censoring what we say, overstating our opinions in anticipation of attack, or deciding not to speak at all. In such an environment, the free flow of ideas is impeded and Consultative results will be limited. Compassion, on the other hand, creates the emotional, spiritual, and thought climate that generates free-flowing interpenetration of ideas, which allows Consultation to flourish and deliver unlimited results.

Love, Fellowship & Compassion

Compassion is one of the manifestations of love. As referenced earlier, 'Abdu'l-Bahá says:

> **True consultation is spiritual conference in the attitude and atmosphere of love. Members must love each other in the spirit of fellowship in order that good results may be forthcoming. Love and fellowship are the foundation.**[43]

It is clear that simply being "nice" to each other during Consultation is not enough; in fact, niceness is woefully inadequate in terms of the requirements for Compassionate Consultation. When 'Abdu'l-Bahá says that "True consultation" must occur "in the attitude and atmosphere of love," the implication is that love must be present in participants' *attitudes* to the extent that it creates an *atmosphere*. 'Abdu'l-Bahá extends these concepts when he says, "Members must love each other in the spirit of fellowship…" Compassion may be seen as the meeting ground between love and *fellow*ship because it is love conveyed through wholeheartedly acknowledging and welcoming another as a *fellow* human being with inherently valuable perspectives, needs, and concerns.

In an effort to grasp the magnitude of the power of love and compassion, let us reflect upon the following words of 'Abdu'l-Bahá:

> **Know thou of a certainty that Love is the secret of God's holy Dispensation, the manifestation of the All-Merciful, the fountain of spiritual outpourings.**
>
> **Love is heaven's kindly light, the Holy Spirit's eternal breath that vivifieth the human soul. Love is the cause of God's revelation unto man, the vital bond inherent, in accordance with the divine creation, in the realities of things. Love is the one means that ensureth true felicity both in this world and the next. Love is the light that guideth in darkness, the living link that uniteth God with man, that assureth the progress of every illumined soul. Love is the most great law that ruleth this mighty and heavenly cycle, the unique power that bindeth together the divers elements of this material**

world, the supreme magnetic force that directeth the movements of the spheres in the celestial realms. Love revealeth with unfailing and limitless power the mysteries latent in the universe. Love is the spirit of life unto the adorned body of mankind, the establisher of true civilization in this mortal world, and the shedder of imperishable glory upon every high-aiming race and nation....

O ye beloved of the Lord! Strive to become the manifestations of the love of God, the lamps of divine guidance shining amongst the kindreds of the earth with the light of love and concord.[44]

This passage makes clear that love has tremendous power. We can begin to understand why true Consultation is so powerfully effective in providing new insights, understanding, and unity when love, the spirit of fellowship, and compassion are the attitude, atmosphere, and foundation for it.

Compassion Burns through Mental & Emotional Fog

Early one morning while writing this chapter, we opened the curtains to see our entire building wrapped in a dense fog. The white, fog-filled air was pressing against the screens of the porch, and the air was dense, damp, chilly, and opaque. Over the next forty minutes, however, we watched the sun rise, gradually warm the air, and cause a radical shift in the environment.

Starting from an almost suffocating closeness of atmosphere in which everything seemed oppressive, unclear, and impenetrable, the sunlight had, at first subtly, gently, and steadily, and later warmly, strongly, and irresistibly, penetrated, dissipated, and then banished the fog. In its place were light, clarity, and warmth. As observers of this process, we had evolved from blindness and disorientation about our setting to clearly discerning and understanding both the terrain around us and the relationships between things.

This example in the natural world has a correlation in the spiritual realm. Whether we are using Compassionate Consultation with a spouse, a family, an organizational group, or a community, the luminary of compassion works very similarly to the sun in opening things up, dissipating the fog of misconceptions and uncertainty, removing stubbornly myopic lenses, revealing the true terrain and situation around us, fostering an atmosphere of warm possibility for Consultation about what is next and what needs to be, and creating readiness for receiving divine illumination. Compassion is transformative.

The Example of Sharon & Ahmad—Compassion Enhances Clarity of Perception

A real life example will serve to illustrate the perception-enhancing dynamics of compassion. Sharon had been aware for many years that she had personal issues around the fear of being abandoned, which had been fostered by experiences in her family of origin. At a time when she was feeling very insecure and anxious, she admitted for the first time to her husband, Ahmad, that she struggled with fears of abandonment.

Ahmad's first thought was that this was ridiculous because Sharon had their children, her friends, and himself—all of whom loved her and were devoted to her; however, he caught himself and did not voice this thought. Because Sharon and he had been consciously developing their compassion muscles when they Consulted together, he had the sense to stop, take a deep breath, and open his heart in compassion. He looked directly into her eyes and asked, "What does that feel like?" After reflecting for a moment, Sharon said, "I suddenly realize that it's not so much a fear of abandonment as a fear that I'm not worthy enough for people to want to be with me." Ahmad then asked her to tell him more about her feelings so that he could better understand her suffering. Sharon said, "If I am not meeting everyone else's needs all the time, then I won't be needed. So, I am always afraid I'll fall short, even with you and the kids."

Sharon's original disclosure to Ahmad followed by his responses voiced in compassionate, curious, open-ended questions had created a compassionate atmosphere that enabled Sharon to get new awareness and clarity about this fear that had shadowed her for many years. Now, she had something specific to reflect upon and work on.

During the following weeks, she asked Ahmad and her children what they liked and loved about her; she reflected on whom she liked to be with and why; she increased her self-esteem by focusing on her attributes that she and others appreciated; and she reflected on what being alone meant to her. She was then able to make dramatic progress in reducing her fear in the months that followed. She and Ahmad also realized that it was his compassionate responses that had enhanced the clarity of her perceptions, enabling her to identify the core beliefs underlying her fear. In time, she learned to come from love rather than fear in her relationships.

Absence of Compassion Causes Absence of Vision

It is common for participants attempting to use Consultation (and other decision-making methods) to confer at length using what seems to be rational discussion in an unsuccessful attempt to achieve clarity and reach a decision. In many cases, the problem is not the lack of enough rational insight and discussion, but *the lack of enough compassion.* The presence of a compassionate atmosphere during Consultation engenders curiosity, the desire to really hear information that is outside our awareness or comfort zone—to take it in, and to ask objective, open-ended, and powerful clarifying questions that go deep enough to reach true understanding. Despite our best intentions, in the absence of a compassionate atmosphere we are likely to become reactive and stuck.

Often in groups the discussion becomes stuck because one person, let's call him Joe, repeatedly expresses the same point, coming at it each time from a slightly different angle. Other participants attempt to make their points with the hope that the discussion will move on, but Joe makes the original point again. Joe is unwilling to let go of his idea because he does not think the other members of the group are hearing or understanding his point since they are not responding in the way he expects and desires. *The missing element in the group's process at this point is compassion.* What can forward the process is for Mary to compassionately say, "It is clear that this is a very important point to Joe. Let's make sure we understand it correctly. The point you want to make sure we get, Joe, is (*Mary reflects back Joe's thoughts and feelings*). Is that correct?" When genuine compassion enters the Consultative atmosphere in this way, Joe will most likely feel heard, understood, and able to let go of his idea and move forward with the group. This compassionate approach also allows other group members to truly hear the idea again in an objective way because Joe's earlier insistence may have caused their ears and minds to close to the idea.

In summary, compassion is more than just a virtue in Compassionate Consultation; it is an *essential, strategic tool.* The luminary of compassion creates perceptual clarity during Compassionate Consultation by enabling thoughts, feelings, and ideas to be truly shared, seen, and heard without the "fog" produced by preconceptions, attachments, and prejudices. In this way, compassion fosters clear vision and deeper understanding. Indeed, Bahá'u'lláh says:

> In this Day whatsoever serveth to reduce blindness and to increase vision is worthy of consideration. This vision acteth as the agent and guide for true knowledge. Indeed in the estimation of men of wisdom keenness of understanding is due to keenness of vision.[45]

Chapter 5

Cultivating Compassion

While wonderful outbursts of compassion occur periodically and temporarily in response to disasters and personal tragedy in the world, as an everyday, consistent, inter-personal attribute, compassion (including the component of taking action to alleviate suffering) does not predominate. This condition has a large impact because cultural norms strongly influence all of us—they powerfully dictate values and behavior. As a consequence, we may struggle as products of our cultures to generate adequate compassion when attempting to use Consultation for making decisions, solving problems, tapping into opportunities, and deepening understanding.

Fortunately, human beings have the capacity to *rise above their cultures*. To build up the luminary of compassion in our lives so that it shines with equal intensity to the luminary of Consultation, it behooves us to *cultivate* compassion in ourselves. A statement often attributed to Mahatma Gandhi is to "be the change you wish to see in the world."[46] Change must start within us. Let's look at some steps and perspectives that may help us cultivate and strengthen our compassion "muscles" so that we are ready for the demands Compassionate Consultation will put on us.

Step 1: Acknowledge & Rely Upon the Existence of a Compassionate God

It is very difficult to generate robust compassion for others or ourselves without a sense of receiving compassionate support from our Creator. If we do not believe that God's compassion is infinite, we may conclude that compassion is a limited resource which must be hoarded rather than shared. Unless we see divine compassion as a deep aquifer with a limitless supply of pure water we can go to for replenishment through prayer, supplication, and meditation, our personal compassion vessel can get depleted and eventually go dry. We find ourselves empty of compassion at the very moment we or people around us need it.

Opening the Door to Compassion

Compassion and love are divine in origin. The Bahá'í Writings state:

> O SON OF MAN!
>
> Veiled in My immemorial being and in the ancient eternity of My essence, I knew My love for thee; therefore I created thee, have engraved on thee Mine image and revealed to thee My beauty.[47]

God's love and compassion for us led to our creation in His image, and to God's promise not to leave us alone, but to reveal His beauty to us through a succession of divine Messengers or Manifestations including Krishna, Moses, Zoroaster, Buddha, Jesus Christ, Muhammad, The Báb, and Bahá'u'lláh. These Manifestations of God have not only modeled the attributes of compassion and love to humanity, but They have clearly called upon us to develop these spiritual attributes (along with many others) as one of the purposes of life. This call can be heard in the Writings of Hinduism.

> That one I love who is incapable of ill will, who is friendly and compassionate.[48]

It is also heard in the Buddhist Writings:

> Compassion is a mind that savors only mercy and love for all sentient beings.[49]

The call for compassion is heard in the Judaic Writings:

> Be of the disciples of Aaron—one that loves peace, that loves mankind, and brings them nigh unto the Law.[50]

And it is heard in the Christian Writings:

> If I give away all I have, and if I deliver my body to be burned, but have not love, I gain nothing.[51]

The call is also heard in the Writings of Islam:

> **A man is a true Muslim when no other Muslim has to fear anything from either his tongue or his hand.**[52]

To whatever degree our upbringing and life experiences have been unloving and uncompassionate, we may need to struggle more to connect with God in a way that allows us to feel His compassion and love in return. This is challenging because we need to learn to love God in order to feel His love. The Bahá'í Scriptures say:

> **O SON OF BEING!**
>
> **Love Me, that I may love thee. If thou lovest Me not, My love can in no wise reach thee. Know this, O servant.**[53]

Humankind has free will, and when we choose to love God we open the door and complete the circuit to experiencing God's love and compassion in return. When we are tapped into God's love and compassion in this way, we are more able to *consistently feel* love and compassion for ourselves and for our fellow human beings.

Conveying Compassion & Love For The Sake of God

Part of the dilemma in exercising a consistent flow of compassion during Consultation is that, for most of us, it is easier to feel compassion for some people than for others; however, the demands of Compassionate Consultation require that we feel compassion for everyone involved. 'Abdu'l-Bahá describes what we must strive for:

> **Humanity is not perfect. There are imperfections in every human being, and you will always become unhappy if you look toward the people themselves. But if you look toward God, you will love them and be kind to them, for the world of God is the world of perfection and complete mercy.**[54]

Compassion sees others with a sin-covering eye, and for most of us, it cannot be developed just by knowing it is important. Rather, it needs exercise to be developed like a muscle over time through prayer *and* through consciously taking action with love and compassion until it becomes a habit of heart and mind. Such exercise polishes and purifies the heart. In

Compassionate Consultation, as each member's heart increases in its ability to reflect God's compassion back to other members, the quality of the Consultation also increases.

Step 2: Acknowledge That *You* Are a Spiritual Being

In our previous book, we discussed how having self-compassion (which is different than self-pity) contributes significantly to the ability to have compassion for others. When we are harsh with ourselves, we tend to be harsh with others as well. Even without much self-compassion, people can generate superficial and selective compassion for people with whom they are comfortable during a casual social exchange; but Compassionate Consultation will require more from us. Without self-compassion, it is very difficult to generate compassion for people with whom we are having a disagreement or struggling to solve a problem. The challenge of Compassionate Consultation is to generate compassion for all people in all their diversity—including ourselves—in difficult and stressful circumstances. So, how can we do this?

Focusing on the Big Picture of Your Life

One key to cultivating self-compassion is learning to focus on the *big picture* of your life. It is easy to become self-critical or to blame others when your focus is on the often stressful details of getting an education, making a living, raising a family, living on a budget, saving for retirement, and the host of other details that must be attended to daily in order to navigate life in the material world. While all these things are important, they relate to the *small picture* of your life. Focusing on the *big picture* of your life involves seeing yourself as a spiritual being struggling through a human experience and visualizing your journeying soul's struggle to pass through this world while attempting to fulfill the three ultimate purposes of life: to know and love God, to acquire spiritual attributes, and to carry forward an ever-advancing civilization.

The goal in focusing on the big picture of your life is not to be self-indulgent, but to regularly observe and honor your own personal spiritual journey as *an epic journey* worthy of notice. You know you are making progress in this regard when you feel your heart being *moved* as you reflect on the heroic struggle of your soul to overcome obstacles, scale walls of personal growth, and do your absolute best in fulfilling the purposes of life. This experience of self-compassion will fuel your ability to feel compassion for everyone else in your life and their journeying souls' struggles.

The True Self

The aspect of yourself that sees the big picture of your life and is focused on your spiritual journey is the true self or soul. In our previous book, we explored facets of the true self at some length, asserted that this is the growth-seeking self, and demonstrated with reference to the world's Holy Books that this is the aspect of each of us to which the Messengers of God speak. We also indicated that it is your true self that has the capacity to *simultaneously* feel compassion for yourself and others and that this is a quick reference indicator to determine whether your true self is engaged or not in the moment. This simultaneous incoming *and* outgoing compassion is one of the reasons that Compassionate Consultation flourishes when participants are operating from their true selves.

Your true self resonates to the summons of the Messengers of God. The Bahá'í Writings express this summons:

> O SON OF SPIRIT!
>
> I created thee rich, why dost thou bring thyself down to poverty? Noble I made thee, wherewith dost thou abase thyself? Out of the essence of knowledge I gave thee being, why seekest thou enlightenment from anyone beside Me? Out of the clay of love I molded thee, how dost thou busy thyself with another? Turn thy sight unto thyself, that thou mayest find Me standing within thee, mighty, powerful and self-subsisting.[55]

This sacred and eternal part of us carries the latent attributes of God, is noble, is made of the essence of knowledge, and is molded out of the clay of love. This is the true self, our higher nature; but it can be distracted by "another," which could represent our lower nature that is preoccupied with worldly status, material wealth, temporal power, and recognition, or other conditions that lead us to busy ourselves with the small picture of our lives.

The Lower Nature and the True Self

Dimensions of our lower nature, their relationship to the true self, and the dynamics between these two aspects of our being during Compassionate

Consultation will be treated in more detail in Chapters 9 and 13. At this point it suffices to say that because our lower nature is preoccupied with material desires, it can cause problems during Consultation when it dominates our true self or higher nature. For example, when I leave my office late to get to an important meeting and find myself caught in heavy traffic, aspects of my lower nature that are impatient and fear failure become so energized that I feel incapable of experiencing compassion for myself, for others in the traffic jam, or for people in the important meeting to which I am driving. My lower nature has me caught in a web of anger, anxiety, shame, and blame and is dominating my true self. I am unfit in the moment for Compassionate Consultation with myself or anyone else.

As we will see, with practice the true self can learn to Consult with and manage the aspects of our lower nature. When this is happening, we will find ourselves fully in touch with compassion. Like a muscle that is called upon regularly, our ability to focus on our spirit's journey, consistently come from our true self, and make our lower nature step back will allow us to be ready for the compassion demands Consultation places on us.

Step 3: Acknowledge That *All* People Are Spiritual Beings

One of the findings in our previous book was that there is multiplicity of guiding intention in the universe and that things are happening all the time to you, me, and everyone else which are meant to guide us along our individual spiritual growth paths. Moving from intellectually entertaining this idea to compassionately acting from it can be expedited by training ourselves to see all other people as spiritual beings struggling through a human experience.

Perceiving the Journeying Soul in Others

Some years ago we were involved in a business relationship with a talented man who was also very controlling and distrustful of everyone with whom he interacted. His need for control and his distrust became so oppressive that we found ourselves swinging between feeling deeply hurt and feeling intensely angry toward him. Eventually, we realized that this difficult relationship was giving us an opportunity to practice accessing our true selves when hurt or angry aspects of our lower nature wanted to lead our beings.

Our first steps were to focus our attention on feeling self-compassion for being in this distressing situation, then to get to know him better from a place of compassion, learning more about his background, life experiences, and perspective on life. This effort led to a new understanding of how he had come to see the world as a very threatening, brutal, and unforgiving place. We tried to "walk a mile in his shoes" and actually felt compassion for the pain he experienced as he tried to navigate his life with the fears that were always with him. In short, we learned to perceive the journeying soul in him. As a result, we were able to come from our true selves most of the time, confer and collaborate with him from a place of compassion rather than hurt and anger, and maintain a longer working relationship with him than he was accustomed to.

The Limiting Effects of Otherness

Much of our cultural learning teaches us to set tight boundaries on the definitions of "us" and "them." Distinctions based on gender, ethnicity, class, race, caste, tribe, religion, country, political perspective, sexual orientation, educational experience, and earning level are generally accompanied by value judgments of good or bad and right or wrong. When we make such distinctions, we conceptually carve off one portion of humanity that is not worthy of compassion from another portion that is.

When these distinctions are made we focus on separateness rather than connection to others, and we restrict the flow of compassion and the possibility of achieving breakthrough results using Consultation. 'Abdu'l-Bahá says:

> O ye lovers of this wronged one! Cleanse ye your eyes, so that ye behold no man as different from yourselves. See ye no strangers; rather see all men as friends, for love and unity come hard when ye fix your gaze on otherness. And in this new and wondrous age, the Holy Writings say that we must be at one with every people; that we must see neither harshness nor injustice, neither malevolence, nor hostility, nor hate, but rather turn our eyes toward the heaven of ancient glory. For each of the creatures is a sign of God, and it was by the grace of the Lord and His power that each did step into the world; therefore they are not strangers, but in the family; not aliens, but friends, and to be treated as such.[56]

When we truly acknowledge that all people are spiritual beings struggling through a human experience, that all are members of a single family and bring this awareness to the Consultation environment, we free the flow of compassion and generate a Consultation atmosphere that optimizes the creation of breakthrough decisions, solutions, and understanding.

Step 4: Be Mindful of Your Own Shortcomings

Many of us live in environments where interpersonal gossip and back-biting—whether face to face, in news and social media, or through other channels of popular culture— make up a large proportion of the conversation. This constant feeding of the human tendency to sit in judgment of others and discuss their failings is a great barrier to building our compassion muscles because, in doing so, we forget entirely about our own shortcomings and elevate ourselves at the expense of others. This attitude can destroy the Compassionate Consultation atmosphere.

Jesus Christ Teaches Mindfulness about One's Own Shortcomings

A Biblical story teaches about the antidote to this problem. In the midst of a crowd of people Jesus Christ is teaching, a woman caught in adultery is brought before Him by the scribes and Pharisees. In accordance with Jewish law, His permission is sought for stoning her. The crowd is seething with righteous indignation and an urge to execute harsh judgment on the woman. Christ's counsel is, "He that is without sin among you, let him first cast a stone at her."[57] With this statement, the energy for stoning the woman evaporates as the focus shifts from her behavior to the behaviors of those sitting in judgment. The atmospheric transformation is dramatic. The scripture says:

> And they which heard it, being convicted by their own conscience, went out one by one, beginning at the eldest, even unto the last: and Jesus was left alone, and the woman standing in the midst.[58]

By shifting the awareness of the people in the crowd from judging the woman to mindfulness about their own shortcomings, Jesus Christ is teaching the power of compassion. Then, having addressed the needs of the crowd, Christ turns to addressing the needs of the woman. The scripture continues:

> When Jesus had lifted up himself, and saw none but the woman, he said unto her, Woman, where are those thine accusers? Hath no man condemned thee?
>
> She said, No man, Lord. And Jesus said unto her, Neither do I condemn thee: go, and sin no more.[59]

Christ's compassionate handling of the situation alleviates her suffering and models the loving attitude we are to cultivate toward others. In addition, He calls on all who would judge to have the humility to consider their own faults. This story illustrates both how compassion can work as a constructive change agent and how the Messengers of God model compassionate behaviors during Their ministries on earth.

Being Mindful of Your Shortcomings & Cultivating Humility

Closely related to compassion, humility includes mindfulness about one's own shortcomings and is an essential attribute in effectively achieving Compassionate Consultation. Without humility, compassion disappears, and stubbornness, contention, and hard-heartedness often take its place. Bahá'u'lláh and 'Abdu'l-Bahá tell us successively:

> Blessed are the learned that pride not themselves on their attainments; and well is it with the righteous that mock not the sinful, but rather conceal their misdeeds, so that their own shortcomings may remain veiled to men's eyes.[60]

And:

> It is my hope that you may consider this matter, that you may search out your own imperfections and not think of the imperfections of anybody else. Strive with all your power to be free from imperfections. Heedless souls are always seeking faults in others. What can the hypocrite know of others' faults when he is blind to his own? ...As long as a man does not find his own faults, he can never become perfect. Nothing is more fruitful for man than the knowledge of his own shortcomings. The Blessed Perfection [Bahá'u'lláh] says, "I wonder at the man who does not find his own imperfections."[61]

Step 5: Build the Muscle of Compassion & Practice CPR

Your ability to feel and express compassion can also be increased by applying the Knowledge + Volition + Action growth model (see Chapter 3). This process begins with increasing your Knowledge about compassion (e.g. what it is, how it is expressed, how it impacts people and situations) to the point that it increases your Volition (or motivation) to take new compassionate Action. Once you are in action, you can practice CPR—**C**onsciously, **P**roactively, and **R**egularly exercising and building the "muscle" of compassion just as you would build a muscle in your body that needs strengthening. There are numerous ways to exercise this muscle and practice CPR. Here are a few.

Studying the Lives & Teachings of the Messengers of God

A good starting point for increasing knowledge about compassion is to study and meditate on the lives and teachings of the Messengers of God that founded the world's great revealed religions. Unlike philosophers who typically espouse certain behaviors, but do not act accordingly, God's Messengers behaviorally model Their teachings through the actions They take during Their ministries. For example, all of the Messengers of God prescribe what has become known as the Golden Rule, which calls for compassion:

> One should not behave toward others in a way which is disagreeable to oneself. This is the essence of morality. All other activities are due to selfish desire.—Hinduism.[62]

> You shall love thy neighbor as thyself.—Judaism.[63]

> Comparing oneself to others in such terms as "Just as I am so are they, just as they are so am I," he should neither kill nor cause others to kill.—Buddhism.[64]

> And as ye would that men should do to you, do ye also to them likewise.—Christianity.[65]

> Not one of you is a believer until he loves for his brother what he loves for himself.—Islam.[66]

Blessed is he who preferreth his brother before himself.—Bahá'í Faith.[67]

Deepening your knowledge and volition on how these Messengers modeled the Golden Rule and then making yourself accountable for putting it into action at home, at work, and in the community consciously, proactively and regularly builds your muscle of compassion.

Observing & Learning From the Lives of Compassionate People

It can be helpful in building the muscle of compassion to carefully observe and learn from people around you who exhibit strong compassion. In addition, you can study biographies and autobiographies of historical figures who have demonstrated a large capacity for compassionate behavior such as Mother Teresa, Nelson Mandela, Martin Luther King Jr., Abraham Lincoln, and 'Abdu'l-Bahá.

Using Film as a Resource to Learn About Compassion

Some films depict and inspire the development of compassionate behaviors. Several that come to mind are *As Good As It Gets*, *It's a Wonderful Life*, *Marvin's Room*, *An Unfinished Life*, *Man In The Moon*, and *Gran Torino*. Studying such films can edify and inspire you in your compassion development process.

Scheduling Compassion Coffees

As an experiment to better understand the power of compassion and to build our compassion muscles, we started scheduling what we call "compassion coffees" during which we practice being consciously compassionate toward each other. Not only do we find these exchanges enjoyable and refreshing, but our relationship becomes stronger and deeper as a result. You can do it with a significant other, friend, or family member. Here are the guidelines we follow:

    1. Take turns talking to each other about your hopes, dreams, fears, struggles, and anxieties—whatever you have energy around;

    2. The listener responds with *compassion* and *curiosity* only, which can include open-ended questions (ones that cannot be answered with a

"yes" or a "no" and which begin with the words "how," "what," "where," and "when") to clarify or deepen understanding about the speaker's thoughts and feelings. The sole goal is to understand, empathize with, and alleviate the distress of the other.

3. The listener must have <u>no agenda</u> for the speaker—that is, no evaluations, judgments, demands, edifying feedback, instructions, or plans for the speaker's improvement unless these are requested by the speaker.

Discussions of this nature consistently generate deep exchanges and breakthroughs in understanding on the part of both speaker and listener. Putting things into words with another human being who is compassionate, non-judgmental, and safe is a liberating and insight-generating experience. This practice builds the compassion muscle and other skills that are beneficial to the Compassionate Consultation process. For an illustration, see "The Example of Gina & David" in Chapter 6.

Step 6: Learn To Replace Anger with Compassion

Dealing with anger and resentment (low-level anger) is important because they prevent or limit the expression of compassion. While anger inhibits the quality of all types of deliberation and decision-making, it can make Compassionate Consultation impossible because true Consultation *requires* the presence of compassion. In other words, if we feel anger or resentment toward a person or situation, it is difficult to simultaneously feel compassion for that person or situation. From ancient to recent times, God's divine Messengers have warned us against anger:

Hinduism

> Why, sir, do you get angry at someone
>
> Who is angry with you?
>
> What are you going to gain by it?
>
> Your physical anger brings dishonor on yourself;
>
> Your mental anger disturbs your thinking.
>
> How can the fire in your house burn the neighbor's house
>
> Without engulfing your own?[68]

Judaism

> A wrathful man stirreth up strife: but he that is slow to anger appeaseth strife.[69]

Buddhism

> Conquer anger by love.[70]

Christianity

> Let not the sun go down upon your wrath.[71]

Islam

> Those who spend (freely), whether in prosperity, or in adversity; who restrain anger, and pardon (all) men; for Allah loves those who do good.[72]

Bahá'í Faith

> Jealousy consumeth the body and anger doth burn the liver: avoid these two as you would a lion.[73]

The Lion of Anger

The last quotation from Bahá'u'lláh is a concise metaphor that instructs us regarding what to do with anger (or jealousy). At first, the instruction "… avoid these two as you would a lion" may seem to suggest that when we feel anger (or jealousy) we should repress it. However, this will not get rid of it. Like other emotions, anger is energy, and you cannot destroy energy; it may move in a different direction, take on a different form, or, if pushed down out of consciousness, cause a physical ailment or generate explosive pressure that awaits an opportunity to escape. If repression is not the antidote to anger, we need to explore the metaphor more closely.

In order to avoid a lion, we would not run toward it, and we certainly would not embrace it. In addition, we would not feed the lion which would only make it stronger and keep it returning to us for nourishment. Instead, we would need to be constantly aware of its whereabouts, notice whenever it became visible or made its presence known, and keep our distance from it. Relaxing our vigilance could lead to our destruction; the lion could devour us and our relationships.

So, anger is like a lion that we want to vigilantly observe from a distance. It can be destructive; it can compromise the immune system and damage our organs; it can cause disunity, destroy relationships, and even cause wars. When we sense anger arising in us, we want to be mindful that it is approaching, realize that we have an issue of some kind that is triggering the anger, and use this important information to identify and constructively deal with the underlying cause of the anger.

Properly Channeling the Energy from Anger

The energy to do this is embedded in the anger itself. Because anger is energy, its approach releases energy in us that can be used to address the situation at hand. Properly channeled anger can provide the energy to develop spiritual attributes, get out of a bad relationship, start a new career, or work effectively against injustice. As physician and mindfulness guru Jon Kabat-Zinn says:

> It's not that feelings of anger don't arise. It's that the anger can be used, worked with, harnessed so that its energies can nourish patience, compassion, harmony, and wisdom in ourselves and perhaps in others as well.[74]

Properly channeled, anger can provide the energy to respond creatively to difficulties and obstacles in our lives that keep us trapped in unhealthy or immature patterns. Like the presence of the lion that alerts us to the fact that we need to take a different path to preserve our well-being, the presence of anger can alert us to the need for making a change in a situation that is causing dissension and distress.

So the constructive way to deal with approaching anger—in life generally and in Compassionate Consultation—is to understand what it is about and then find a way to change it into what is required for clear thinking, feeling, and decision-making. To do this, we need to be mindful of some aspects of the human mind.

The Mammalian Brain

Why is it that I may experience big anger when, for example, my spouse does not greet me at the door, or my supervisor does not compliment me, or my friend has been too busy to have lunch with me for three weeks? Some understanding of the brain clarifies this. The part of the brain associated with anger is the mammalian or, in terms of evolution, our "old" brain. Because this instinctual part of the brain focuses on safety and survival, it recognizes patterns that it associates with danger or loss. In humanity's early days, it was this mammalian brain that generated fear and anger to protect a human being during an encounter with a saber-toothed tiger. A person needed to remember life-threatening encounters so that she or he would build up survival skills and be able to quickly shift into fight-or-flight mode.

Today, of course, we don't encounter saber-toothed tigers, but the mammalian brain can still instantly send us into fight-or-flight mode over anything we perceive as a threat—regardless of the magnitude of the threat. This means, for example, that I may interpret my spouse not greeting me at the door as a sign of danger in the relationship, my boss not complimenting my work as an indicator of job insecurity, and my friend being too busy to see me as a precursor to being alone in the world.

Additionally, this also means that someone criticizing a project I did at work may feel as threatening as not being able to find my mother at the grocery store when I was three years old. This is because the mammalian brain will have the intensity of our emotional responses to such triggers be equal to the *combined total* of all our previous fears about safety and survival in life. Ideas and emotions generated in this part of the brain exist out of time, are triggered by like circumstances, and are designed to get our attention.

The Cerebral Cortex

Another part of the brain called the cerebral cortex, however, knows that not every alarm requires a big reaction and can determine, for example, that it would not be appropriate to react to the person who criticized our project at work by throwing a wastebasket or screaming personal insults.

We all have the capacity to shift out of the mammalian part of the brain to the cerebral cortex, the problem-solving and rational decision-making part of the brain. When confronted by distressing feelings, the cerebral cortex is able to consider the anger or any other emotion in context, decide whether it warrants any response, and, if so, make a conscious decision about how to respond. Maturation as a human being is at least partly about learning to respond thoughtfully and responsibly in a way that is congruent with our beliefs, values, needs, and wants rather than reacting without thought in a knee-jerk fashion; and the cerebral cortex is *the resource* for developing this ability.

If you think of the brain as a filing system, the mammalian part of the brain is the "blame" file; all you can find in that file is whatever there is, or has been, to blame in your life. The value of the "blame" file is that it keeps you alert for what might be dangerous and prepares you to fight or take flight in a given situation in order to protect yourself. The disadvantage of the "blame" file is that when you're in that part of the brain, you cannot find ways to make things better because you are not in the right file. To make things better, you need to shift into the cerebral cortex to make sense of the feeling you are having, put it into perspective, and make a conscious decision about how to respond. *The key to making this shift is learning to replace anger with compassion by identifying the true source of the anger.*

Seeing Core Hurts behind Anger

We have acknowledged that anger and resentment are the lions that we need to be vigilantly attentive to and avoid in order to Consult effectively because they can constrict compassion and cause distortions in our perspective. However, we have also concluded that anger and resentment are valuable emotions that let us know when something is not right and change is needed. Positive change might mean altering the way we think about something or rearranging our outer circumstances. Anger and resentment (and other forms of low-level anger such as frustration or irritation) are the indicators that let us know we need to pay attention to something in our lives. Progress occurs when we look behind or beneath the anger or resentment at the source, which is usually a *core hurt*.

Psychologist Steven Stosny says that one or more core hurts are behind all anger. He lists core hurts from the least serious to the deepest and most serious[75] as follows.

CORE HURTS

A feeling that I am…

>   Disregarded/unimportant
>   Accused: guilty or mistrusted
>   Devalued
>   Rejected
>   Powerless
>   Unlovable

The concept is that anger is generated by our conscious or unconscious experience of a core hurt. The deeper the core hurt is, the more intense is the resulting anger. We want to be able to recognize the core hurt that is the cause of the anger so that we can deal with the cause effectively. To do this, it is necessary to shift out of the mammalian brain (which means we do not latch onto the anger) and move to the cerebral cortex by asking ourselves the question, *"Which of the core hurts are behind this anger I am starting to experience?"* When we ask ourselves an open-ended question (one that cannot be answered with a yes or a no), we engage the cerebral cortex, the problem-solving part of the brain.

The very act of trying to identify the core hurts we are experiencing is an expression of self-compassion. We are recognizing and validating that we are experiencing emotional pain. When we can identify the deepest core hurt we are experiencing, we instantly begin the process of healing from the core hurt even as we gain awareness of the underlying cause of our anger. Not only do we have something specific to work with when we turn our attention to core hurts, but by showing compassion to ourselves in identifying our core hurts we dilate our heart, and a dilated heart is able to feel and express compassion for others as well, which makes us more able to listen to, and understand, another person's perspective. All of these factors contribute to our ability to be more objective and Consult effectively.

The Example of Mike, Rochelle & Lauren

Let's look at an example of how this all works. Mike and Rochelle are married with a fifteen-year-old daughter, Lauren. Lauren asked Mike if he wanted to go to a rock concert with her. Usually, this would make Rochelle feel pleased because she puts great value on the relationship between her husband and daughter. However, when she heard about the invitation, she was filled with anger. In her head, she was thinking *How could they leave me out?* and *How could they be so thoughtless?*

She was distressed and in tears when she asked Lauren how she could be so inconsiderate. Lauren defended herself saying that she might get teased by her peers if she went with her mother or her father and mother, but going with Dad alone was more acceptable. Nevertheless, she added that if it meant that much to Rochelle she could go too. That did not console Rochelle. Her awareness was firmly planted in the mammalian part of her brain. Rochelle said she wanted Lauren to want her to go—not just give in and take her by default. Having heard this exchange, Mike came into the room and spoke to Rochelle in a compassionate tone. "This just isn't like you. What is really going on with you?" Rochelle took a deep breath, accepted his hug, and cried even harder. She realized that her angry reaction, which was out of character, indicated something deeper going on inside her.

Mike's compassionate question was enough to help Rochelle use the energy from her anger to shift herself out of her blame files into the problem-solving part of her brain. She identified the deepest core hurt she was feeling, which was feeling *powerless*. She was now able to apply self-compassion and Consult within herself about what was really going on. And she instantly realized that her sense of powerlessness was not just about the concert.

Rochelle surveyed the past year of her life and recognized that her eldest daughter had gone away to college, her father had passed away, her mother had been scheduled for cancer surgery in the coming weeks, and Lauren would be going to college in another few years. All of these changes were things Rochelle was *powerless* to stop. Her self-compassion allowed her to move out of the anger about not being invited to the concert and to go deeper and recognize the core hurt, which carried a great wave of emotional pain and sadness.

Staying in the anger/resentment mode would have kept Rochelle stuck with deep, painful feelings and no additional understanding of herself and her life situation. As a result of experiencing compassion from her husband followed by self-compassion, however, she was able to discover the deepest of her core hurts, powerlessness, and a degree of two other core hurts, rejected and disregarded. These deep feelings had caused her to react in an uncharacteristic way and with an intensity that—on the surface—seemed unwarranted in the circumstances. From the standpoint of core hurts, however, it all made perfect sense. That Lauren and Mike were going to leave her for the concert, even though it would only be for a few hours, felt like a huge loss, and it triggered all of her accumulated feelings of powerlessness and abandonment.

With her deepened understanding, Rochelle could fully experience compassion for herself that was self-nurturing and healing. And almost simultaneously, her self-compassion overflowed into compassion for Lauren who had been the unwarranted recipient of her anger. She explained the source of her feelings to Lauren, apologized for reacting as she had, and the two of them ended up hugging, crying, and laughing together. Thus, their relationship was deepened and strengthened by this experience.

The pathway to understanding is always away from anger and toward compassion, and practitioners of Compassionate Consultation need to habitually choose this path.

Chapter 6

Putting Compassion into Action

In the last chapter we explored some ways to cultivate compassion as a primary resource for Compassionate Consultation and growth-seeking. Because using compassion in tense situations when differing opinions are involved can be a challenge, we will now more fully address compassion in action.

Growth-Seeking & Conflict

Seekers of growth can expect resistance and challenging obstacles as they wade into the swamp of change. And since most change and growth entails human interaction (with other people or ourselves), growth-seekers need to move proactively toward Compassionate Consultation. When they do so, they also move proactively toward conflict. But they move toward *constructive* conflict rather than *destructive* conflict—and they need to know the difference.

Constructive Conflict

The root meaning of the term conflict is "to strike together." Constructive conflict occurs when ideas, opinions, concepts, strategies, and perspectives strike together, and the parties involved are committed to resolving the conflict collaboratively. This seems to be the kind of positive Consultative conflict that 'Abdu'l-Bahá is referring to when He says, "The shining spark of truth cometh forth only after the clash of differing opinions."[76]

In constructive conflict during Consultation, we willingly allow our opinions and thoughts to clash together, but we reserve the greatest part of our attention for the sparks of truth that emerge from these clashes. Constructive conflict leads to truth by deepening awareness, increasing understanding, providing a clearer view of possibilities, and revealing the spiritual principles involved.

Destructive Conflict

Destructive conflict occurs when personalities, egos, or people strike together, and they are committed to winning or gaining advantage over each other. 'Abdu'l-Bahá refers to this kind of conflict during Consultation when He says:

> They must in every matter search out the truth and not insist upon their own opinion, for stubbornness and persistence in one's views will lead ultimately to discord and wrangling and the truth will remain hidden.[77]

Destructive conflict leads away from truth by narrowing our awareness, reducing our understanding, and obscuring possibilities and spiritual principles.

Compassion & Conflict

When we experience destructive conflict in our efforts to make decisions through the use of Consultation, it is due to a shortage of compassion. While solutions to even the most complex problems may be reached through the "clash of differing opinions" when compassion is present, a shortage of compassion on even simple problems often results in destructive conflict that leads to the hardening of one position against another and the inability to reach solutions.

The Conflict Choice Map

The Choice Map shown in Figure 6.1 was developed by Management Associates[78] and illustrates the choices we can make in conflict situations about what is going to be "struck together." Will it be personalities and egos, issues and positions, or underlying interests and concerns that are struck together? Conflicts that begin and stay at the shallowest awareness level where *personalities and egos* strike together are the most destructive and intractable. Some conflicts reach a deeper awareness level where *issues and positions* strike together, and these conflicts are only somewhat less destructive and intractable. Other conflicts that go to an even deeper awareness level where *underlying interests and concerns* surface and strike together are the most constructive and least intractable.

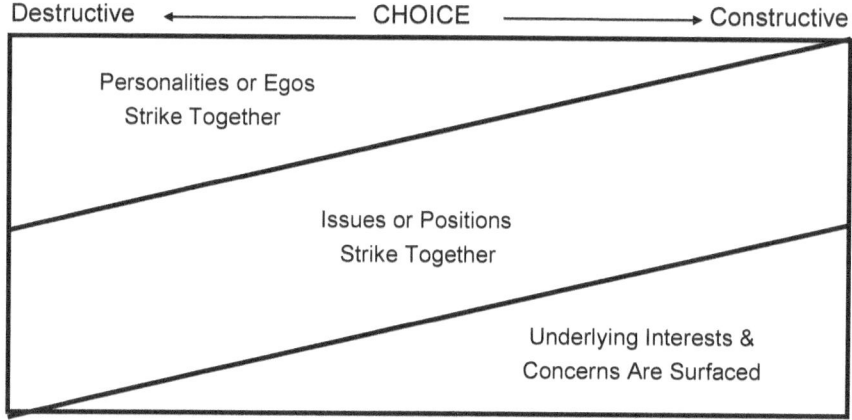

Figure 6.1

The Choice Map helps us understand that underneath each *position* that a person or group in conflict takes about an *issue* lies *interests* and *concerns.* For example, say that my *position* is that I am opposed to increasing immigration quotas in the United States. The *concerns* underlying my position are 1) I am already having trouble finding work, and 2) pay rates in my field of work are already too low. The value in going beneath our positions to identify each party's *underlying interests and concerns* is that even if our *positions* are in conflict, we may discover shared and compatible *interests* and *concerns.* If we surface the concerns and interests beneath our positions, we can creatively search for areas of common concern and possible agreement. We may, for example, be able to discover and agree on a way to increase immigration quotas and still assure good jobs and pay rates for existing citizens.

The Choice Map & Internal Conflicts

The Choice Map also has relevance for an individual's internal conflicts.

An individual can have very harsh self-talk going on inside of his or her head that corresponds (in The Choice Map) to *personalities and egos striking together*. There can be conflict within a person around assumptions and core beliefs (that have been learned from the family of origin or culture such as "I'll always be single because I am not an interesting person" or "I am nothing if I don't earn at least $100,000 per year") that correspond in The Choice Map to *issues or positions striking together*. There can also be internal conflicts around personal values, a sense of life purpose, issues of faith, the language of the heart, and ultimate aspirations, and these dimensions correspond to *underlying interests and concerns* in the Choice Map. Whether the conflict is within the individual or between members of a group, going deeper to identify underlying interests and concerns is the most effective way to move toward constructive conflict resolution.

Choosing To Move To the Right on the Choice Map

Overall, The Choice Map shows that the more each individual chooses to work toward the right-hand side of the map, where only issues and positions and underlying interests and concerns strike together, the more objectively the conflict will be handled, the more creative the solution will be, and the more positive the aftermath of the conflict will be. The more each individual chooses to work toward the left-hand side of the map, where only personalities and egos and issues and positions strike together, the more subjective, emotional, and destructive the dynamics, outcome, and aftermath will be.

The Choice Map & Compassion

What the Choice Map does *not* show is that the ability to move to the right and toward positive resolution is determined by the presence or absence of *compassion*. When both self-compassion and compassion for others are present, the group's process will naturally move toward the right. Compassion makes it possible to omit the focus on egos and personalities, to move sensitively through issues and positions, and to dilate hearts so that underlying issues and concerns are revealed and explored on the path to constructive and creative resolution.

Without compassion, further discussion of an issue may simply crystallize the arguments, positions, and opinions into two or more opposing sides resulting in a stalemate, the escalation of emotions, and adversarial strategizing on how to win. This would represent moving to the left on the Choice Map where only personalities and egos and issues and positions strike together. In other words, without compassion, attempting to Consult about an issue that involves differing opinions can make a situation worse. In the absence of compassion, it is common for no solution to be reached, for feelings to be hurt, and for participants to resolve not to be honest or open with each other in the future in order to protect themselves. In the absence of compassion, *Compassionate Consultation has not been experienced.*

This is a great loss, because destructive conflict causes differing opinions and perspectives, which are inherently rich in creative possibilities, to lose their subtle nuances and complexities and become over-simplified, rigid, and lifeless. Rather than making insightful discoveries, creating helpful solutions, and forging stronger connections between participants, destructive conflict causes barriers to be erected and people with opposing opinions to become angry, self-righteous, and judgmental. Whether in a family, work, or community environment, lack of compassion generates distrust, defensiveness, and hyper-vigilance—a climate that is the opposite of what is needed for effective Consultation.

Circumstances Requiring Pre-Loading of Compassion

There are times when even a seemingly innocuous suggestion about a topic for discussion or Consultation can create an emotionally-charged situation; this calls for an output of compassion *before* any Consultation can take place. When a situation, a topic, or a problem triggers intense emotions, we have what is commonly called an "issue." An issue may involve:

- experiencing uncomfortable, unwanted feelings
- experiencing feelings that are bigger than the situation warrants
- experiencing conflicting feelings or wants
- doing or saying something that we know is inappropriate
- not doing or saying something we wanted to do or say
- having disturbing, confusing thoughts

Issues can prevent us from making Consultative decisions because they indicate the presence of blind spots, which are areas of incomplete understanding or lack of awareness that are surrounded by defensive emotions. Generally speaking, when we encounter an issue, we have come to a wall. We then have a choice about whether we want to scale the wall and go over it or treat the wall as a dead-end—that is, choose a no growth path by becoming defensive rather than determining what is going on inside of us. Let's look at an example for clarification.

The Example of Jan & Wayne—Pre-Loading Compassion

Jan told her husband of fifteen years, Wayne, that she was going to the grocery store and asked if there was anything he wanted her to get for him. He replied, "You know, I think we should start to eat differently so we will be healthier." Jan was taken aback; she was visibly angry. She said sarcastically, "Thanks a lot!" She added, "Haven't I always been mindful about our health when it comes to food preparation?" Noticing her anger, Wayne responded, "You are too sensitive!" This made Jan even angrier, and Wayne, in turn, was puzzled and angry that Jan was responding with such intensity.

From this point, the exchange could escalate, with each party verbally attacking the other and moving even further to the left on The Choice Map. Alternatively, they could both withdraw and try to distract themselves to get rid of the uncomfortable feelings (e.g. Jan might go shopping, and Wayne might watch a football game on TV). In either case, no one would really understand what the strong feelings were about, and from then on they would probably avoid the "hot" topic of changing their eating habits. Both partners would probably feel resentful and might carry the resentment indefinitely, adding it to the resentment carried from other seemingly trivial and unresolved incidents. When we avoid dealing with an issue in our lives, the spiritual growth lab of life tends to keep resurfacing it for us in different contexts. If Jan and Wayne continue to avoid the issue, they will stay stuck at that level of awareness indefinitely and continue to have tests around the same issue until they are willing to deal with the issue, pass the test, and move to a new level of awareness.

Another possibility is that they could approach the situation with a growth-seeking perspective from the start. They could recognize the uncomfortable situation as an opportunity for growth as individuals and as a couple—as well as an opportunity to discuss how they might make dietary changes to ensure optimal health and wellness. Jan might recognize that her big feelings indicate she has encountered an "issue" and a resistance force in the form of her own husband whose reaction to her question feels unexpectedly strong and judgmental. Big feelings *could* prompt her to stop and reflect. She has a choice between becoming angry with the resistance force or welcoming it and recognizing that the situation offers an opportunity for growth.

> *A Note to the Reader: The positive monologue and dialogue examples in the following pages may sound idealized to some readers, but they are actually examples taken from real life that reflect the power of compassion and other Compassionate Consultation resources and tools. The more we practice using these resources and tools, the better we get at interacting in compassionate ways and using Compassionate Consultation.*

The best way for Jan to discover the issue or wall she has encountered is to *pre-load compassion*—that is, come from self-compassion followed by compassion for Wayne—which allows her to respond with judgement-free awareness and say:

> "I am feeling strong emotions in response to what you said. I guess I am feeling anger because your comment that we need to change the way we eat gives me core hurts—it makes me feel devalued as a cook and homemaker, roles I work very hard at and in which I take great pride. For fifteen years, I've been the primary menu developer in our family and assumed I was doing a good job of it, but now I'm feeling like I've been accused and found guilty of not doing it well enough. But even as I say that, I realize that I am feeling a little tired of our eating patterns, which are the same ones my mother taught me twenty-five years ago. And I am curious about what is behind your comment—maybe there is something there that I need to hear and think about."

Jan's self-compassion is clearing up the emotional fog arising from the exchange between Wayne and her and is allowing her to get in touch with the core hurts underneath her anger. Her self-compassion is also generating a compassion-softened feeling toward Wayne and helping her see the early outlines of a wall she may need to scale so that she can go over it into new awareness.

Wayne has his own growth-seeking drama unfolding. In the weeks preceding the intense exchange with Jan, he had been thinking about their health, but had mentioned nothing about it to Jan. He is surprised by how rapidly the exchange with Jan intensified and by his quick, insensitive response to Jan ("You are too sensitive!"). It would be easy for him to drop the subject in order to avoid a blow-up with Jan, but he recognizes in Jan's intense reaction that there is an issue to deal with—Jan is a resistance force or obstruction calling him to discover a wall that is separating him from some kind of growth and new awareness. He applies compassion to himself to get in touch with the feelings under his anger, then experiences compassion for Jan who is visibly upset. He articulates his thoughts:

> "I am sorry to have upset you by what I said—I was also a little surprised by what I said. You've been a great cook and homemaker through all the years we have been married. It's just that after my co-worker Paul had a heart attack last month, I've been thinking and worrying a lot about our health. You and I are the same age as Paul and his eating patterns are a lot like ours. I am also carrying around the same amount of extra weight as Paul, and I find I am short of breath when I use the stairs instead of the elevator at work. A few weeks ago, I read an article about nutrition and health that really got my attention, and just now when you said you were going to the store, I suddenly realized I am ready to start making some changes to lose some weight and reduce my fat intake. I should have said something about this to you sooner, but I've just been ruminating about it in the back of my mind until now."

Wayne's self-compassion and compassion for Jan have cleared up his confusion about the intense exchange and help him reflect upon, and reveal to Jan, what has been going on silently inside him. The triggering obstructions in the swamp of change for Wayne are his friend Paul's heart attack, Wayne's shortness of breath, the article he read, and now Jan's intense response to his comment; they have helped to define a wall. The wall he needs to scale may involve taking full responsibility for his nutrition and health. Jan may discover that she has the same wall (Jan taking full responsibility for her nutrition and health), and she and Wayne may decide as a result of their Consultation to adopt the behaviors that will help them scale the wall together.

Using Compassion to Create the Consultative Atmosphere

It is evident that, after the original tense exchange between Wayne and Jan, the atmosphere was too emotionally charged for them to Consult. Compassion was needed before they would be able to Consult effectively and avail themselves of the growth possibilities inherent in the situation. 'Abdu'l-Bahá says that for effective Consultation to take place and lead to a robust decision, participants need to weigh their opinions "with the utmost serenity, calmness, and composure."[79] Jan's and Wayne's emotionally-charged states would not initially permit that to happen. A shift in perspective and atmosphere was needed, and compassion was the attribute that enabled such a shift to occur—compassion for self and other.

Compassion Does Not Equal Agreement

To have compassion for another does not necessarily mean that we agree with that person's perspective. It does mean that we are able to hear the other person's thoughts, feelings, assumptions, expectations, and beliefs in an open, non-judgmental way; that we "try on" her or his perspective and understand how and why that person thinks and feels the way he or she does; and that we are moved to alleviate the person's distress. Strong feelings in response to another person or an idea can get in the way of our ability to do this.

Tapping into the Motivation to Manifest Compassion

When destructive conflict breaks out, it can be very difficult to access compassion. Tapping into the motivation to manifest compassion is partly about using the tools and resources described in the last chapter, "How to Cultivate Compassion." But the motivation to manifest compassion also comes from the inherent growth-seeker within you that is eager to progress, deepen your understanding, draw closer to God, and fulfill the purposes of life. This inherent growth-seeker is the true self. When our true self is in the lead, we are moved to respond with an open heart and mind so that positive interactions occur, and calm, measured solutions are reached.

Consulting compassionately is highly rewarding. It removes the fear and anger that can trigger when an emotionally charged situation arises. Going forward, Jan and Wayne make efforts to look at emotionally-charged incidents in their lives as opportunities for growth. They joke with each other about putting on their "growth-seeker hats" when problems or concerns arise. This image helps them detach from their egos and engage their compassion. With compassion engaged, they find that situations which create strong feelings are defused, and that they are able to be curious and non-judgmental with each other. They have learned that exchanges as apparently trivial as the one about buying different groceries can yield increased individual awareness, improved communication, and a deepened relationship.

Bias Blocks Compassion

What often gets in the way of compassion is the tendency for each of us to believe that we have "the truth," that our reality is "the true reality," and that we know what is right or wrong, good or bad, appropriate or inappropriate. The fact is that much of what we believe to be "the truth" is simply what we learned from the environment in which we grew up. Had we grown up in a different family or culture, what we believe to be "truth" could be different; what we see as good or bad, right or wrong, correct or incorrect, or appropriate or inappropriate could be different. These presumptions we have about "truth" can be biases that block our compassion. *Compassion is unbiased.* If we are to be compassionate, we need to divest ourselves of biased learning, because compassion calls for us to be non-judgmental, accepting, and curious. If we are not able to activate our compassion toward another, we have a bias toward him or her, and *biases prevent productive Consultation*. Whereas compassion fosters connection and unity, bias fosters separation and adversarialism. Let's look at an example of how compassion can bring unity and harmony to an otherwise adversarial situation triggered by bias.

The Example of Elana & Her Parents—Replacing Bias with Compassion

Fourteen-year-old Elana wanted to wear a navel ring, which was the style among her peers. She asked her mother and father for permission to have her navel pierced. Her father promptly said, "Absolutely not—end of discussion!" Her mother said, "In our family we don't do things like that." Elana was hurt and angry. She thought her parents neither cared about her nor understood her. She distanced herself from them and drew closer to her peers, whom she felt understood her better. At this point, Elana's parents brought Elana in for counseling because they were distressed that Elana no longer communicated as much with them.

Elana was right about her parents not understanding her. They had made no effort to see the issue from Elana's point of view. In the counseling session, when we explored the parents' reasons for their negative responses, they cited such things as "only cheap girls do that," "her grandparents would think she was a bad girl," "it is indecent and encourages promiscuity," etc. They were adamant in their opinions—navel rings were definitely bad, wrong, and inappropriate. Elana was just as adamant in her opinion. In terms of the Choice Map, both Elana and her parents were locked at the "issues and positions" level and seemed unable to go deeper to reach "underlying interests and concerns."

After discussing with the family the importance and power of compassion when making decisions and solving problems, we asked Elana to share what was so important to her about having a navel ring. The basis of her thinking was that wearing a navel ring was a way to fit in with her peers. She got good grades, did not use drugs or alcohol, and did not want a sexual relationship—unlike many of her peers. The navel ring was a way she could fit in with her peers without compromising on behaviors that were not safe and could have long-term negative consequences. Her parents were able to generate enough compassion to listen in a non-judgmental way so that they could understand Elana's perspective. Their compassionate stance created the safety and softness that allowed Elana to reveal her underlying interests and concerns, and their compassion demonstrated to her that they understood she had valid reasons for her strong feelings. For her parents to understand Elana's perspective and see how her desire to have a navel ring made sense to her did not mean they agreed with her. It simply meant that they understood her and wanted to alleviate her distress.

After this sharing of feelings and ideas by Elana and the application of compassion by her parents, Elana said she felt they had heard her; she felt good that they had cared enough to really want to understand her thinking. When the family left the counseling session, they had not made a decision about the navel ring, but they had started to Consult effectively about it. Elana's parents had moved away from their initial knee-jerk biases, and Elana had successfully and compassionately responded to her parents when they revealed their underlying interests and concerns. As a family they were considering the issue from a more objective perspective arising from the interplay of their honest thoughts and feelings in an atmosphere of compassion. They recognized that their concerns involved whether the procedure for piercing was safe, whether Elana would wear less modest clothing in order to show the ring, what judgments were made about girls who have navel rings by students who do not have them or by teachers, and how Elana would feel about those judgments.

A Rush to Judgment Blocks Divine Guidance and Causes Destructive Conflict

When there is a rush to judgment (as in the case of Elana's parents), the one who is judged before being heard and understood feels discounted, rejected, not taken seriously, not considered important, and powerless—in short, she or he experiences a number of core hurts and the pain of being a victim of bias. And when we experience one or more of these hurt feelings, we tend to respond in defensive ways, one of which is to get angry and withdraw. Another is to get angry and counter-attack—to attack the attacker in a way that is as hurtful to the other person as his or her attack was to us. Either way, the absence of compassion leads to destructive conflict. And this, in turn, seems to prevent the Consultative parties from being divinely guided to any effective solution to the problem. In addition, the absence of compassion damages relationships. So, it is extremely important that we learn to engage our compassion because lack of compassion prevents Consultative breakthroughs and leads to increasing disunity.

Cultural Learning Can Undermine Compassion

The environment in which we grow up impacts the nature of our spiritual growth struggles. Early experiences condition us to think and behave in certain ways that lead to either spiritual strengths or weaknesses. Consequently, some spiritual attributes and virtues will seem like second nature to us, while others will come only with hard work. Compassion is one of those attributes that requires hard work for most people. This is at least partly because the competitive cultures of Western Civilization foster the opposite of compassion—gossiping, criticism, fault-finding, and blaming. In addition, in families where gossiping, criticism, fault-finding, and blaming are the norm, children learn that it is not okay to be who they are and that there is a very narrow range of acceptable ways of thinking, feeling, and behaving. In the process, children tend to internalize the critical, fault-finding, and blaming voices that surrounded them in their early years. This undermines self-esteem and fosters self-protective behaviors. Protection might take the form of attacking others through blaming and criticism or withdrawal. Compassion is undermined in this climate. As a result, changing these divisive patterns of thinking and behaving into compassionate patterns requires intention, courage, and hard work.

To truly mature in the growing-up process, we need to decide which of the beliefs, expectations, and assumptions we learned in our families-of-origin and in our larger culture we want to keep and which we want to discard.

The Example of Gina & David—Transcending Cultural Learning with Compassion

Gina and David are a married couple. They use some compassion in their Consultative discussions, but usually do it in hurried and stunted ways. A typical exchange would be:

David: You are being grumpy—like you're mad at me.
Gina: I feel grumpy. I've been working too much. I have been so busy at the office.
David: Maybe you just need to relax. Let's go to a movie.

David shows some compassionate concern about Gina, but what results is a hurried and temporary quick-fix. In the exchange David makes an observation about Gina, Gina replies, and David comes up with a quick solution. While Gina might feel better for a short time if she follows this advice and goes to a movie, there has been no significant increase in self-awareness or understanding, and therefore, true Consultation has not occurred. There is some compassion present, but it is too stunted and inadequate for true Compassionate Consultation to have taken place.

What follows is a second version of the exchange that begins the same way, but has a very different outcome because David has learned how to apply compassion more fully as he tries to understand what Gina is experiencing. This prompts Gina to STOP and use self-compassion to take a closer look at her grumpy mood and what is behind it.

David: You seem grumpy—like you're mad at me.

Gina: I feel grumpy. I've been working too much. I have been so busy at the office.

David: I hear you. You've been working very hard at the office. I'm trying to understand how you're feeling. How are you feeling because of having to do so much work?

Gina: Well, I'm enjoying my work. But, I did lash out at a co-worker yesterday when he put an additional responsibility on my plate. I guess I felt angry.

David: To what degree was it the proverbial "straw that broke the camel's back"—you were maxed out and just couldn't take one more responsibility?

Gina: I'm not sure. I guess it made sense that I would be assigned the task. But I think I was hurt—yes, I was hurt that he would dump that on me when I was already struggling with the heavy load I'm carrying. I feel unappreciated—like my extra hard work lately isn't being noticed, like I'm not being treated as a person with feelings and not being considered important or valuable.

David: So, you feel hurt that your efforts aren't being noticed or appreciated at the office.

Gina: Yes. And come to think of it, I'm not feeling appreciated around here either. It seems like the kids dump their problems on me the minute I come through the door. It feels like I'm not important except to be used to meet everyone else's needs. No wonder I have been feeling down and have been grumpy.

David: I can see why you would too. You feel unappreciated, like you're not treated as if you're important and valuable at work and at home.

Gina: Yes, that's it. But I also feel guilty and upset with myself for talking like this.

David: Say more about that.

Gina: I am *supposed* to be doing all these things—helping everyone at the office and helping everyone at home—but I can't seem to be the person I want to be when I am doing all this.

David: Who says you are supposed to be doing all this?

Gina: I have the voices of my mom and dad in my head, and the culture certainly gives me the message that a good woman is self-sacrificing.

David: So the voices of your parents and voice of the culture are saying to do all of this and be self-sacrificing. But a moment ago you said, "I can't seem to be the person I want to be when I am doing all this." What kind of person do you want to be?

Gina: Instead of feeling resentful and agitated and wanting to be left alone most of the time, I want to feel happy and loving when I'm doing things for the kids or you. I want to feel enthusiastic and excited when I'm asked to do any tasks at work, and I want to be peaceful and loving and even joyful most of the time.

David: What would it take to be that?

Gina: I would need to scale things down—not really change what I am doing, but set some boundaries as to how much of each thing I am willing to do.

David: What's stopping you from doing this?

Gina: I guess I would need your help in sorting things out, and, most of all, I need to give myself permission not to have to be all things to everyone and to take care of myself the way I take care of others.

Debriefing the Gina & David Example

In this example, David begins a true Consultative process by applying compassion, by not having an agenda for Gina, by reflecting on the feelings Gina is expressing, and by asking open-ended questions to bring focus and depth to what Gina is experiencing. She then uses the compassionate space David has created to apply self-compassion, to look more deeply at her feelings and experience, and to begin to understand how she wants to transcend her cultural learning. Together, they are identifying and agreeing upon the facts and beginning to clarify and agree on the issue with which Gina is struggling. From a growth-seeking standpoint, the obstacles or triggers in her tailored environment are the burdensome amount of work she has at the office, the co-worker who gave her an additional task at work, the children's and David's relentless needs, the agitating thoughts generated by her cultural learning, and David probing to understand why Gina is so grumpy. By having the courage to step into the compassionate space available to her and not shift attention away from herself by changing the subject, Gina has begun to see not only a wall that separates her from a more authentic way of being, but what the wall represents and what she has to do to scale it.

While the Consultative process between Gina and David is not complete, the presence of a compassionate atmosphere has already enabled Gina to discover that she needs to set boundaries around her *doing* activities and manage her time in a way that will enable her to avoid becoming overwhelmed and stay balanced so that she can feel good about who she is *being*. Since she is the only one who will know when she has achieved a balance that allows her to feel good about the way she is *being*, she realizes that she needs to be the one to set boundaries with others.

The next step is for Gina to continue the Compassionate Consultation process with David to determine what specific changes she needs to make in order to be able to manifest the personal attributes and virtues she values so highly. Based on their discussion, Gina and David articulate the following statement of Gina's issue: *"How to achieve balance of my body, mind, and spirit (get my needs met) while meeting my office and home responsibilities."* In many respects, this issue or problem statement actually articulates the wall that Gina wants to go over. The results of Gina's and David's further Consultation on this issue can be found in Chapter 14 (see section title, "The Example of Gina & David Continued"), and a structure for compassionately unfolding feelings and going deeper as David demonstrated can also be found in Chapter 14 (see section title, "The Example of Dane & Ellen Revisited").

The Example of Maya—Using Self-Compassion to See the Obstacles & the Wall

When a person commits to growth-seeking, she or he commits to proactively searching for the walls that need to be scaled to grow spiritually, intellectually, and socially. Self-compassion is critically important in this process because without it we may find ourselves unable to identify the triggering obstacles or walls. Self-compassion enables us to honestly face our own shortcomings and weaknesses and begin the process of change.

The following example of Maya illustrates how self-compassion can be used to rapidly clarify both the sources of resistance and the opportunity for growth.

Maya is in a group at work that meets and confers regularly, and she finds herself having negative feelings toward a male member of the group. While the group at work follows a consensus decision-making process rather than a formal Compassionate Consultation process, Maya believes in the power and importance of Consultation combined with compassion and is working on developing the skills and attributes necessary to practice it. Even though the other group members seem to be unaware of her negative feelings about the male member of the group, Maya realizes that she is an invisible impediment to the work group's decision process because she does not feel accepting of one of the group members. In fact, she feels no compassion for him. She cannot hear what he says from an objective perspective, and she is not able to give the same consideration to his contributions as she gives to those of others.

Using the growth-seeking perspective, Maya recognizes that this co-worker may be serving as a trigger for growth in her life. She also realizes that where there is resistance, it may be related to a wall she needs to scale. She does some compassionate and honest introspection about what is preventing her from being accepting and non-judgmental toward her co-worker; she discovers that the thing that troubles her about him is that he speaks to her in a condescending tone of voice. Because of this, it seems to Maya that he does not respect or value her as a person or a professional. She acknowledges to herself that she feels angry and that under the anger is the core hurt of feeling devalued by this co-worker. As she experiences self-compassion, she notices a softening in her feeling toward the co-worker and a sense of compassion for him as a spiritual being struggling through his own human experience.

From this compassionate space, Maya can see clearly that this co-worker with his condescending tone of voice is a triggering obstruction for her. She then asks herself, *what is the wall that I need to scale and go over?* Because Maya is in a space of compassion for self and others, her true self is already engaged. She turns to God and asks for assistance to understand what she needs to work on to grow as a spiritual being. After being meditatively and compassionately present with these questions for a few minutes, she recognizes that what her co-worker threatens is her self-worth. His tone of voice, her angry reaction to it, and the hurt she experiences are all calling her attention to her fragile sense of self-worth. She realizes that the wall she needs to go over is to develop her sense of self-worth to the point that it will not be subject to the approval of others.

Maya's next step would be to use the Consultation process with a trusted friend or by herself to determine what to do with this new awareness and how to scale the wall she has identified.

Emotions Are Clues to Triggering Obstructions That Are Clues to Walls

The process of Maya's growth began with her recognition that she was not able to be accepting of her co-worker's ideas because she had a negative feeling toward him. This bothered her because her apparent inability to listen to him in a non-judgmental way prevented her from using her emerging Consultation skills to help her work group become more effective. Rather than simply blaming the co-worker, Maya was willing to see him as a triggering obstruction and *look at herself first* as the one who needed to change. This is a growth-seeking attitude. Another growth-seeking attribute she demonstrated was the ability to use self-compassion to look at feelings she was not proud of and follow those feelings back to discover a wall. Clearly, Maya had a choice to make about whether she would work alone on the issues she had with her co-worker, or whether she also wanted to be a triggering obstruction to him, bring his condescending tone to his attention, and try to work with him on joint growth.

Emotions or feelings are the growth-seeker's clues to triggering obstructions that, in turn, are clues to walls. Self-compassion enables our true self to look *objectively* at feelings we have and with which we are not happy, as Maya did. In this way, feelings can act as guides to help us go deeper, discover attitudes and beliefs that are not working for us or that we are not honoring, and make life decisions that will move us toward fulfillment of the purposes of life. However, if *the emotions have us* (rather than *us having the emotions*) and we are not able to muster self-compassion to understand them, our emotions will confuse us rather than guide us.

Disowning Emotions—Breaking Patterns Through Self-Compassion

Our life experiences may not have taught us how to use our emotions and feelings as guides to making good decisions. It is common to disown emotions and feelings—to not acknowledge that we even have them. In fact, we may not be conscious that we have them.

The Example of John—Recognizing Constriction of Feelings

We may have been socialized in our family of origin to act in ways that undermine our self-awareness, leaving us emotionally handicapped. Let's look at the case of John. One of the "truths" he learned in his family of origin was that only certain emotions are "acceptable" and that even for these "acceptable" emotions there is an "appropriate" range which you "shouldn't" exceed. His family taught him that anger was the one emotion that was appropriate for boys and men to show. His parents would criticize him for getting excited and happy about his success in sports or his excellent grades, because they believed that "pride goes before the fall" and "the axe will soon fall." This restricted his joy. After repeatedly having his spontaneous emotions blunted, the pattern was set for a lifetime of restricted feelings. As John started to work on owning his emotions, he said he felt as if he had a "strait-jacket" on his feelings. He had a hard time determining how important something was to him or how much something meant to him because he had learned to not trust his feelings. As a child, when he did express his feelings, his parents would often say they were not the "right" feelings to have (i.e., "You shouldn't feel sad," "You're not hurt," and "Only sissies feel like that," etc.).

When a child's affective expression is stifled as was John's, the internal experience of knowing what you want or need is also stifled, which inhibits the progress that can come from *knowing* what you want and need, using *volition* to set a goal, and taking *action* to achieve it (as in the K + V + A change model referred to in Chapter 3). The stifling of affective expression also limited John's ability to make choices. For example, later in life when he was trying to decide between two jobs, he did not have access to the range of his feelings that would enable him to choose the job that would bring him the most satisfaction and fulfillment. He would wonder whether he had the "right" feelings or whether he "should" be feeling something different. The one feeling he always had access to was anger (which was alright for boys to express according to his family's rules). Consequently, he found himself expressing anger, even in situations that might elicit only irritation, disappointment, or frustration in other people. However, although the other emotions were outside of his conscious awareness, he still carried them inside.

Gradually, through consistent practice in the application of self-compassion, John was able to overcome the constriction of his feelings, gain access to a fuller range of emotions, and use them as guides to better understand himself and navigate growth.

The Example of Kendra—Stifled Emotions Pop Up Unexpectedly

Emotions that are outside of our conscious awareness can get us into trouble because they influence how we perceive things and how we react even though we are not aware of those emotions. The example of Kendra illustrates how this works.

Kendra had an encounter with a salesperson early in the day who was condescending, rude, and sarcastic toward her. While at the moment she was uncomfortably aware that her face was turning red and that she felt embarrassed and angry, she just took a deep breath and walked away. Kendra had learned to avoid conflict, so she tried not to be upset, which is often referred to as "stuffing" feelings. She distracted herself by calling a friend in the hope that just hearing a friendly voice and talking about plans for the weekend would make the uncomfortable feelings go away. Although this did make her feel better for the moment, the anger, embarrassment, and hurt she had experienced earlier were not gone forever. The energy of these feelings was stuffed inside her only to surface later in the day, at a time and with a magnitude that the situation at hand did not warrant.

That afternoon was a normal afternoon in terms of job stress, but Kendra found herself feeling irritated and resentful, and, as a result, she acted short-tempered toward some of her co-workers. Two of them criticized Kendra for having a bad attitude, which surprised Kendra because she thought everything at work was going well. In reality, even though the resentment and hurt Kendra carried inside from feeling devalued and shamed earlier in the day were out of her conscious awareness, they were still affecting her mood and behavior. If Kendra had paid attention to, and compassionately processed, the feelings she was experiencing during or shortly after the rude encounter with the salesperson, she could have dealt with them then. The healthy thing to do is to put your feelings where they belong—with the original incident. When you do this you are more likely to see the triggering obstruction and wall patterns that can help you make new choices and accelerate your growth.

For Kendra, processing the feelings as they occurred could have involved any number of options including telling the salesperson that her attitude was inappropriate and uncalled for, talking to a friend about how she was feeling, or deciding not to take the bad attitude of the sales clerk personally—that is, interpreting the rude behavior as an indication the salesperson was having a bad day.

Seeing and Using Emotions for What They Are

Emotions are not good or bad—they are simply pieces of information that let you know about your interpretation of a situation. If you have been ignoring your emotions for a long time, you might begin by compassionately observing what is happening in your body ("my neck and shoulders are tight"), what you are thinking ("I can't handle this"), and what you are feeling ("I am feeling a surge of anger"). When you become aware of these sensations, thoughts, and feelings, you are in a position to pose the growth-seeking questions of "What are the triggering obstructions?" and "What is the wall I need to scale?"

Dealing with your emotions in this compassionate, intentional way empowers you because it is your true self that is in control of your attitude, mood, or emotion. It will be hard for someone to "push your buttons" when you condition yourself to respond with compassionate intention rather than reacting without thought. You end up *having the emotions* rather than *the emotions having you*. When you regulate your emotions in this way and make discoveries by using them as guides, self-esteem increases.

This inner work is not easy, and while it may be accomplished working alone, many people may benefit from working with a trusted friend, coach, or counselor. However the work is accomplished, it is a key element of walking the path of a growth-seeker, and it is liberating. With self-compassion we are able to look at what we have experienced—no matter how painful or uncomfortable; to understand how it has impacted us; to validate our feelings; and decide what changes we can make to improve ourselves and our situation.

Without self-compassion, much of what we feel may stay hidden from our conscious awareness. Aspects of our lower nature may try to distract us, immobilize us with guilt, or put blame on others in order to avoid being overwhelmed by painful feelings. In fact, the internal conflict we create through our resistance to painful, vulnerable, and uncomfortable feelings is what causes much of our struggle in life. Trying to escape these feelings is often the underlying reason for mood altering addictions such as drugs, alcohol, shopping, food, sex, compulsive work, or gambling.

By becoming compassionately aware of all of our feelings and accepting them, our energy can move freely. When we accept and integrate all that we are, we become whole. This does not mean that we *act* on all of our feelings. It simply means that we are open to the experience of our feelings—that we are self-accepting. We then use this awareness to mindfully walk the growth-seeking path and make changes where we find unhealthy, destructive currents that contradict our beliefs, values, purposes, and growth goals.

The Example of Carlos—Feelings Are the Main Clues to What We Are Thinking

Some people are more in touch with their feelings than their thoughts. However, since feelings arise from thoughts, feelings are the clues to what we are thinking. To make constructive, healthy changes it is necessary to become aware of our habitual self-defeating, self-sabotaging, or irrational thoughts.

Let's look at an example. Carlos became aware that he was feeling anxious and angry, but he was not sure why. He thought back over his day and remembered that he was feeling calm until after he had lunch with a co-worker. During the lunch, the co-worker had mentioned that he and their boss had ordered Chinese food the night before when the two of them were working late on a project. Carlos realized that he had felt anxious and angry toward the co-worker after that. He had begun worrying about whether the co-worker would get a promotion and maybe even get his (Carlos') job because the boss probably liked the co-worker better.

Carlos applied self-compassion and focused on the triggering exchange with his co-worker to identify the hidden thought inside of him that had generated the anxiety and anger. He realized that the thought was, "If you are not constantly currying favor with people in authority, they will turn against you." He was startled to discover this thought in his mind but simultaneously and intuitively sensed that this thought ran through his mind regularly. Given his childhood experiences, Carlos could understand why he had this habitual thought/belief. He also realized how this thought could generate feelings and actions driven by self-protection, fear, anger, and competitiveness.

Still holding his compassionate perspective, Carlos decided to look at the facts to determine how likely it was that he needed to constantly curry favor with his boss to prevent the boss from turning against him. The facts were: 1) Carlos and the boss had worked late on many projects together; 2) the boss was consistently appreciative of Carlos' work; and 3) Carlos had a track record of being competent, reliable, and responsible. These facts indicated to Carlos that his fear and anger were unfounded.

As a result, Carlos realized that his co-worker had been a triggering obstruction and that the feelings that emerged within himself as a result of the co-worker's comments during lunch had enabled Carlos to identify a wall—an habitual thought/belief that was limiting him and preventing him from seeing things clearly. This belief had been with Carlos for many years; it triggered habitual thoughts and feelings that put him in a negative mindset, and it inhibited his spiritual growth. It was a wall that Carlos committed to scaling.

The Example of Bob—Defensive Thoughts Can Hide Primary Thoughts

We all want to think well of ourselves, and this is constructive unless it prevents us from looking at aspects of ourselves that need improvement. Clearly, we cannot work on improvement if we do not recognize a weakness. Sometimes, we may be blind to a weakness because we have adopted defensive thoughts, feelings, and behaviors in order to mask a primary thought or belief we do not want to face.

Let's look at an example to clarify this point. Bob habitually kept his schedule so full that he was constantly busy. As a result, he did not have adequate time to study and work on papers for his college courses until the last minute, and he would end up receiving low grades. After becoming a growth-seeker, Bob resolved to improve his grade point average (GPA). After applying self-compassion, he reasoned that the solution was to drop some activities so he would have more time to study and work on his papers. Consequently, he cleared his calendar. However, time went by, and he still was not studying and working on the papers more. What was going on? Bob began to suspect that he had not penetrated deeply enough to identify the underlying problem. By applying self-compassion again, he started to recognize that keeping himself busy was a defensive behavior he had adopted to give himself an acceptable reason for not doing well in his studies. He became aware that he must have some *primary underlying thought or belief* that was creating insecurity and fear around not doing well in school.

Bob continued to use self-compassion in an effort to determine the primary reason for his procrastination. As he listened and noticed in order to become increasingly familiar with his habitual self-talk, he discovered a critical internal voice that said, "I am stupid. I'm not smart enough to get good grades." He immediately recognized that it had been less painful and shameful for him to believe he did not do well in school because his numerous responsibilities prevented him from having adequate study time than to believe he did not do well because he was not smart enough. Bob realized that this thought and belief pattern, uncomfortable or painful as it might be, had to be dealt with in order to improve his GPA. This thought pattern was preventing him from achieving his goals, and it had been operating *behind* his defensive thoughts.

Compassionately Identifying and Rationally Countering Blanket Beliefs

Blanket thoughts and beliefs such as "I am stupid" are irrational and can be countered with rational statements. Bob approached his situation from several different angles. First, he came from his true self and recalled occasions when he was labeled "stupid" by a parent, a sibling, or a classmate (i.e., when he got mud on the carpet, dropped his books in a puddle getting off the school bus, etc.). He focused on the situations he remembered and analyzed them to see whether his behavior merited the label "stupid." Bob realized that in no case was that label accurate, but he had internalized it as truth. He discovered that he had developed an inner critic that called him "stupid" whenever he made a mistake or had an accident. This internal voice and his defensive behavior surrounding it had kept him recycling through the same ineffective behavioral patterns for years. Bob concluded that this internal voice was so persistent in his internal thoughts that, if left alone, it could become a life-long internal obstacle to growth.

As a growth-seeker, he committed to becoming consciously aware of it, looking at it compassionately and rationally, and replacing it with positive self-talk.

Bob made several changes in order to go over the wall that was hindering him from doing his best in school. If he caught himself silently calling himself "stupid" when he made a mistake, he talked back to that critical voice saying, "I am intelligent. It was only a mistake and everyone makes mistakes," or "I'm smart, and I wasn't thinking clearly at that moment." Secondly, Bob recalled times that he had received good grades. He determined that what he had done differently on those occasions was to spend more time studying and preparing. So, he studied and prepared longer in order to raise his GPA. Third, he made a list of things he was proud of accomplishing in his life and his personal qualities and attributes that contributed to those achievements. By consciously focusing more on these positive accomplishments and attributes, his self-esteem improved. As a result of these changes, not only did he do better on his college papers, but he made strides in other areas of his life as well.

Habitual Thoughts Behind Limiting Feelings & Behaviors Can Be Elusive

As the experiences of Bob and Carlos indicate, discovering the habitual thoughts and beliefs behind limiting feelings and behaviors is seldom easy. In fact, most of our self-talk is unconscious, and even if we make the effort to become aware of it, we may avoid probing deeper for fear that we will discover something truly negative about ourselves. We may fear that the motive behind some of our behavior could be ignoble, that we could be embarrassed if anyone knew this thing about us, or that our sense of self-worth could be undermined if we acknowledged our shortcomings.

However, growth-seekers develop the courage to examine negative self-talk and determine if there is any validity to it. If there is some validity, they develop virtues to overcome it. If there is no validity, they replace it with *affirmative* self-talk. Bahá'u'lláh says, "… man should know his own self and recognize that which leadeth unto loftiness or lowliness, glory or abasement, wealth or poverty."[80] The quality that allows one to do this is self-compassion.

Chapter 7

Creating the Compassionate Consultation Atmosphere

Before we look more closely at possible procedural *steps* for Compassionate Consultation in Chapter 10, we will examine in this and the next chapter *what compassion looks like behaviorally* during the steps of Consultation and in the diverse contexts in which Consultation can be used. Because Consultation is a transformative decision-making resource designed for the building and operation of a new, spiritually-centered world civilization, these diverse contexts include the self, marriage, the family, the neighborhood, the community, work groups, businesses, institutions, and government bodies. Required compassionate behavioral standards are the same for all these contexts.

Compassion Is a "Mother" Word

The Writings of Bahá'u'lláh, 'Abdu'l-Bahá, and Shoghi Effendi offer abundant detail describing the behavioral qualities that must inform those who strive to practice Compassionate Consultation. When Bahá'u'lláh says, "The heaven of divine wisdom is illumined with the two luminaries of consultation and compassion,"[81] compassion is a "mother" word[82] in the sense that it gives birth to a prolific offspring of behavioral virtues and attributes required for Compassionate Consultation practitioners. When combined with the *procedure* of Consultation, these behavioral virtues and attributes create a compassionate climate or *atmosphere* of interaction in which things conducive to finding deeper understanding, wise solutions, and unity flourish, while unconducive things disappear. In addition, these behavioral virtues and attributes create the *group culture* that must under-gird the steps of Consultation.

The 7 Prime Requisites

A distilled and comprehensive statement of the qualities group members should have to most effectively combine Consultation and compassion can be found in the following statement made by 'Abdu'l-Bahá:

> The prime requisites for them that take counsel together are purity of motive, radiance of spirit, detachment from all else save God, attraction to His Divine Fragrances, humility and lowliness amongst His loved ones, patience and long-suffering in difficulties and servitude to His exalted Threshold. Should they be graciously aided to acquire these attributes, victory from the unseen Kingdom of Bahá [Glory] shall be vouchsafed to them.[83]

A requisite is a requirement—that is, something that is necessary or essential to the occurrence or existence of something else. The following requisites are therefore necessary or essential to the occurrence or existence of true Consultation or Compassionate Consultation in any deliberative setting:

The 7 Prime Requisites

1. Purity of motive
2. Radiance of spirit
3. Detachment from all else save God
4. Attraction to His divine fragrances
5. Humility and lowliness amongst His loved ones
6. Patience and long-suffering in difficulties
7. Servitude to His exalted Threshold

The 7 Prime Requisites as Spiritual Attributes

The 7 Prime Requisites that need to be "acquired" by those who would Consult are clearly very lofty, refined, and highly challenging *spiritual* attributes. Indeed, the Universal House of Justice[84] refers to the need to "develop skill in the difficult but highly rewarding art of Bahá'í consultation" and indicates that it is "a process which will require great self-discipline…" as well as reliance on God.[85] Consequently, for most people who combine Consultation with compassion, the 7 Prime Requisites represent both a *current vision* of what they seek to manifest in any given session of Compassionate Consultation and a highly refined *future vision* of what they aspire to manifest more fully in the future after they have sought and gone over additional walls of personal development. We are capitalizing the words "Prime Requisites" to refer to these qualities prescribed by 'Abdu'l-Bahá.

The 7 Prime Requisites & 12 Behavioral Standards

From the guidance of Bahá'u'lláh, 'Abdu'l-Bahá, and Shoghi Effendi, we have identified an additional twelve Behavioral Standards which contribute to the effective practice of Consultation. One can think of these 12 Behavioral Standards as stepping-stones on the path to fully embodying the 7 Prime Requisites. We are capitalizing the words "Behavioral Standards" to refer to the attitudes and actions we have identified from various other passages in the Bahá'í Writings which we believe contribute to the achievement of the 7 Prime Requisites identified by 'Abdu'l-Bahá. Figure 7.1 describes the concept for these relationships.

In the left-hand column are the 12 Behavioral Standards to be honored in order to create a climate and culture conducive to Compassionate Consultation. Consistent application of these Behavioral Standards can contribute to the members' acquisition of the 7 Prime Requisites as spiritual attributes. *In the listing below, no specific correlation is intended between the same numbered items in the two columns.*

The Compassionate Consultation Behavioral Standards that Lead to Embodying the Prime Requisites	The Prime Requisites of Compassionate Consultation
1. Having absolute love & harmony	1. Purity of motive
2. Praying collectively for divine assistance	2. Radiance of spirit
3. Honoring the inherent value of each member	3. Detachment from all else save God

4. Treasuring Diversity	4. Attraction to His divine fragrances
5. Seeing the group as an instrument for receiving divine guidance	5. Humility and lowliness amongst His loved ones
6. Arriving at a unanimous decision	6. Patience and long-suffering in difficulties
7. Having unity in implementing decisions	7. Servitude to His exalted threshold
8. Detaching one's ego from one's ideas	
9. Disagreeing dispassionately	
10. Having the attitude of an investigator of truth	
11. Using perfect liberty in expression within a context of courtesy, moderation & patience	
12. Praising others & thinking of oneself as evanescent	

Figure 7.1

The first six of the 12 Behavioral Standards will be explored in this chapter in the context of creating the *atmosphere* for Compassionate Consultation; and the second six in the next chapter in the context of creating the *group culture* for Compassionate Consultation. In order to clarify and draw attention to the developmental relationships between the 12 Behavioral Standards and the 7 Prime Requisites, references to the Prime Requisites will be in ***bold italics***. The description of each Behavioral Standard begins with a growth-seeker situation that illustrates the need for the Standard.

Compassionate Consultation Behavioral Standard #1:

Having Absolute Love & Harmony

Growth-Seeker Situation: Ralph notices that he always sits next to Jenna and Juan at staff meetings and realizes he does so because he feels comfortable with them and somewhat uncomfortable with, and alienated from, the other members of the group.

Compassionate Consultation Resource Needed: A deepened understanding of Behavioral Standard #1 and commitment to addressing the barriers to honoring it.

The First of the Two Essential Requirements

The first of the two essential requirements specified by 'Abdu'l-Bahá for successful Consultation is contained in the following quote:

> The first condition is absolute love and harmony amongst the members of the assembly. They must be wholly free from estrangement and must manifest in themselves the Unity of God, for they are the waves of one sea, the drops of one river, the stars of one heaven, the rays of one sun, the trees of one orchard, the flowers of one garden.[86]

Absolute Love & Harmony

Having absolute love and harmony is a tall order. Striving to attain it requires that we scale the walls that limit our ability to experience absolute love and harmony toward each other. It requires that we learn to see the other members as parts of a diverse family in which estrangement and coolness have been banished by the vitalizing presence of love. This kind of love would need to spring from *purity of motive* and *radiance of spirit* (Prime Requisites numbers 1 and 2) or it could not be one that is "wholly free from estrangement." Such love and harmony would need to arise from loving the members for the sake of God and feeling "*attraction to His divine fragrances*" (Prime Requisite #4). 'Abdu'l-Bahá tells us:

> Be in perfect unity. Never become angry with one another. Let your eyes be directed toward the kingdom of truth and not toward the world of creation. Love the creatures for the sake of God and not for themselves. You will never become angry or impatient if you love them for the sake of God. Humanity is not perfect. There

are imperfections in every human being, and you will always become unhappy if you look toward the people themselves. But if you look toward God, you will love them and be kind to them, for the world of God is the world of perfection and complete mercy. Therefore, do not look at the shortcomings of anybody; see with the sight of forgiveness. The imperfect eye beholds imperfections. The eye that covers faults looks toward the Creator of souls. He created them, trains and provides for them, endows them with capacity and life, sight and hearing; therefore, they are the signs of His grandeur.[87]

Explanatory Images

Phrases 'Abdu'l-Bahá uses to describe the first essential requirement such as "absolute love and harmony" and "manifesting in themselves the unity of God" may at first seem impossible to fully comprehend. The limits of language start to be felt. What would it look like for a group to have these attributes, and how would such a group function? 'Abdu'l-Bahá uses metaphors to answer these questions. He says the Consulting members need to be:

> ...the waves of one sea, the drops of one river, the stars of one heaven, the rays of one sun, the trees of one orchard, the flowers of one garden.[88]

In all of these images individual differentiation exists, but it is merged into a larger unity and harmony; the parts exist, but they are *being* or *moving as one*. Like the complex but coordinated flocking patterns of birds, or the shoaling patterns of a school of fish gliding and turning as one through the ocean currents, potentially separate elements move collaboratively in response to a larger unity and purpose.

The Promise of Unlimited Results & Divine Bestowals

One functional benefit of absolute love and harmony as a requirement for Compassionate Consultation is that it releases the power and potential of the group. 'Abdu'l-Bahá says:

> The unity which is productive of *unlimited results* is first a unity of mankind which recognizes that all are shel-

tered beneath the overshadowing glory of the All-Glorious; that all are servants of one God; for all breathe the same atmosphere, live upon the same earth, move beneath the same heavens, receive effulgence from the same sun and are under the protection of one God. This is the most great unity, and its results are lasting if humanity adheres to it…[89] (emphasis added)

This deep definition of unity combined with Behavioral Standard #1 defines a new paradigm. "Absolute love and harmony," a sense of absolute unity among the Consulting members, *makes possible results that are unlimited*. For some, the use of the term "absolute" in the articulation of this Behavioral Standard may make it seem impossible to accomplish. It helps to think of it on a continuum so that, as a group grows in its sense of unity, as it progresses toward "absolute love and harmony," the results it is capable of achieving become less and less limited.

Another functional benefit of absolute love and harmony among the Consulting members is that it is conducive to receiving divine assistance. Speaking to a group about the conditions for receiving divine assistance, 'Abdu'l-Bahá said:

There is no discord here; all is love and unity. When souls are gathered together in this way, the divine bestowals descend.… When the souls become separated and selfish, the divine bounties do not descend, and the lights of the Supreme Concourse are no longer reflected even though the bodies meet together. A mirror with its back turned to the sun has no power to reflect the sun's effulgence.[90]

It appears that both unlimited results and divine assistance are made possible by absolute love, harmony, and unity among the members.

The Condition for Good Results

That 'Abdu'l-Bahá calls absolute love and harmony a "first condition" in order to Consult effectively is significant. A condition is something that must be present for success. When 'Abdu'l-Bahá says elsewhere that, "The first duty of the members is to effect their own unity and harmony in order to obtain good results,"[91] it suggests that if something is blocking unity and harmony, the Consulting members need to address and resolve the block before dealing with other issues, "...in order to obtain good results." 'Abdu'l-Bahá instructed members of Bahá'í assemblies to postpone or take time out from the discussion of issues that are generating destructive conflict:

> **The honored members of the Spiritual Assembly should exert their efforts so that no differences may occur, and if such differences do occur, they should not reach the point of causing conflict, hatred and antagonism, which lead to threats. When you notice that a stage has been reached when enmity and threats are about to occur, you should immediately postpone discussions of the subject, until wranglings, disputations, and loud talk vanish, and a propitious time is at hand.[92]**

Anything that creates separation and disintegration is counter-productive. This does not mean that difficult, highly controversial issues must be avoided. The key is not *what* is discussed, but *how* it is discussed. Therefore, the important work of removing divisive blocks of hearts and minds must be attended to. And compassion is the attribute that each person must call on to address these problems. As 'Abdu'l-Bahá says:

> **Therefore true consultation is spiritual conference in the attitude and atmosphere of love. Members must love each other in the spirit of fellowship in order that good results may be forthcoming. Love and fellowship are the foundation.[93]**

Compassionate Consultation Behavioral Standard #2:

Praying Collectively For Divine Assistance

Growth-Seeker Situation: Jack, Karen, and their three adolescent children have begun having Compassionate Consultation family meetings once per week to address family issues, make plans for the future, and make sure family tasks are getting done satisfactorily. While everyone has been willingly attending the meetings so far, every issue seems to be met with five different and irreconcilable opinions. The family is gridlocked, with each person becoming more and more attached to his or her preference.

Compassionate Consultation Resource Needed: An increased honoring of Behavioral Standard #2 by focusing more on praying for assistance together at the start, or in the midst, of meetings.

The Second of the Two Essential Requirements

'Abdu'l-Bahá also specifies the second of the two essential requirements for Consultation:

> **They must, when coming together, turn their faces to the Kingdom on High and ask aid from the Realm of Glory.**[94]

This injunction is the basis for the first step of the "6-Step Consultation Model" which specifies collective prayer as a prerequisite step for entering into Compassionate Consultation. The quote does not say, "Each member should pray before starting to Consult." It says, "They must, when coming together, turn their faces to the Kingdom on High and ask aid from the Realm of Glory." There is a value placed on the Consulting members praying *together* to God for aid, assistance, and guidance.

Opening the Door to Divine Love, Guidance & Assistance

The Holy Writings tell us that God will assist us if we ask Him. As referred to earlier, Bahá'u'lláh says, "Love Me, that I may love thee. If thou lovest Me not, My love can in no wise reach thee."[95] Clearly, divine assistance is always readily available to us, but we must open the door and invite it in. Consequently, the members entering into Compassionate Consultation must collectively request divine assistance in order for it to flow to and through them. This is an act of humility that prepares their hearts and minds to be open to divine assistance and to the other members' thoughts and feelings which may represent that assistance. This contributes to their ability to manifest the Prime Requisite of ***humility and lowliness amongst His loved ones***.

Ideas as Tokens of Divine Assistance

Because the members have consciously and collectively sought to open this divine assistance channel, each thought shared during Compassionate Consultation has the potential to be a token of divine assistance and deserves careful, even reverential, scrutiny. Keeping this in mind provides the incentive for members to intensify their listening to and reflection on all the ideas expressed.

Aligning the Members in Relationship with Their Maker

Turning to God in prayer has the effect of *aligning* both the individual members and the Consulting group in the proper relationship with their Maker. Not unlike a chiropractic adjustment at the physical level, sincere prayer tends to put everything in its proper place on the spiritual, psychological, and intellectual levels. The act of prayer, and the accompanying request for assistance, demonstrates the members' individual and joint recognition that they are the created ones bowing in humble servitude before the single, almighty Creator. This act calls forth each member's true self, which, by its very nature, submits and resonates to the influence of its Maker. Clearly, the act of prayer contributes to our ability to manifest the Prime Requisites of **attraction to His divine fragrances** and **servitude to His exalted threshold**.

While the act of collective prayer to God is an acknowledgement of the limiting boundaries implicit in being human, it also optimizes the members' abilities to be creative and inspired within those boundaries. Prayer calls forth our highest powers for use in addressing whatever issue is at hand. 'Abdu'l-Bahá says:

> Prayer...creates spirituality, creates mindfulness and celestial feelings, begets new attractions of the Kingdom and engenders the susceptibilities of the higher intelligence.[96]

Seeing Each Other as if in the Presence of God

Collective prayer generates feelings of reverence toward the Compassionate Consultation process. 'Abdu'l-Bahá encourages members to, "...see each other as if in the presence of God."[97] Approaching the Consultation process in this manner helps evoke all of the Prime Requisites: ***purity of motive, radiance of spirit, detachment from all else save God, attraction to His divine fragrances, humility and lowliness amongst His loved ones, patience and long-suffering in difficulties***, and ***servitude to His exalted threshold***.

A Release from Cares & Burdens

Collectively turning to God in prayer also helps release the Consulting members from any preoccupation with worldly cares and burdens—whether they be cares in their personal lives, partisan political impulses, or entanglements with vested interests—so that they can focus equitably on the present task. Just as warm sunlight can unburden evergreen branches weighed down with heavy winter snow, turning to God in prayer and humbly asking for assistance can lighten the load of the Consulting members so that they can open to, and concentrate on, the work of combining Consultation and compassion.

Compassionate Consultation Behavioral Standard #3:

Honoring the Inherent Value of Each Member

Growth-Seeker Situation: Alicia and Bob admire Jamal because he is so articulate and seems very self-confident. Consequently, they give his opinions more weight than those of others in the group.

Compassionate Consultation Resource Needed: An increased emphasis on, and monitoring of, Behavioral Standard #3: Honoring the inherent value of each member.

Fundamentally, "honoring the inherent value of each member" requires that each member be treated with dignity and respect. Protecting human dignity is essential to any successful human interaction and Compassionate Consultation is no exception. However, even when treating others with dignity and respect outwardly, it is still common to attribute more value to some members than to others. Biases based on such things as educational level, gender, rank, race, age, ethnicity, and personality create filters that affect how much or how little credence we give to others' ideas.

The Poison of Status & Preference Filters

Bias is poison to Compassionate Consultation. This is true for at least two reasons. First, discriminating between members based on our perception of their inherent value is an ego-based practice based on seeing the human family as essentially separate rather than as one. Bahá'u'lláh has proclaimed the oneness of humankind. He states:

> Ye are the fruits of one tree, and the leaves of one branch. Deal ye one with another with the utmost love and harmony, with friendliness and fellowship. He Who is the Day Star of Truth beareth Me witness! So powerful is the light of unity that it can illuminate the whole earth.[98]

Because the bias inherent in using status and preference filters places us in opposition to the spiritual principle of the essential oneness of humankind, it blocks the reception of divine bounties and assistance. Secondly, because we never know through which group member divine assistance may come, if we are listening selectively based on our value filters, we may miss the comments that carry guidance. Alternatively, comments that would carry divine assistance may never get voiced because bias is felt, and it does not feel safe or welcoming to speak up. Commenting on the impossibility of anticipating through which group member divine assistance will come, Shoghi Effendi says:

> Not infrequently, nay oftentimes, the most lowly, untutored and inexperienced among the friends will, by the sheer inspiring force of selfless and ardent devotion, contribute a distinct and memorable share to a highly involved discussion in any given Assembly.[99]

Check Your Status at the Door

In organizational settings where different levels of authority exist, group members are often accustomed to hearing each other at an intensity multiplier of one and the boss or leader at an intensity multiplier of ten. Whereas this can work adequately using the command decision-making method, it is anathema to Compassionate Consultation. To work effectively, each Consulting member must hear *each other member* at an intensity multiplier of ten regardless of their rank or position in the organization. To achieve Compassionate Consultation, the inherent value of each member must be vigilantly honored. Consequently, just as in the frontier days of the old American West where the rule was "Check your gun at the door," so here the operating principle must be "Check your status at the door."

Overcoming Issues of Personality Style, Self-Image and Self-Worth

Honoring the inherent value of each member also means that the group—whether a couple, family, professional, or community group—flexes toward the various communication styles of its members and maintains an atmosphere of interpersonal inclusion, encouragement, acceptance, and safety. For example, group members who are introverted (as measured in the Myers Briggs Type Indicator®)—preferring to process their ideas internally before they speak—may need more time to formulate their ideas and find it difficult to jump in because the conversation flow is so fast that the issue they want to address has already passed. In such cases, members who are extroverted (as measured in the MBTI®)—preferring to jump in and process their ideas out loud—may need to talk less and/or slow the discussion down. As another example, less confident members may be inclined to edit or stifle their ideas for fear of being judged, and other members may need to invite and encourage their participation. In both examples, the group risks being deprived of perspectives that could be pivotal to the Consultative discussion at hand. Honoring Behavioral Standard #3 means, on the one hand, that sensitive and persistent accommodation to other members is habitual. On the other hand, it also means that *each person feels habitually duty-bound to honor and contribute her or his own ideas and perspectives* to the Consultation process.

How Honoring Manifests Itself

Honoring the inherent value of each member means first that we identify any limiting preconceptions we have about another member, recognize that we have a personal wall to scale, and then scale it. It also means that we proactively notice when someone is not being treated with respect and compassionately correct the situation. For example, when a member notices that someone has been interrupted it would be appropriate to say, "I believe we may have cut off Maria before she was finished, and I want to hear what she was going to say." Or, when someone has been silent during an extended discussion, another member could check in with that member saying, "We have not yet heard from Adib in this discussion, and I would like to hear his thoughts."

Honoring this Behavioral Standard creates an atmosphere in which all members feel valued because every idea is attentively heard and given genuine consideration by all the other members. Clearly, there also needs to be an absence of prejudicial or undercutting comments and body language as ideas come forth. Each person's thoughts and ideas need to get an equally open-minded initial hearing. Only after that are the ideas dealt with on the basis of their relevance and usefulness to the issue at hand.

Ultimately, honoring the inherent value of each member ensures the full and open *interpenetration* of ideas that is required to move the group members—individually and collectively—to the walls that must be scaled in order to discover deeper understanding, breakthrough ideas, and the wise path forward.

When group members honor Behavioral Standard #3 with integrity, they facilitate their ability to manifest the Prime Requisites of ***humility and lowliness amongst His loved ones, patience and long-suffering in difficulties***, and ***servitude to His exalted threshold***.

Compassionate Consultation Behavioral Standard #4:

Treasuring Diversity

Growth-Seeker Situation: Janine's way of looking at things is different from the way Sabra sees things. Instead of asking Sabra to explain her views until she understands them, Janine has gotten into the habit of just not listening intently when Sabra speaks.

Compassionate Consultation Resource Needed: An increased emphasis on Behavioral Standard #4, treasuring diversity, demonstrated by intensified curiosity and listening.

The world has evolved from a place where people could easily avoid encountering diversity to one where people are unavoidably confronted with diversity every day. This can be a challenge, but the advancement of human society increasingly requires that we acknowledge, and not just tolerate, but value diversity. Individuals and groups that want to make use of Compassionate Consultation must evolve still further to the point that they *treasure* diversity.

Pragmatic Factors

Beyond the moral and ethical dimensions of *valuing* diversity, there is a very pragmatic reason for group members using Compassionate Consultation to *treasure* diversity. The greater the diversity of genders, races, ethnicities, personalities, ages, personal histories, and backgrounds that exist among the Consulting members, the wider the range of knowledge bases, life experiences, vantage points, and resources that can be drawn upon by the group to reach solutions, decisions, and outcomes that are innovative and transformative.

Without such diversity, conferring members can easily miss critical issues and overlook possible options, pitfalls, and innovations. When members are homogeneous, their decisions are more vulnerable to being "blind-sided" further down the road by circumstances they did not anticipate due to the limited perspective and experience bank provided by the group members. This is true whether the term "members" refers to a government body, a community, an organizational group, a couple, a family, or even the different internal aspects of an individual.

In addition, by engaging and embracing the full range and diversity of the human resources in any given group, we increase the trust in, and mutual commitment to, the plan of action resulting from the deliberations.

Impatience as an Indicator

Until group members are skilled in Compassionate Consultation, the presence of diversity will invariably slow things down as people struggle to understand and accept perspectives, approaches, and styles different from their own. Most of us will discover our own challenges with diversity through feelings of impatience with others—impatience with member A's failure to get to the point, member B's tendency to be emotional, or member C's reliance on life experience rather than formal research. When impatience manifests itself as a voice in our head that says, "This isn't the proper way to approach things," the growth-seeker in each of us must respond with, "This may be an opportunity for me to scale a wall toward personal growth."

Growth could be encouraged by asking oneself, "What kind of diversity am I having trouble treasuring right now?" This kind of honest, searching question generates new insights and opportunities for personal and relationship growth. Through it we may discover that the member we *least want* to hear from is precisely the one we *most need* to hear from to gain breakthrough insights, to grow personally, and to resolve the issue being addressed. It is issues such as these that call out for the use of the Prime Requisite of *patience and long-suffering in difficulties*.

Treasuring Diversity by Embracing the Oneness of Humankind

Because *patience and long-suffering in difficulties* is most challenging when very different perspectives are present, it helps when all members acknowledge and embrace the oneness of humankind. The goal is to *treasure* diversity by seeing and welcoming each perspective as one aspect of a single whole rather than as something alien. Bahá'u'lláh states that in this era it is God's intent to establish this sense of oneness:

> God hath verily purposed to bring the hearts of men together, though it require every means on earth and in the heavens.[100]

Compassionate Consultation can be one of the means to accomplish this end if we commit to treasuring diversity. 'Abdu'l-Bahá describes how intense our commitment must be:

> It is incumbent upon everyone to show the utmost love, rectitude of conduct, straightforwardness and sincere kindliness unto all the peoples and kindreds of the world, be they friends or strangers. So intense must be the spirit of love and loving-kindness, that the stranger may find himself a friend, the enemy a true brother, no difference whatsoever existing between them. For universality is of God and all limitations earthly. Thus man must strive that his reality may manifest virtues and perfections, the light whereof may shine upon everyone. The light of the sun shineth upon all the world and the merciful showers of Divine Providence fall upon

all peoples. The vivifying breeze reviveth every living creature and all beings endued with life obtain their share and portion at His heavenly board. In like manner, the affections and loving-kindness of the servants of the One True God must be bountifully and universally extended to all mankind. Regarding this, restrictions and limitations are in no wise permitted.[101]

Finding the Treasure in Diversity

When we treasure diversity during Compassionate Consultation, all kinds of diversity are embraced, relished, welcomed, invited to come forth, solicited, deferred to, waited upon, and supported. As a divergent perspective is expressed, it should be received by the other members with energetic attention and curiosity. It should be carefully entertained, examined, tried on, and reflected upon. In the same way that we will treasure the unique vision and experience of the first person to walk upon Mars, we must treasure the unique vision and life experience of *each* member in Compassionate Consultation. It is then that Consultation may give us "insight into things" and enable us "to delve into questions which are unknown."[102]

When the members of a group treasure diversity, the Consultative atmosphere created seems to *draw down* divine assistance, and *draw forth* the best in the diverse members to make their indispensable contributions to the process of Compassionate Consultation.

Compassionate Consultation Behavioral Standard #5:

Seeing the Group as an Instrument for Receiving Divine Guidance

Growth-Seeker Situation: David decides not to attend a committee meeting which he would normally attend as a member. While he considers the topic on the agenda important, he cannot see how anything edifying will come from it because he knows that the other people attending the meeting are not as knowledgeable about the topic as he is.

Compassionate Consultation Resource Needed: Internalization of Behavioral Standard #5 and the related research.

The Compassionate Consultation members' collective request for divine assistance (Behavioral Standard #2) finds its complement in Behavioral Standard #5 where the members must actually *see the group as an instrument* for receiving divine guidance in relation to the issue being addressed.

The 75/25 Rule & the Wisdom of Consensus Decision-Making Groups

To begin to explore Behavioral Standard #5 it is helpful to look at some of the research relating to group decision-making. Research shows that groups using *consensus* processes to make decisions and solve problems consistently and reliably outperform individuals making decisions (as in command decision-making). This is not true of groups that use majority rule or advisory decision-making processes even if they rely heavily on a gifted member.

Consensus decision-making involves the members of a group thoroughly discussing an issue and then agreeing on the wisest decision that every member of the group can live with. Our term "75/25 Rule" refers to the statistical results from the research demonstrating the superiority of group consensus decision-making over individual decision-making. This research is relevant to Compassionate Consultation because, while most forms of consensus decision-making are not Compassionate Consultation, Compassionate Consultation can be seen as a very refined, supercharged form of consensus decision-making.

The research demonstrating the 75/25 Rule[103] involves people in organizations and communities who were first asked to make decisions and solve problems individually so that the effectiveness and creativity of their decisions and solutions could be evaluated. Problems addressed in the research were the kinds of limited resource problems that we most often encounter in our daily personal and professional lives, such as how to accomplish an objective within certain time and/or financial constraints. The result of the evaluations of individual decision-making quality was a normal distribution of abilities (a bell-shaped curve) with some very competent individual decision-makers and problem-solvers at the high end, some much less competent at the low end, and the majority falling in the middle.

These same individuals were then randomly organized into groups in which they made decisions and solved problems using consensus decision-making. These consensus group decisions and solutions were then evaluated for effectiveness and creativity. The results were consistent. The consensus decision-making groups outperformed the best individuals in the groups in terms of decision and solution quality and creativity 75 percent of the time. The other 25 percent of the time, the groups did virtually as well as the best individual decision-makers and problem-solvers in the groups—hence our term, 75/25 Rule.

Going beyond the 75/25 Rule with Compassionate Consultation

The foregoing research shows that human beings can usually be assured of achieving higher decision-making quality on common limited resource type issues simply by using consensus (or Compassionate Consultation) methods. 'Abdu'l-Bahá prefigured these findings long before the research was done when He said:

> The purpose of consultation is to show that the views of several individuals are assuredly preferable to one man, even as the power of a number of men is of course greater than the power of one man.[104]

But we have said that Compassionate Consultation is a very refined, supercharged form of consensus decision-making, and the Writings of Bahá'u'lláh and 'Abdu'l-Bahá suggest that we can expect considerably more from it than the results promised by the 75/25 Rule. For example, 'Abdu'l-Bahá suggests that there are no limits or inappropriate applications for the use of Consultation combined with compassion:

> Man must consult on all matters, whether major or minor, so that he may become cognizant of what is good. Consultation giveth him insight into things and enableth him to delve into questions which are unknown. The light of truth shineth from the faces of those who engage in consultation.[105]

The suggestion here seems to be that Consultation can lead to transformative results in all arenas—above and beyond common limited resource type issues—including, for example, areas of primary research such as finding a cure for cancer.

To understand this claim requires that we consider what distinguishes Compassionate Consultation from conventional consensus decision-making. The spiritual component would appear to be the distinction. In particular, the difference seems to rest on the efforts of the Consulting members to prayerfully *request* divine guidance and then spiritually align themselves with their Creator as they address an issue so that they can *receive* divine guidance.

Seeing the Group as an Instrument for Receiving Divine Guidance

Seeing the group as an instrument for receiving divine guidance clearly goes beyond mere reliance on the synergy generated by a group of people as they reach a consensus decision. In Compassionate Consultation, the members try to access *divine* assistance, guidance, and bestowals as they address an issue. 'Abdu'l-Bahá says:

> …The bestowals of God are moving and circulating throughout all created things. This illimitable divine bounty has no beginning and will have no ending. It is moving, circulating and becomes effective wherever capacity is developed to receive it.[106]

It appears that this "capacity is developed" in the Consulting members by their prayerful request for divine guidance and their creation of a compassionate atmosphere. "Capacity is developed" when the members long for connection and strive to purify themselves in order "to receive it." 'Abdu'l-Bahá says:

> The bestowals of the Almighty are descending from the heaven of grace, but capacity to receive them is essential. The fountain of divine generosity is gushing forth, but we must have thirst for the living waters. Unless there be thirst, the salutary water will not assuage. Unless the soul hungers, the delicious foods of the heavenly table will not give sustenance. Unless the eyes of perception be opened, the lights of the sun will not be witnessed. Until the nostrils are purified, the fragrance of the divine rose garden will not be inhaled. Unless the heart be filled with longing, the favors of the Lord will

not be evident....Therefore, we must endeavor night and day to purify the hearts from every dross, sanctify the souls from every restriction and become free from the discords of the human world. Then the divine bestowals will become evident in their fullness and glory....[107]

When this capacity is successfully developed, a circuit is completed that energizes the Compassionate Consultation process. Referring to the "Supreme Concourse," a term for the divine realm, 'Abdu'l-Bahá is reported to have used a metaphor to describe the effect of this receptivity:

> In these meetings...we should be in connection with the Supreme Concourse. Between the Supreme Concourse and us there should be telegraphic communication, one end of the wire in the breast of each one here and the other in that Concourse on high, so that all we might say or do would be inspired.[108]

Accessing the Bestowals of God through Reliance, Surrender & Humility

'Abdu'l-Bahá also provides advice on the manner in which we should receive divine guidance during Compassionate Consultation. He says:

> Likewise in larger issues, when a problem ariseth, or a difficulty occureth, the wise should gather, consult, and devise a solution. They should then rely upon the One true God, and surrender to His Providence, in whatever way it may be revealed, for divine confirmations will undoubtedly assist. Consultation, therefore, is one of the explicit ordinances of the Lord of mankind.[109]

The appropriate response to receiving divine guidance is to "*rely* on the One true God, and *surrender* to His Providence, in whatever way it may be revealed..." (emphasis added). When we become the humble servant to God's guidance, "...divine confirmations will undoubtedly assist." These behaviors encourage the development of the Prime Requisites of **purity of motive**, **radiance of spirit**, **detachment from all save God**, **humility and lowliness amongst His loved ones**, and **servitude to His exalted threshold**.

Recognizing Unripe Decision Environments

Even after a thorough discussion of an issue, there may be times when a group feels no clear sense of guidance; the group may be leaning in one direction or another, but there is no resolve or enthusiasm to commit to a path. While this may indicate the need to Consult further, it could be a sign that the decision environment is unripe—that the time is not yet right for a decision to be made. In this case, the group may need to table the issue and come back to it at another time recognizing that the divine guidance has been to wait.

There is a poignant scene in the film *Dances with Wolves* that illustrates this idea. In the middle of the nineteenth century, a solitary soldier is occupying a US Army outpost within the territory of a Native American tribe. In the scene, a tribal chief and his leadership council confer on what to do about the soldier. Some tribal members see the soldier as a threat and advocate killing him. Others say he is not a threat and recommend leaving him alone. Still others are torn between these two positions. After facilitating a long discussion, the chief says that the issue is very complex, that they should reflect and sleep on it and return to confer further on it at a later time. The tribe appears to accept the conferring group as an instrument for receiving guidance, and when guidance is not felt, the members delay the decision trusting that the guidance will be forthcoming. While they are in this delay mode, events demonstrate that the soldier, far from being a threat, is actually a friend and a blessing to the tribe. Waiting proves to be a wise and guided decision.

Compassionate Consultation Behavioral Standard #6:

Arriving at a Unanimous Decision
(With Majority Rule Voting Only as a Last Resort)

Growth-Seeker Situation: Rod is at a group meeting where an issue is being addressed. He looks at his watch and sees that it is getting late. There are several possible solutions still being intensely considered by the group despite the weariness of the members. Rod says, "Let's just take a vote and go with whatever solution gets the most votes because it's getting late and we all have to go to work tomorrow." The group members are evenly split over whether to continue Consultation or simply go with the vote of the majority.

Compassionate Consultation Tool Needed: A deepened understanding of the options inherent in Behavioral Standard #6.

When using Compassionate Consultation, the goal is a unanimous decision. While the Bahá'í Writings relating to Consultation provide for the use of majority rule voting, there is a strong preference indicated for reaching unanimous decisions among the members of the group. 'Abdu'l-Bahá says:

> The shining spark of truth cometh forth only after the clash of differing opinions. If after discussion, a decision be carried unanimously well and good; but if, the Lord forbid, differences of opinion should arise, a majority of voices must prevail.[110]

The root words of "unanimous" literally mean "to be of one mind," which echoes Bahá'u'lláh's admonition to "Be united in counsel, be one in thought."[111]

These distinctions clarify a difference—whereas the standard for a consensus decision is that all of the group members are *willing to live with it*, the standard for a Compassionate Consultation decision is that all of the members *will wholeheartedly support it*. In general, the members' attempts to manifest all 7 Prime Requisites and to honor all 12 Behavioral Standards foster the ability to "be united in counsel" and "one in thought." More specifically, this ability is fostered by the members honoring Behavioral Standard #6, arriving at a unanimous decision with majority rule voting only as a last resort.

Shoghi Effendi gives further clarification on the behavioral attributes that contribute to the ability to reach unanimity when he says:

> Indeed it has ever been the cherished desire of our Master, 'Abdu'l-Bahá, that the friends in their councils, local as well as national, should by their candor, their honesty of purpose, their singleness of mind, and the thoroughness of their discussions achieve unanimity in all things.[112]

The Majority Rule Option

As previously noted, 'Abdu'l-Bahá characterizes the reaching of a unanimous decision as "well and good" while differences of opinion requiring a resort to majority rule voting is accompanied by the exclamation, "the Lord forbid." Therefore, Consulting members should continue searching for "the shining spark of truth" until true unanimity can be reached in the majority of cases and only as a last resort use majority rule voting. The existence of an imminent deadline for a decision could be one example of a case where a Compassionate Consultation decision-making group that has not reached unanimity would need to resort to a majority rule vote. But there are also other options available.

The Three Attempts Method of Reaching Unanimity

Bahá'u'lláh's strong preference for unanimity is reflected in what we might call the "three attempts method" of achieving unanimous agreement. He says:

> If consultation among the first group of people assembled endeth in disagreement, new people should be added, after which persons to the number of the Greatest Name (9), or fewer or more, shall be chosen by lot. Whereupon the consultation will be renewed, and the outcome, whatever it is, shall be obeyed. If, however, there is still disagreement, the same procedure should be repeated once more, and the decision of the majority shall prevail. He, verily, guideth whomsoever He pleaseth to the right way.[113]

Using Majority Rule Voting as a Tool for Reaching Unanimity

In some circumstances, the absence of unanimity is an indication that the Consulting members must simply persevere in the process; but in other circumstances a *test* majority vote can be taken as a way to gauge the tentative direction in which the group is leaning, and this indication can then be used as a basis for more rapidly reaching a unanimous decision.

In some situations, because the Consulting members are seeing the group as an instrument for receiving divine guidance, the *tentative* majority direction may be interpreted by the minority voting members as the wiser path, and they can proactively realign themselves in the majority direction making the *final* majority rule vote unnecessary.

In still other circumstances, the tentative majority rule vote may trigger a deeper discussion that leads back to an embrace by all members of the original minority opinion or to an altogether different unanimous decision.

Members must keep in mind that whenever the *final* decision is reached through a majority rule vote, it immediately becomes a unanimous decision. Referring to such a situation, Shoghi Effendi says:

> As soon as a decision is reached it becomes the decision of the whole Assembly, not merely of those members who happened to be among the majority.[114]

Using Majority Rule Voting as a Tool for Reaching Hybrid Decisions

Another option is possible. When a Compassionate Consultation group gauges the tentative leaning of the members through the use of a test majority rule vote, the absence of adversarialism in the Consultative environment can sometimes help foster a new unanimous decision that is a hybrid of the majority and minority positions. This emerges not as a compromise, but as a manifestation of 'Abdu'l-Bahá's words that, "…the light of reality becomes apparent when two opinions coincide."[115] Often hybrid decisions reflect the members' recognition that the majority and minority positions actually represent a false dichotomy, and a decision is reached in the previously unexplored middle.

For example, we worked with a product development group that focused on designing an after-market, hand-operated automobile sunroof. The members went back and forth for some time about whether the sunroof should "tightly seal" to keep out rain or be "easy to use" when cranking it open and closed—with the assumption that one could not have both.

After gauging the group's leaning with a majority vote, the close vote helped the members realize that they were dealing with a false dichotomy. They quickly reached a unanimous decision to design the sunroof at the "sweet spot" where both "easy to use" and "seals tightly" met—meaning both attributes would be present in the product. Of course, such hybrid decisions often occur during the use of Compassionate Consultation without the aid of a majority rule vote.

Submitting to the Majority & Surrendering To Providence

It is important to keep in mind that prior to reaching a unanimous or majority rule vote decision, the Consulting members have passed through a stage of Consultation where it has been:

> ...not only the right but the sacred obligation of every member to express freely and openly his views.[116]

But after the full expression of views, the spirit of sensitivity and submission to divine guidance must intensify. Members must detach from their views to the extent that they are able to sense where the group is trying to go in response to divine guidance and then yield to its influence. Even in situations where majority rule voting needs to occur as a last resort, 'Abdu'l-Bahá indicates that the proper response of outlying members is to support the emerging decision in a spirit of unanimity:

> ...and should differences of opinion arise a majority of voices must prevail, and all must obey and submit to the majority.[117]

While one might "obey" the majority decision *halfheartedly* and according to the *letter* of the law only, to also "submit" to the majority means to surrender one's will and to obey the decision *wholeheartedly* and according to the *spirit* as well as the letter of the decision. Elsewhere, and as previously referenced, 'Abdu'l-Bahá emphasizes the importance of surrendering one's will at this stage of the Consultative process and suggests that it opens the way to experiencing divine confirmations when he says:

> They should then rely upon the One true God, and surrender to His Providence, in whatever way it may be revealed, for divine confirmations will undoubtedly assist.[118]

Clearly, honoring Behavioral Standard #6, arriving at a unanimous decision, calls on members to manifest all seven of the Prime Requisites—namely, **purity of motive, radiance of spirit, detachment from all else** *save God, attraction to His divine fragrances, humility and lowliness amongst His loved ones, patience and long-suffering in difficulties,* and *servitude to His exalted threshold.*

Chapter 8

Creating the Compassionate Consultation Culture

Growth-Seeker Situation: Marion owns a business and has introduced Compassionate Consultation to the eight-member leadership team as the decision-making procedure she would like to use in the team's meetings. The leadership team members have been receptive to the use of Compassionate Consultation, but all too often, Marion finds herself and her team members slipping back into old behaviors. Most of the time, the team's atmosphere is characterized by competitiveness and disunity.

Compassionate Consultation Resources Needed: Introduction of the 7 Prime Requisites and the 12 Behavioral Standards of Compassionate Consultation as on-going accountability tools for use by the team.

All twelve of the Behavioral Standards—the six discussed in the last chapter and the six to be discussed in this chapter—contribute to the creation of both the atmosphere and the group culture of Compassionate Consultation. However, the first six especially fortify the climate or atmosphere while the second six especially fortify the group culture.

The Nature of Culture

One definition of culture is "the set of shared attitudes, values, goals, and practices that characterizes an organization."[119] A couple, a family, a business, an institution, a community, or the world may be considered as an organization. The different aspects or perspectives within an individual may also be seen as an organization. In all these senses, the dictionary definition of culture applies.

A practical way to think of culture is that it is "the way we do things around here." In this sense, the nature of a culture is dictated by what is and is not valued, and commonly held values dictate acceptable behaviors of the culture. These values and behaviors become deeply embedded to create the nature of the culture. As the "Growth-Seeker Situation" above illustrates, when it comes to the culture that encourages Compassionate Consultation, it tends to require *different* values and behaviors than we are accustomed to, regardless of the "organization" to which we are referring. In other words, our individual (internal), couple, family, business, institutional, community, and world cultures are often at variance with the culture that fosters Compassionate Consultation.

The Writings of Bahá'u'lláh, 'Abdu'l-Bahá, and Shoghi Effendi are aimed at unifying and advancing the best aspects of human culture. A purpose behind these Writings is to create an ever-advancing, spiritually-centered world civilization in which the spiritual, material, social, and technological aspects of culture are in balance. Compassionate Consultation is a primary tool to expedite this progressive and transformational process; and the behavioral and interpersonal standards required to use it call upon us to embrace a much larger portion of our potential as spiritual beings.

In Figure 8.1 below, the left-hand column contains the 12 Behavioral Standards to be honored in order to create a climate and culture conducive to Compassionate Consultation. Consistent application of these Behavioral Standards can contribute to the members' acquisition of the 7 Prime Requisites as spiritual attributes. *In the listing below, no specific correlation is intended between the same numbered items in the two columns.*

The Compassionate Consultation Behavioral Standards that Lead to Embodying the Prime Requisites	The Prime Requisites of Compassionate Consultation
1. Having absolute love & harmony	1. Purity of motive
2. Praying collectively for divine assistance	2. Radiance of spirit

3. Honoring the inherent value of each member	3. Detachment from all else save God
4. Treasuring diversity	4. Attraction to His divine fragrances
5. Seeing the group as an instrument for receiving divine guidance	5. Humility and lowliness amongst His loved ones
6. Arriving at a unanimous decision	6. Patience and long-suffering in difficulties
7. Having unity in implementing decisions	7. Servitude to his exalted threshold
8. Detaching one's ego from one's ideas	
9. Disagreeing dispassionately	
10. Having the attitude of an investigator of truth	
11. Using perfect liberty in expression within a context of courtesy, moderation & patience	
12. Praising others & thinking of oneself as evanescent	

Figure 8.1

Creating a Sub-Culture Conducive to Compassionate Consultation

Consequently, aspiring to use Compassionate Consultation in today's world involves learning how to create a group sub-culture within our existing cultures that is conducive to the use of this process—at least for the span of time during which we want to use Consultation. This means allowing the 7 Prime Requisites and the 12 Behavioral Standards (see Figure 8.1 repeated from the previous chapter for easy reference) to dictate the values and behaviors that will become deeply embedded in our Compassionate Consultation sub-culture.

Compassionate Consultation Behavioral Standard #7: Having Unity in Implementing Decisions

Growth-Seeker Situation: A family of seven is deciding where to go on winter vacation. Two family members want to go to the ocean in a warm climate, another two want to go to the mountains to ski, and three others want to go to Chicago to visit the art and science museums. The discounted travel rates are about to expire, so the parents cut short discussion and force a decision based on where the majority wants to go. However, in the aftermath of the decision, there are hard feelings that threaten to undercut the primary purpose of the vacation, which is to provide an experience that will refresh and bond the family members.

Compassionate Consultation Resource Needed: An understanding of, and commitment to, Behavioral Standard #7, having unity in implementing decisions.

Arriving at a Unanimous Decision (Behavioral Standard #6), flows naturally into Behavioral Standard #7, Having Unity in Implementing Decisions. Compassionate Consultation involves not only the ability to be "as one soul and one body" while *making* decisions, but also the ability to be "as one soul and one body" while *implementing* decisions. A letter written on behalf of Shoghi Effendi regarding appropriate practices in Consultative groups uses the word "faithfully" to describe the spirit that needs to be present during implementation of a decision:

> Through the clash of personal opinions, as 'Abdu'l-Bahá has stated, the spark of truth is often ignited, and Divine guidance revealed… But once the opinion of the majority has been ascertained, all the members should automatically and unreservedly obey it, and faithfully carry it out.[120]

To "faithfully" carry out a decision while "automatically and unreservedly" obeying it is to *wholeheartedly* implement it. Having unity in implementing decisions obviously prohibits active and passive resistance as well as half-hearted support for the decision and its implementation, which are common practice in response to decisions in today's world.

Unity in Making & Implementing Decisions Springs from Consecration

When both Behavioral Standards #6 and #7 are being honored by a Consultative group, a culture is created in which the spirit of unanimity that informs the decision naturally carries through into the implementation process that follows. The members of such a group will have a uniformly higher level of unalloyed, enthusiastic commitment and dedication to the decision and the resulting plan of action than exists with any other decision type. This unity of purpose springs from a sense of *consecration* to seeing the decision through because of the prayers for divine assistance that preceded it.

Fostering a True Continuous Improvement Culture

Having such unity in implementing decisions fosters a true continuous improvement culture, a culture where high learning and improvement are occurring at an accelerated and continuous rate. Such cultures are acutely needed in the world today, and they occur as a result of Compassionate Consultation for several reasons.

First, because everyone is unitedly and wholeheartedly supporting the decision, the set of ideas embedded in the decision is given an optimum opportunity to take root, grow, and have its effect. By comparison, in an implementation environment where there is disunity, the set of ideas forming the decision will never get a fair test because adversarial attitudes and behaviors will prevent it from fully taking root, growing, and bearing fruit.

Secondly, when unity in implementing decisions is being honored, the *variable* of human support has been turned into a *robust constant*. As a result, the members implementing the decision experience accelerated learning. They can more rapidly and objectively learn the degree to which the decision is having the *desired* effect because the decision's robustness can be assessed in an *optimum and clear,* rather than a *partisan and confused,* context. Any elements of the decision that are working effectively or ineffectively become starkly apparent, and any necessary adjustments can be rapidly noted, considered, and implemented.

Thirdly, after Compassionate Consultation, the group's revisiting and revising of decisions can be done in harmony. Because a culture of faithfulness, consecration, and unity has driven both the decision-making *and* the implementation, if evidence starts to come in that the decision, or an aspect of the decision, is not working optimally, the members, having preserved harmonious relations, will find themselves in an ideal situation to reconvene in unity, adjust the decision, and then wholeheartedly support that revised decision.

In contrast, when the level of support for the decision continues to vary among members during implementation as it usually does with other decision-making types, it is difficult to tell whether a sub-optimal decision implementation is being caused by a flawed decision, the variability of member support, or some combination of the two. This limits learning and increases confusion; and frustration, distrust, and disunity grow in such a decision-making culture. Consequently, when members attempt to revisit and discuss possible adjustments to the decision, the frustration, distrust, and disunity lead to recriminations and friction, and decision adjustments either cannot be agreed upon or are made adversarially and poorly. Invariably, time and energy are wasted.

Unity Is More Important Than Rightness—and Leads to Truth

'Abdu'l-Bahá further clarifies the meaning and importance of unity in implementing decisions:

> It is again not permitted that any one of the honored members object to or censure, whether in or out of the meeting, any decision arrived at previously, though that decision be not right, for such criticism would prevent any decision from being enforced. In short, whatsoever thing is arranged in harmony with love and purity of motive, its result is light, and should the least trace of estrangement prevail the result shall be darkness upon darkness.[121]

The guiding spiritual principle is that unity and harmony are even more important than rightness because anything that is generated from harmony, love, and purity of motive is life-giving and leads toward illumination. Conversely, anything that is generated from conflict, division, or estrangement is life-subtracting and leads toward darkness.

'Abdu'l-Bahá clarifies how the Consultative process works when we choose unity in implementing decisions:

> If they agree upon a subject, even though it be wrong, it is better than to disagree and be in the right, for this difference will produce the demolition of the divine foundation. Though one of the parties may be in the right and they disagree that will be the cause of a thousand wrongs, but if they agree and both parties are in the wrong, as it is in unity the truth will be revealed and the wrong made right.[122]

That disunity and ultimate disagreement "will produce the demolition of the divine foundation" is a striking concept. One possible interpretation of this concept is that if we have a right decision, but are in disunity during the implementation, our fractured relationships will prevent the decision from leading to successful outcomes.

An Ultimate Goal of Unity & Truth

Mindfulness about protecting the "divine foundation" leads us to an entirely different cultural stance during Compassionate Consultation. Our cultural assumptions—regardless of the diversity characterizing the members—must be that *we are already in unity*, that we will vigilantly guard our unity, that we will seek truth and rightness, and that we will find the truth either now as a consequence of the immediate decision, or in the near future as a consequence of our learning during our unified implementation of the decision. There needs to be a *hard focus on unity* and *a soft focus on seeking truth and rightness*. When this occurs, the great majority of decisions are both unified *and* right, while a small minority of decisions are unified and wrong. 'Abdu'l-Bahá refers to this phenomenon when he says:

> I swear by the One true God, it is better that all should agree on a wrong decision, than for one right vote to be singled out, inasmuch as single votes can be sources of dissension, which lead to ruin. Whereas, if in one case they take a wrong decision, in a hundred other cases they will adopt right decisions, and concord and unity

are preserved. This will offset any deficiency, and will eventually lead to the righting of the wrong.[123]

The principle of valuing unity more highly than rightness seems counter-intuitive and may make us wonder if this is really the most expedient path. As if to put to rest such concerns, 'Abdu'l-Bahá says, "This will offset any deficiency, and will eventually lead to the righting of the wrong." Clearly, having unity in implementing Consultative decisions *is the most direct path* to achieving truth and rightness.

Honoring the Behavioral Standard of having unity in implementing decisions calls upon the members' ability to manifest all seven of the Prime Requisites—*namely,* **purity of motive, radiance of spirit, detachment from all else save God, attraction to His divine fragrances, humility and lowliness amongst His loved ones, patience and long-suffering in difficulties,** *and* **servitude to His exalted threshold.**

Deciding Where to Go on Vacation

Now let's go back to the example of the family of seven trying to decide where to go on winter vacation in the "Growth-Seeker Situation" that opened this section. The situation clearly calls for a better understanding and honoring of having unity in implementing decisions. Consultative groups need to develop the discipline and detachment to wholeheartedly support the majority view when time has run out and a decision must be made.

However, the difficulties in the aftermath of the "Growth-Seeker Situation" are also a function of their *having cut short discussion* on the issue. There would have been a preferable outcome if the family had Consulted together until all members felt heard, understood, and validated. Extending their Consultation could have enabled them to consider whether there was a location that could accommodate all preferences, to decide to drive and spend a short time at a series of places that would meet each of the sub-group's preferences, or to plan future trips which would accommodate the sub-groups' preferences which were not being addressed in the immediate trip. Members are assisted in their ability to achieve unity in implementing decisions when the Consultation has been combined with *compassion* so that all input, views, and preferences are heard, understood, and fully considered. Put another way, having unity in implementing decisions does not stand alone—it integrates with the other 11 Behavioral

Standards and the 7 Prime requisites to create a *compassion stronghold* that protects the unity and welfare of all.

Compassionate Consultation Behavioral Standard #8:

Detaching One's Ego from One's Ideas

Growth-Seeker Situation: After the group meeting, Michael finds himself in a bad mood. After reflection, he realizes that he feels humiliated because his ideas were not adopted in the decision of the group. He wonders whether anyone respects him.

Compassionate Consultation Resource Needed: Going over the wall implicit in honoring Behavioral Standard #8—detaching one's ego from one's ideas.

Behavioral Standard #8 is about detachment, a spiritual quality that has been extolled in the scriptures of all the world's major religions. In Compassionate Consultation, the attribute of detachment is expressed as the ability to share an idea clearly and succinctly without championing it, to fully articulate an idea without being a partisan for it, and to effectively convey an idea without arguing for it. This ability is rare in today's world, but is essential in Compassionate Consultation. It contributes to the members' abilities to manifest the Prime Requisites of *purity of motive, detachment from all else save God, and humility and lowliness amongst His loved ones.*

Making Ideas Group Property

Detaching one's ego from one's ideas means that one shares an idea and then immediately makes the idea "group property." The object is to be comfortable letting the group do with the idea what it will and to have what the group does with the idea in no way add to, or subtract from, one's sense of self-worth. Whether the group accepts, rejects, or rearranges the idea does not influence the outlook or attitude of the contributor. 'Abdu'l-Bahá says, "If another contradicts him, he must not become excited..."[124] and "Should any one oppose, he must on no account feel hurt..."[125] He also makes clear that separating our egos from our ideas expedites the discovery of truth:

> In order to find truth we must give up our prejudices, our own small trivial notions; an open receptive mind is essential. If our chalice is full of self, there is no room in it for the water of life. The fact that we imagine ourselves to be right and everybody else wrong is the greatest of all obstacles in the path toward unity, and unity is necessary if we would reach truth, for truth is one.[126]

When all members of a group using Compassionate Consultation detach their egos from their ideas in this way, it creates a culture in which the group will achieve not only the benefits of the 75/25 Rule, but also unlimited results.

When one or more group members do not detach their egos from their ideas, problems tend to occur. For example, if I am holding on tightly to my ideas, it may lead you to challenge my idea, hurt my feelings, and strain our relationship, or it may lead you to avoid confronting my idea in order to protect our relationship. Either way leads to our exchanges becoming less authentic and effective and to our decision-making process becoming less compassionate, less focused on the investigation of truth, and less informed by divine guidance as egos clog the channel.

Ego attachment to an idea may also manifest itself as people withholding their ideas for fear of criticism or non-acceptance. In such cases, members' failure to detach their sense of self-worth from their ideas and think of them as group property robs the group of perspectives needed to reach wise, robust decisions.

Separating one's ego from one's ideas is expedited by honoring Foundation Principle #5, seeing the group as an instrument for receiving divine guidance. When we think of ourselves as instruments for receiving divine guidance, we can visualize the ideas coming down from above us into our hearts and minds. Our job is to verbally channel these ideas to our group colleagues as part of the flow of thought that needs to come to the discussion. Rather than attaching to and trying to own the data, we simply serve as intermediaries who receive, articulate, and thereby deliver the data so that the group can use it in the Compassionate Consultation process. Freeing ourselves from owning the data we personally deliver allows us to remain objective enough to entertain all the perspectives and data being shared while taking notice of where the divine guidance may be leading us.

If You Have an Idea, You Are Duty-Bound to Share It in a *Detached* Way

The guideline to keep in mind is that if you have a relevant idea, you are duty-bound to share it in a succinct, courteous, and *detached* way with the other members because it could either *be* the idea, or *lead* to the idea, that resolves the issue which the Consulting members are addressing.

Compassionate Consultation Behavioral Standard #9:

Disagreeing Dispassionately

Growth-Seeker Situation: Henry can feel himself getting very emotional whenever differing ideas and opinions are clashing together during Compassionate Consultation. He gets preoccupied with his feelings during what he sees as the competition of ideas and is often startled when the group moves in a new direction away from the initial idea clash. In such situations, he has to work at getting his emotions under control so that he will not lose track of the direct line of reasoning the group is following. At such times, he feels like he is trying to catch up to the group.

Compassionate Consultation Resource Needed: Learn to disagree dispassionately and follow the sparks emerging from the clash of ideas into new terrain.

Learning to honor the previously-discussed Behavioral Standard, detaching your ego from your ideas, is excellent preparation for honoring Behavioral Standard #9, *disagreeing dispassionately*. Being dispassionate involves being calm, objective, and fair rather than being influenced by strong emotions and bias. When human passion and strong feeling enter into disagreements, issues get clouded. 'Abdu'l-Bahá says:

> ...the pursuit of passion and desire will wrap the eyes in a thousand veils that rise out of the heart to blind the sight and the insight as well.[127]

The goal of detachment from strong feelings does not relate to the *subject*, but to the *thoughts and opinions* being expressed; one can feel strongly about the subject while dealing dispassionately with the thoughts and opinions clashing around it. In a group culture of dispassionate disagreement, the dispassion allows the members to focus not on a *competition* of thoughts, but on the *collision, confluence,* and *interpenetration* of thoughts out of which something new will emerge.

Discovery in the Terrain around Thought Collisions

In discussing the relationship between dispassion and thoughts in the process of Consultation, some of the shorter quotes we have already referenced are integrated in the following statement by 'Abdu'l-Bahá:

> The members thereof must take counsel together in such wise that no occasion for ill-feeling or discord may arise. This can be attained when every member expresseth with absolute freedom his own opinion and setteth forth his argument. Should any one oppose, he must on no account feel hurt for not until matters are fully discussed can the right way be revealed. *The shining spark of truth cometh forth only after the clash of differing opinions* (emphasis added).[128]

Here, the clash or collision of differing thoughts and opinions creates shining sparks; the light from these sparks illuminates the terrain and possibilities around the issue being discussed, and the truth or right way is revealed.

Consciously & Intentionally Using the Tool of Dispassionate Disagreement

Dispassionate disagreement involves the skill of *consciously* recognizing disagreement as a tool for discovering truth. A tool is something we take up with intention to achieve a desired outcome. A tool for raising children is embedded in the phrase, "One should never get mad when one is angry." The idea is to use anger as a calculated tool to achieve a constructive end rather than being carried away by emotion and losing control of one's self, which could be counter-productive and harmful.

This concept can also be applied to the intentional and dispassionate use of disagreement during Consultation. While it is common in most decision-making groups for members to express frustration and even anger during disagreements, the process of combining Consultation with compassion requires a conscious and craftsman-like approach to disagreement.

The essence of this principle can be found in the preceding quote from 'Abdu'l-Bahá. Until the last sentence, 'Abdu'l-Bahá appears to be specifying only that members detach their egos from their ideas (Behavioral Standard #8). However, the last sentence, "The shining spark of truth cometh forth only after the clash of differing opinions,"[129] seems to broach another challenging skill with the introduction of the vivid image of clashing and sparks—like the striking of *flint and steel* to start a fire. In this image, 'Abdu'l-Bahá has differing opinions in the role of the flint and steel and truth in the role of the spark produced. 'Abdu'l-Bahá's image bears closer scrutiny.

Starting a Fire with Flint & Steel

Some of us will remember the first time we saw a scout leader or other adult start a fire by striking together flint and steel. Although it might be expected that the striking action would be very powerful, in actuality striking the flint and steel together is done in a very controlled, mindful, craftsman-like way. The striking itself is almost gentle, and the focus is not on the flint and steel, but on the sparks that come forth from the striking. The flint and steel are only tools to produce the sparking, and once a substantial spark flies out and lands on the straw-burning medium, the flint and steel are immediately dropped, and the spark-infused straw, looking like the nest of a small songbird, is carefully picked up and gently blown upon until smoke emerges, and finally, flame bursts forth. As the straw bursts into full flame, it is placed at the base of the wood kindling, which, in turn, begins to burn so that everyone present can be warmed and illuminated by the campfire. The whole process is very mindful, intentional, controlled, and craftsman-like.

The Flint & Steel Concept Applied To Disagreeing Dispassionately

This fire-starting method relates to the manner in which disagreement should be handled in Compassionate Consultation. As with the striking together of the flint and steel, "the clash of differing opinions" is not harsh disagreement, but dispassionate, even gentle, disagreement. The dispassion in relation to the ideas and opinions is supported by the compassionate atmosphere maintained by the group members and their ability to separate theirs egos from their ideas. As a result, the members let their ideas and opinions collide with *mindfulness* and *a sense of craft*. With intention, the members share their differing ideas and opinions and watch with curiosity to see what sparks will issue forth from the clashes. The members' preoccupation is not with their clashing opinions, but with the new insights and ideas that are sparked *by* the clashes.

In this environment group members are ready to drop their opinions (the flint and steel) the moment they see a promising idea spark forth from the opinion clash. A promising idea is one that has the potential, if nurtured, to burst into flame and illuminate a better path or decision for the group. The better path or decision is the one that, in the context of the issue being addressed, best reveals and aligns the members with reality, unity, and truth. 'Abdu'l-Bahá says:

> …the light of reality becomes apparent when two opinions coincide. A spark is produced when flint and steel come together.
>
> Man should weigh his opinions with the utmost serenity, calmness and composure. Before expressing his own views he should carefully consider the views already advanced by others. If he finds that a previously expressed opinion is more true and worthy, he should accept it immediately and not willfully hold to an opinion of his own. By this excellent method he endeavors to arrive at unity and truth.[130]

In our discussion of Behavioral Standard #7, Unity in Implementing Decisions, we emphasized that unity is more important than correctness or truth even while the ultimate goal is to achieve unity *and* truth. In the foregoing quotation, 'Abdu'l-Bahá provides a method to achieve both for He says, "By this excellent method he endeavors to arrive at unity and truth." The method involves realizing that at the point where "two opinions coincide" and "a spark is produced," rather than "willfully" challenging or resisting the newly emerging idea or direction, the members must treat it like a fragile thing—like a spark in the straw—and nurture it into fuller life and dimension.

Breathing Life into Newborn Ideas

Like the scout leader blowing on the fragile spark that has landed in the nest of straw, Compassionate Consultation decision-making members must establish a culture in which they habitually breathe life into newborn ideas that have emerged from the clash of differing opinions and landed in the "straw" provided by a compassionate atmosphere. It is the compassion of the Consulting members, the "attitude and atmosphere of love" that they create, that provides the dilation of heart and the welcoming, ego-free intellectual culture that are conducive to both the sharing and nurturing of ideas. Behavioral Standard #9 might just as appropriately be called "*compassionately* disagreeing" as dispassionately disagreeing.

Sparks Illuminate the Path

Since no one knows from which clash of differing opinions or from whose mouth the better idea or path will emerge, the culture co-created by Compassionate Consultation decision-making members will tend to have an air of mindful, excited expectation to see what will be revealed. Dispassionately disagreeing also involves the ability of each member to be mindful (in the words of 'Abdu'l-Bahá) of "a previously expressed opinion" which "is more true and worthy" and to "accept it immediately" without "willfully hold[ing] to an opinion of his own."[131] When dispassionate disagreement prevails in the group culture, it expedites the ability to move through ideas gracefully and to efficiently follow the illuminating sparks to what is most "true and worthy." Indeed, 'Abdu'l-Bahá's statement that, "…not until matters are fully discussed can the right way be revealed,"[132] seems to indicate that many times the Consultation process is a *revelation process* in the sense that it can make apparent and illuminate the better path. Bahá'u'lláh says:

> Take ye counsel together in all matters, inasmuch as consultation is the lamp of guidance which leadeth the way, and is the bestower of understanding.[133]

Think of the Truth as a Refined & Hidden Thing

It may be helpful to think of the truth, the right way, the good result, the solution that aligns us with spiritual reality, or whatever we may call it, as a refined and hidden thing that will not show itself unless the culture and climate are right. 'Abdu'l-Bahá says:

> They must in every matter search out the truth and not insist upon their own opinion, for stubbornness and persistence in one's views will lead ultimately to discord and wrangling and the truth will remain hidden.[134]

Clearly, maintaining both dispassionate disagreement and an atmosphere of compassion creates a culture, climate, and energy-frequency conducive to truth-seeking and truth-finding. In addition, maintaining these cultural and atmospheric qualities helps the members to manifest the Prime Requisites *purity of motive*, *radiance of spirit*, *detachment from all else save God*, and *servitude to His exalted threshold*.

Compassionate Consultation Behavioral Standard #10:

Having the Attitude of an Investigator of Truth

Growth-Seeker Situation: Leticia's friends tell her that she has a strong opinion about everything and a very persuasive personality. Usually this works in Leticia's favor, but during Compassionate Consultation decision-making meetings, she can sense that her persuasiveness is not always appreciated by the other group members.

Compassionate Consultation Resource Needed: Develop the skill of having the attitude of an investigator of truth.

'Abdu'l-Bahá says:

> ...consultation must have for its object the investigation of truth. He who expresses an opinion should not voice it as correct and right but set it forth as a contribution to the consensus of opinion.[135]

What is it to be an investigator of truth? A good investigator must have an open mind because investigating truth requires an ability to consider data, objectively entertain different possibilities and perspectives, and avoid prematurely drawing conclusions. Often we think of investigators patiently "building a case" until they have reached a conclusion. Similarly, Compassionate Consultation participants who are investigators of truth keep an open mind, gather and look at data, consider the issue from different perspectives, follow intuitions and hunches, stay attuned to feelings, and patiently, gradually "build the case" for what the reality or truth seems to be.

Making Contributions to the Consensus of Opinion

It is common in decision-making groups to hear members express opinions in a tone that conveys, "This is the truth, and you would see it as such if you were not so blind and ignorant!" This tone is antithetical to a Compassionate Consultation culture. 'Abdu'l-Bahá's admonition in the preceding quote that "He who expresses an opinion should not voice it as correct and right but set it forth as a contribution to the consensus of opinion" suggests that a group member who has the attitude of an investigator of truth would share her or his ideas in a tone that conveys, "Here is an idea which may have elements in it that we could use to get closer to the truth or reality. I submit it for the consideration of the group." This is an approach that Leticia, the woman in the "Growth-Seeker Situation" opening this section, needs to learn to use during Consultation in place of her high-powered persuasion skills. Ideas are to be submitted with humility and in a spirit of service to the group in its investigation of truth. When this is done, it helps group members manifest the Prime Requisites of ***humility and lowliness amongst His loved ones***, ***purity of motive***, ***radiance of spirit***, ***detachment from all else save God***, and ***servitude to His exalted threshold***.

Investigating the Truth or Reality of a Situation

'Abdu'l-Bahá helps us further understand the process of investigating the truth or reality of a situation when He says:

> Man must consult on all matters, whether major or minor, so that he may become cognizant of what is good. Consultation giveth him insight into things and enableth him to delve into questions which are unknown.[136]

The first sentence of this quotation suggests that one way of thinking about investigating the truth is that it reveals to us "what is good." Whether we are using Consultation to wisely make decisions, solve problems, assess situations, or align material conditions with spiritual reality, we are seeking "good" remedies to the needs arising out of an issue.

The second sentence of the quotation, "Consultation giveth him insight into things and enableth him to delve into questions which are unknown," adds further dimension to an understanding of the process of investigating truth. The word "insight" refers to the power or act of seeing into or penetrating a situation. It also refers to the act of apprehending the inner nature of things or of seeing intuitively. So combining Consultation and compassion enables us to penetrate situations and apprehend the inner nature of things using rational thought, intuition, and divine assistance.

When we say that Compassionate Consultation can help align the material reality with spiritual reality, one meaning is that the *outer* nature of things can be aligned with the *inner* nature of things. For example, when one of our clients used Compassionate Consultation with his spouse to discuss the significance of his recurring back troubles, the understanding emerged that he was trying to carry too much of the weight of the world on his shoulders single-handedly. Consulting as a couple in the spirit of investigators of truth led the inner reality behind an outer condition to become evident to them.

Similar combinations of rational thought and intuition supported by divine assistance during the Consultative process can lead groups to breakthroughs in scientific research or new product development where the attempt is being made to move from a guess, theory, or proposition to certainty about the truth, possibilities, or reality of a situation. Bahá'u'lláh's previously referenced words are relevant again:

> Consultation bestoweth greater awareness and transmuteth conjecture into certitude...For everything there is and will continue to be a station of perfection and maturity. The maturity of the gift of understanding is made manifest through consultation.[137]

Compassionate Consultation Behavioral Standard #11:

Using Perfect Liberty in Expression within a Context of Moderation, Courtesy & Patience

Growth-Seeker Situation: At the weekly family meeting, eleven-year-old Jimmy complained loudly about his sister to his parents. He said, "Cara is so lazy—you let her lie around and talk to her creepy friends on the phone while I have to mow the lawn." Cara made a face at Jimmy and began planning a way to get back at her brother.

Compassionate Consultation Resource Needed: Learning to use perfect liberty in expression within a context of moderation, courtesy, and patience.

Perfect Liberty

At the heart of Compassionate Consultation is the right of the individual group member to freedom of expression. 'Abdu'l-Bahá says:

> When meeting for consultation, each must use perfect liberty in stating his views and unveiling the proof of his demonstration.[138]

To many, including Jimmy in the Growth-Seeker Situation above, the term "liberty" implies a no-holds-barred, let-it-all hang-out attitude that would accept the expression of blunt, long-winded, and even insulting views. However, 'Abdu'l-Bahá' uses the term *"perfect* liberty." Bahá'u'lláh defines "true" and "perfect" liberty:

> Say: True liberty consisteth in man's submission unto My commandments, little as ye know it. Were men to observe that which We have sent down unto them from the Heaven of Revelation, they would of a certainty, attain unto perfect liberty. Happy is the man that hath apprehended the Purpose of God in whatever He hath revealed from the Heaven of His Will that pervadeth all created things. Say: The liberty that profiteth you is to be found nowhere except in complete servitude unto God, the Eternal Truth. Whoso hath tasted of its sweetness will refuse to barter it for all the dominion of earth and heaven.[139]

Clearly, human beings are happiest and most effective when they live according to this definition of liberty. In the context of Consultation, "perfect liberty" means that the members have freedom of expression but exercise it in the context of moderation, courtesy, and patience.

Moderation

'Abdu'l-Bahá says:

> The honored members must with all freedom express their own thoughts, and it is in no wise permissible for one to belittle the thought of another, nay, he must with moderation set forth the truth....[140]

Moderation is an attribute that lessens the intensity or extremeness of things, which would include stating one's thoughts briefly and concisely rather than with excess and verbosity. When moderation is present, intense manifestations of passion-driven behavior disappear. Instead, we find equanimity, balance, and composure even under stress. Honoring the Behavioral Standard of moderation helps Consulting members to manifest the Prime Requisites of *purity of motive*, *radiance of spirit*, and *patience and long-suffering in difficulties*.

For those learning the process of Consultation, moderation may be achieved initially through an act of will, but habitual moderation during Consultation results from cleaving to compassion in all its forms. As a result, moderation becomes an attribute of the compassionate culture created by mature practitioners.

Compassionate moderation tends to neutralize ego-based passion in which a person attempts to elevate himself or herself above another. In the quotation above, 'Abdu'l-Bahá's counsel that "...it is in no wise permissible for one to belittle the thought of another" is a case in point. Simply through an immoderate tone of voice or facial expression, one can belittle the thought of another. However, this would never occur in the culture of moderation, equanimity, and composure that arises out of compassion. Compassion creates an atmosphere and culture of softness and receptivity that is conducive to all ideas being brought forward by the members without fear of rebuff or denigration. Indeed, Shoghi Effendi states that one of the keynotes of Bahá'u'lláh's teachings is "...the spirit of frank and loving consultation."[141]

Courtesy, Dignity & Care

'Abdu'l-Bahá says:

> They must then proceed with the utmost devotion, courtesy, dignity, care, and moderation to express their views.[142]

While the attribute of devotion has been addressed in several other Behavioral Standards, courtesy, dignity, and care have not. Courtesy is behavior that is distinguished by respect for and consideration of others. Courtesy protects human dignity, and protecting dignity is essential for getting anything effectively accomplished with human beings. Dignity refers to the quality of being worthy, honored, or esteemed, and it could relate to both protecting the dignity of others and maintaining one's own dignity during the Consultative process.

Courtesy also informs care. Care implies having a painstaking concern during Consultation that everything about ourselves—our language, demeanor, body language, facial expressions, and efforts to effectively address the issue—advance rather than retard the Consultative process.

Bahá'u'lláh clarifies the importance of courtesy, dignity, and care by emphasizing the power of human speech to lead us toward or away from understanding:

> A kindly tongue is the lodestone of the hearts of men. It is the bread of the spirit, it clotheth the words with meaning, it is the fountain of the light of wisdom and understanding.[143]

A lodestone is something that strongly attracts, as with a magnetic force. Thus, kind, courteous, and caring speech used during Compassionate Consultation attracts human hearts and opens them to a full consideration of what is being said so that communication and understanding are optimized, and agreement is more easily achieved. Conversely, the meaning of words expressed without kindliness will be lost on the listeners and agreement will be elusive.

In the Growth-Seeker Situation at the beginning of this section, Jimmy's unkind and discourteous outburst is likely to reduce rather than enhance understanding. Young people, like adults, can learn to use "perfect liberty"—especially if everyone else in the family is demonstrating that they too are struggling to learn it. If his parents and his sister asked him to restate his feelings in the context of courtesy, dignity, and care, he might say, "I am really angry because it seems like I always have to do more chores than Cara. It does not seem fair or just to me."

Finally, when we demonstrate courtesy and care and protect the dignity of others, we create an atmosphere that allows all participants' best selves to come forth in Compassionate Consultation. A colleague once said:

> "Growing up, my perception was that my fellow family members were very critical and judgmental. Even if I said, "It's a beautiful day," a fellow family member was likely to say, "It's not a beautiful day, it's a gorgeous day!" It felt like I couldn't say anything right. Because of this kind of discourtesy, I more often experienced undercutting correction rather than affirming agreement. To this day, when someone responds to me in this way, the child in me either feels punctured or angered. If this happens during Consultation, I am not at my best."

We all have triggers like this. Courtesy, care, and kindliness soothe the human interface, protect dignity, and prevent these triggers from firing during Consultation. In addition, honoring the Behavioral Standards of courtesy, dignity, and care help the Consulting members manifest the Prime Requisites of **attraction to His divine fragrances** and **humility and lowliness amongst His loved ones**.

Patience

'Abdu'l-Bahá specifies patience as one of the 7 Prime Requisites for effective Consultation, but he pairs it with another attribute in the phrase "...*patience and long-suffering in difficulties*..."[144] This is an instructive combination of terms. With patience we bear trials calmly, steadfastly, and without complaint in spite of difficulty or adversity. "Long-suffering" takes the requirement up a notch; it refers to patiently enduring offense or hardship that is long-lasting. The implications are that effectively using Compassionate Consultation may require more patience from us than we are accustomed to mustering, and that the challenges could include both hardship generally and possibly perceived offense from our fellow Consulting members at times.

The Contagious Effect of Modeling Patience & Long-Suffering in Difficulties

In our work facilitating organizational and community groups, we often find that the quality of *patience and long-suffering in difficulties* is the attribute in shortest supply when dealing with difficult issues. Nevertheless, we find that if we, as facilitators, do our best to model *patience and long-suffering in difficulties*, it palpably changes the culture, climate, and self-image of the group. Modeling *patience and long-suffering in difficulties* means that we are unflappable, imperturbable, unconditionally constructive, unwilling to take offense, and relentlessly confident in the group's capacity to do its work and reach agreement. We react to *each* idea with the *same* openness, impartiality, and attentiveness. If the group seems to be going in circles, we may name what we see, but do it in a tone that conveys willingness to continue in the circular pattern if the group needs to do so.

While it is sometimes easier to model patience and long-suffering in difficulties as a facilitator than as a member of a group, we notice that when we set this example, the members of the group increasingly adopt it as well. This also means that if members of a group set this example in the absence of a facilitator, the other members of the group will increasingly adopt it. The combination of having patience and being long-suffering is like a positive virus that, if modeled by one or a few, becomes a healthy contagion that spreads to others too.

In terms of the culture and climate of the group, having patience and being long-suffering focuses the energy of the group, increases listening levels, and helps maintain moderation by decreasing knee-jerk reactivity in the members. In terms of the group's self-image, demonstrating *patience and long-suffering in difficulties* is a powerful way to show faith in, and commitment to, both the group's capacity to handle its work and the divine guidance that will ultimately reveal itself through the instrumentality of the group.

Engendering Spiritual Sight

Using perfect liberty in expression within a context of courtesy, moderation, and patience (Behavioral Standard #11) protects and maintains the compassionate atmosphere that fosters absolute love and harmony among the members (Behavioral Standard #1). Put another way, the combination of perfect liberty, moderation, courtesy, and patience cools and soothes the human relations environment even while ideas are generating heat by clashing together and producing sparks. Bahá'u'lláh tells us:

> One word is like unto springtime causing the tender saplings of the rose-garden of knowledge to become verdant and flourishing, while another word is even as a deadly poison. It behoveth a prudent man of wisdom to speak with utmost leniency and forbearance so that the sweetness of his words may induce everyone to attain that which befitteth man's station.[145]

Similarly, in the early part of the twentieth century, Mary Hanford Ford reported an experience with 'Abdu'l-Bahá in Paris:

> Holding out in His hand a piece of very thin paper before His eyes, 'Abdu'l-Bahá said: "See what a slight thing will shut off our physical sight; so will a slight indiscretion, a cross word, an adverse criticism shut off the delicate spiritual sight."[146]

Being *Tough* on Ideas & *Easy* on Each Other

To summarize, the spirit and group culture of "perfect liberty" involves speaking openly and freely, but doing so with an attitude and behavior that are informed by reverence, dignity, courtesy, care, moderation, and patience. The full power of Compassionate Consultation cannot be accessed without this refined form of perfect liberty existing within and between the members. A culture must be created that allows the members to be *tough* on ideas and opinions ("the clash of differing opinions") while being *easy* on each other ("the first condition is absolute love and harmony amongst the members…"). As the members create and maintain this group culture, they will raise the frequency level of their Compassionate Consultation process to the point where they become unencumbered receivers of incoming divine assistance.

In addition to the Prime Requisites already mentioned in connection with this Behavioral Standard, doing the foregoing things will contribute to the members' ability to manifest the Prime Requisites of **detachment from all else save God** and **servitude to His exalted threshold**.

Compassionate Consultation Behavioral Standard #12:

Praising Others & Thinking of Oneself as Evanescent

Growth-Seeker Situation: Maria and Pierre are newlyweds who have committed to getting skilled in the process of Compassionate Consultation decision-making together. One day Maria suggests to Pierre that they should sit down together and agree on a budget for their household expenses. Pierre agrees to Consult but inside harbors the thought that, since he has the business degree and makes more money than Maria, he should decide how the money will be spent and by whom.

Compassionate Consultation Resource Needed: A deepened understanding of Behavioral Standard #12 and an ability to honor it in practice.

Behavioral Standard #12 is largely about humility to which Bahá'u'lláh calls all of us when He says:

> Know you not why We created you all from the same dust? That no one should exalt himself over the other. Ponder at all times in your hearts how ye were created.[147]

Speaking to groups (referred to here as "the friends") attempting to use Consultation, 'Abdu'l-Bahá states:

> Every one of the friends should highly praise the other and each should regard himself as evanescent and as naught in the presence of others.[148]

'Abdu'l-Bahá is clearly calling Consulting members to manifest Prime Requisite #5, *humility and lowliness amongst His loved ones*. But His words in the preceding quote describe more than just the desired *outcome* of humility and lowliness. He seems to give us a glimpse of the *procedure* for achieving humility and lowliness when he says that each Consulting member "should regard himself as evanescent and as naught in the presence of others." To be "evanescent" is to have no permanence, to be on the point of vanishing, becoming imperceptible, or passing away;

it is to think of oneself as "naught" or nothing in the presence of others. One could think of oneself as the vapor in a meadow that disappears in the morning sun, as the rainbow that disappears even as we try to focus on it, as the dream that slips away from memory the moment we open our eyes following sleep, or as a spiritual being having a temporary and fleeting physical experience in this transient, material world.

One might think that to be evanescent means to be silent and without a self. However, 'Abdu'l-Bahá's admonition is not to *be* evanescent, but to "*regard*" or *think of one's self as evanescent and as nothing* in the presence of others. The goal is to express one's thoughts and opinions with "perfect liberty" *while thinking of one's self* as evanescent and as nothing in the presence of others.

A Dual Dynamic Process of Drawing Forth Each Other's Spirit or True Self

At the same time, 'Abdu'l-Bahá says that each Consulting member "should highly praise the other…" It appears that the desired group process has a dual dynamic in which all Consulting members are supported by the encouragement they are receiving from the other members to freely express their thoughts while, at the same time, they are all detached from the ideas they are personally expressing because they are thinking of themselves as being evanescent or as nothing in the presence of the others. This dual dynamic seems to create an ideal culture for *drawing forth* each member's spirit or true self so that it can *contribute* the idea, feeling, or guided insight in the most authentic way. In addition, the dual dynamic appears to create the ideal culture for each member to *receive* the gift of the other person's spirit or true self in terms of insights, ideas, and incoming guidance.

When 'Abdu'l-Bahá states that Consultation is "spiritual conference in the attitude and atmosphere of love,"[149] He confirms that Compassionate Consultation is conference between the spirits of the members; and members can contribute significantly to the creation of the optimal space for the intermingling of spirits and the interpenetration of ideas when they honor Behavioral Standard #12. In addition, praising their colleagues and regarding themselves as evanescent provides the Consulting members with a prerequisite for accessing divine guidance—a humility that is mystical as well as practical and proactive. Bahá'u'lláh states:

O SON OF MAN!

Humble thyself before Me, that I may graciously visit thee...[150]

The Atmosphere & Culture Conducive To Receiving Divine Guidance

In the end, the 12 Behavioral Standards and the 7 Prime Requisites create an atmosphere and group culture conducive to receiving divine guidance. They assure that Consultation will take place in the presence of compassion so that Compassionate Consultation will result. In effect, they attune both the individual members and the group to the "sound waves" of divine guidance so that the members vibrate in cycle with that guidance and receive it in a pure form.

The Subtle Interplay between the 12 Behavioral Standards

There is subtle interplay and interdependency between the 12 Compassionate Consultation Behavioral Standards. Clearly, if group members are *not* honoring Behavioral Standard #3 (Honoring the Inherent Value of Each Member), it will make it all the harder for group members to honor Behavioral Standard #8 (Detaching One's Ego from One's Ideas). If, in a group setting, you do not appear to be listening to my ideas, considering my input, and including me as a valued member of the group, I will probably hold onto my ideas and push them ever harder upon the group in an effort to have my ideas heard and my value acknowledged by the group. This, in turn, will lead to a contentious atmosphere and make it harder for us to honor Behavioral Standards #1 (Having Absolute Love & Harmony) and #4 (Treasuring Diversity). When it comes to arriving at a decision, festering resentments will make it very difficult for us to honor Behavioral Standards #6 (Arriving At A Unanimous Decision) and #7 (Unity in Implementing Decisions).

The strong interrelationships between the 12 Behavioral Standards mean that those who Consult need to be holding themselves accountable *to all* of the Behavioral Standards, not picking and choosing between them. Inattentiveness to one can negatively affect all the others and prevent the emergence of the 7 Prime Requisites as well.

Striving Is Required, Not Perfection

Clearly, we are not going to be perfect in modeling the Compassionate Consultation Behavioral Standards and manifesting the Prime Requisites, but we do need to be *progressively striving* to develop and hold ourselves accountable to them all. We are promised that divine assistance will come to our aid as we humbly strive to develop these attributes and behaviors. 'Abdu'l-Bahá says:

> Should they endeavour to fulfill these conditions the Grace of the Holy Spirit shall be vouchsafed unto them....and they shall day by day receive a new effusion of Spirit.[151]

Unlimited Results Become Incrementally Available

'Abdu'l-Bahá's words in the preceding quote and experience suggest that the unlimited results possible with Compassionate Consultation become incrementally available to us as we progress in our ability to embody the 7 Prime Requisites and the 12 Behavioral Standards. "New effusion[s] of Spirit" will "day by day" become available to us, and the transformative power and potentialities of Compassionate Consultation will gradually open to us. 'Abdu'l-Bahá says:

> Should they be graciously aided to acquire these attributes, victory from the unseen Kingdom of Baha [Glory] shall be vouchsafed to them.[152]

Chapter 9

Accessing the True Self & Quieting the Lower Nature

Considering the demands of the twelve Behavioral Standards described in the last two chapters, it is clear that one's ability to contribute to the creation of a compassionate atmosphere and culture for Consultation—as well as successfully confer with other members—is a function of one's ability to reliably access one's higher nature while quieting the influence of one's lower nature. This chapter focuses on the dynamics of our inner world as an arena to expand our compassion, Consultation, and growth capacities.

In Chapters 5 and 6, we described the dimension of human beings that has the ability to rise above our lower nature and manifest the attributes of our higher nature as the true self. In our previous book, we cited numerous quotations from a great variety of the world's Holy Books that attest to the reality of this dimension of the human being. For example, in the Judaic Writings we find these words:

> God said, "Let us make man in our image, after our likeness."[153]

The Christian Writings say:

> I am in my Father, and you in me, and I in you.[154]

The Islamic Writings say:

> I have breathed into man of my spirit.[155]

And the Writings of the Bahá'í Faith say:

> Turn thy sight unto thyself, that thou mayest find Me standing within thee, mighty, powerful and self-subsisting.[156]

Given the universal recognition of the true self in the world's Scriptures, how do we go about evoking the true self and quieting the influence of our lower nature during Compassionate Consultation and in our lives generally?

The Messengers of God Call Forth the True Self in Each of Us

The Messengers that God has sent to humankind through the ages have confirmed that part of our purpose in life is to develop spiritual virtues and attributes—the intrinsic, but latent, characteristics of the true self. These great Beings have modeled the very attributes of God to humanity, revealed the Creative Word that imbues souls and civilization with new life and capacity, and founded the world's major religions. We learn about the qualities of the spirit latent within us through the exemplary character, behavior, and teachings of God's Messengers; and furthermore, the eternal, unchangeable truths in Their Holy Writings enumerate, and motivate us to acquire the virtues latent within us. Describing this process, the Writings of the Bahá'í Faith say:

> The Prophets and Chosen Ones have all been commissioned by the One True God, magnified be His glory, to nurture the trees of human existence with the living waters of uprightness and understanding, that there may appear from them that which God hath deposited within their inmost selves.[157]

These Great Beings have brought us into touch with this "inmost" true self, which has been endowed with all that is best and noble in human beings and is associated with the spirit or soul, the dimension of each of us that is eternal.

Without the Divine Messengers, We Would Be Ignorant of the True Self

We might assume that humans have an innate, conscious awareness of the true self and its latent capacities. However, the truth is that without these Holy Messengers providing the resources for us to become aware of and draw forth the true self, humankind would not progress spiritually or socially; we would not know what we are capable of and would remain captives of our lower or animal nature. 'Abdu'l-Bahá explains:

> For the world of nature is an animal world. Until man is born again from the world of nature -- that is to say, becomes detached from the world of nature, he is essentially an animal, and it is the teachings of God which convert this animal into a human soul.[158]

The True Self—Compassionate, Consulting & Growth-Seeking

Gaining a deeper understanding of the true self is critically important because the true self, when aligned with its Creator, is at once the self that is inherently compassionate, the self that excels at Consultation, and the growth-seeking self. In order to consistently and effectively use Compassionate Consultation, we must not only know how to *access* our true self, but increasingly *reside* in it. Accomplishing this also requires that we better understand our lower nature and its relationship to our higher nature.

Recognizing the Tension Between the True Self & the Lower Nature

Through the ages, the Holy Scriptures have gradually awakened us to our dilemma *and* potential in terms of the lower and higher nature within us; and the dilemma and potential are highly relevant to Compassionate Consultation. The Hindu Writings state:

> I know what is good
>
> But I am not inclined to do it;
>
> I know also what is bad,
>
> But I do not refrain from doing it.[159]

The Christian Writings describe these dynamics similarly:

> So I find it to be a law that when I want to do right, evil lies close at hand. For I delight in the law of God, in my inmost self, but I see in my members another law at war with the law of my mind and making me captive to the law of sin which dwells in my members.[160]

The Zoroastrian Writings also refer to these inner conflict dynamics:

> Yes, there are two fundamental spirits, twins which are renowned to be in conflict. In thought and in word, in action, they are two: the good and the bad. And between these two, the beneficent have correctly chosen, not the maleficent.[161]

Distinguishing Between Our Lower & Higher Natures & Energizing the True Self

'Abdu'l-Bahá helps us to understand the differences between our lower and higher natures when he states:

> Know that there are two natures in man: the physical nature and the spiritual nature... The first is the source of all imperfection; the second is the source of all perfection.[162]

'Abdu'l-Bahá describes the imperfections of our physical or lower nature:

> All the imperfections found in the animal are found in man. In him there is antagonism, hatred and selfish struggle for existence; in his nature lurk jealousy, revenge, ferocity, cunning, hypocrisy, greed, injustice and tyranny. So to speak, the reality of man is clad in the outer garment of the animal, the habiliments of the world of nature, the world of darkness, imperfections and unlimited baseness.[163]

Animal attributes are not blameworthy in animals because they are the captives of nature and instinct; however, animal attributes are blameworthy in human beings because we have been equipped with a higher nature that enables us to rise above nature and instinct. Unlike adversarial modes of decision-making, Compassionate Consultation is a process that requires its practitioners to rise above nature and instinct.

'Abdu'l-Bahá also explains how our lower or animal nature can take control of our existence:

> This physical world of man is subject to the power of the lusts, and sin is the consequence of this power of

the lusts, for it is not subject to the laws of justice and holiness. The body of man is a captive of nature; it will act in accordance with whatever nature orders. It is, therefore, certain that sins such as anger, jealousy, dispute, covetousness, avarice, ignorance, prejudice, hatred, pride and tyranny exist in the physical world. All these brutal qualities exist in the nature of man. A man who has not had *a spiritual education* is a brute.[164] (emphasis added)

In contrast, 'Abdu'l-Bahá also explains how "a spiritual education" causes our true self—our higher or spiritual nature—to emerge:

This spiritual nature, which came into existence through the bounty of the Divine Reality, is the union of all perfections and appears through the breath of the Holy Spirit. It is the divine perfections; it is light, spirituality, guidance, exaltation, high aspiration, justice, love, grace, kindness to all, philanthropy, the essence of life. It is the reflection of the splendor of the Sun of Reality.[165]

Commenting further on the nature of the "spiritual education" which can draw forth our true self, 'Abdu'l-Bahá says:

...The Word of God is the cause of spiritual life. It is "a quickening spirit," meaning that all the imperfections which come from the requirements of the physical life of man are transformed into human perfections by the teachings and education of that spirit.[166]

It is evident that daily prayer, meditation, study of the Word of God, and taking action in alignment with the Creative Word free our inherent spiritual, intellectual, and social capacities from the pull of our lower nature and energize the true self. These practices also increase our capacity for Compassionate Consultation because coming from our true self enables us to tap the full potential of this decision-making methodology.

Our True Self is the Life Force within Us That Seeks Change, Growth and Transformation

In the second preceding quotation above, 'Abdu'l-Bahá states that our true self or spiritual nature is characterized by "high aspiration" and is "the essence of life." This suggests that our true self is the dynamic life force within us that seeks change, growth, and transformation.

The vegetable kingdom offers an excellent illustration of the dynamic force of life. Living things in this kingdom invariably stretch upward and outward to draw closer to the sun and are in a constant and dynamic state of change and growth. Even in the harshest and most inhospitable environments, living things in the vegetable kingdom find a way to gain a foothold and commence the process of change, growth, and transformation. The true self demonstrates these same qualities. It is not satisfied with the status quo, but constantly seeks to stretch upward and outward to draw nearer to its Creator. Despite experiencing resistance and inhospitable conditions, this growth-seeking self determinedly gains a foothold, sees obstacles as potential guides, and views set-backs as potential teachers. Rather than coming from confusion and frustration, the true self tends to ask, "What is the significance of what is happening here, and how can I learn and grow from it?" These qualities contribute mightily to the successful use of Compassionate Consultation because they translate problems and challenges into opportunities for spiritual, social, and material advancement.

It is often said with a degree of cynicism that people hate change. But this characteristic is more typical of our lower nature than it is of the true self. The true self sees life as a spiritual adventure and has an intrinsic curiosity about all of creation as a result of its eagerness to achieve greater understanding and proximity to its Creator.

Our True Self Has a Sense of Connectedness to All Living Things

'Abdu'l-Bahá states in the second preceding quotation that our spiritual nature is characterized by "kindness to all." This suggests that our true self recognizes its spiritual kinship with all other human beings and has a sense of custodianship for all created things. When we see a person treating others with disdain or hostility or treating the environment with disrespect and carelessness, these are not manifestations of that person's true self or higher nature, but of their worldly or lower nature. When we are feeling disconnected from other living things, our lower nature is in the lead; when we are feeling connected to other living things, our higher nature is in the lead. When engaged during Compassionate Consultation, the true self's sense of connectedness to all living things assures that the Consulting members will deliberate attentively and respectfully and seek solutions that are fair and just to all the parties impacted by each decision.

Our True Self Is Attracted to & Able to Resonate to Spiritual Realities

'Abdu'l-Bahá describes our spiritual nature in the second preceding quotation as "light, spirituality, guidance..." and as "...the reflection of the splendor of the Sun of Reality." It seems evident from this that our true self knows that it is a divine trust and is attracted to, and able to resonate with, spiritual realities. The presence of these attributes of the true self is also essential during Compassionate Consultation because it prevents the Consulting members from giving undue weight to the purely material realities of a situation being considered and inspires them to both identify and align their decision with the spiritual principles involved in the situation, thereby assuring the advancement of civilization at the micro and/or macro level.

Our True Self Is Endowed with Enlightened Leadership Qualities

We have already discussed some of the true self's enlightened leadership qualities such as its compassion (for self and others), its perspective (the ability to see the small picture of our lives in the context of the big picture of our lives), and its curiosity and aspiration in conjunction with seeking change and growth. In further describing the qualities of the true self, 'Abdu'l-Bahá says:

> ...We find...justice, sincerity, faithfulness, knowledge, wisdom, illumination, mercy and pity coupled with intellect, comprehension, the power to grasp the realities of things and the ability to penetrate the truths of existence.[167]

These qualities enable the true self to create a vision of a preferred future state (in terms of self-development or collective development) and the courage and insight to work creatively toward making that vision a reality. In addition, rather than sitting in judgment of other people, our true self is characterized by the "justice, sincerity, faithfulness," "wisdom," and "mercy" to value and accept the perspectives, talents, and conditions of other people and excels at collaboration with others. Finally, our true self has confidence in its ability to navigate its path through life when relying on the "illumination" coming from the guidance of its Creator.

Throughout the world, there is intense need for the leadership qualities of the true self in all arenas of society—in the family, community, organizations, institutions, and government agencies. *Decisions* in all these arenas can be optimized if we can learn to manifest these latent attributes more consistently in our individual and collective decision-making.

Mastering the Challenge of Coming from the True Self

Fostering the emergence of our true selves requires that we understand how our inner resources are constituted. Shoghi Effendi has clarified the nature of our inner being as explained in a letter from the Universal House of Justice:

> Shoghi Effendi, in a letter dated 25 May 1936, written on his behalf, identifies man's "true self" with "his soul". In describing the nature of "man's inner spiritual self or reality", he notes that the "two tendencies for good or evil are but manifestations of a single reality or self", and that the self "is capable of development in either way."[168]

'Abdu'l-Bahá also clarifies the constitution of our inner resources and the challenge of being human:

> ...This human reality stands between the higher and the lower in man, between the world of the animal and the world of divinity. When the animal proclivity in man becomes predominant, he sinks even lower than the brute. When the heavenly powers are triumphant in his nature, he becomes the noblest and most superior being in the world of creation. All the imperfections found in the animal are found in man... All these great perfections are [also] to be found in man. Therefore

we say that man is a reality which stands between light and darkness. From this standpoint of view, his nature is threefold, animal, human and divine. The animal nature is darkness; the heavenly is light in light.[169]

From Shoghi Effendi's and 'Abdu'l-Bahá's descriptions, we can infer a diagram shown in Figure 9.1. The human reality has the capacity to move in either direction—left or right. When we refer to the true self, we refer to occupying the right-hand circle. When we refer to the worldly self, we refer to occupying the left-hand circle. We all occupy either circle—or somewhere between them—based on the habit patterns established by our decisions and choices in life.

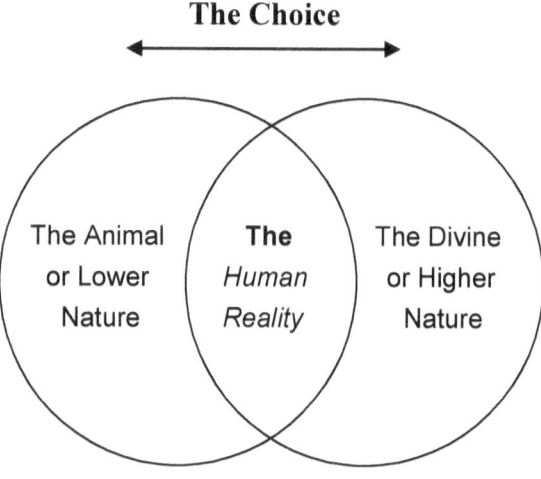

Figure 9.1

Sorting Your Proper from Your Improper Education

Bahá'u'lláh explains the rarity of finding people who fully occupy the right-hand circle:

> Man is the supreme Talisman. Lack of a proper education hath, however, deprived him of that which he doth inherently possess... The Great Being saith: Regard man as a mine rich in gems of inestimable value. Education can, alone, cause it to reveal its treasures, and enable mankind to benefit therefrom.[170]

Merriam-Webster's Dictionary defines a "talisman" as an object that acts as a charm to avert evil and bring good fortune and as something producing magical or miraculous effects. So, we could conclude that if men and women had "a proper education," they would have the supreme capacity among created beings to avert evil, bring good fortune, and produce magical or miraculous effects. Furthermore, this education would allow human beings to manifest "gems of inestimable value" which would profit all created things.

Clearly, this "proper education" draws forth our higher nature (the true self), and anything at variance to this education would be an "improper education" that draws forth our lower nature. We want to unlearn and replace attitudes and behaviors fostered by improper education with attitudes and behaviors fostered by proper education. This guidance comes from the teachings of the divine Messengers. 'Abdu'l-Bahá says:

> The holy Manifestations of God come into the world to dispel the darkness of the animal or physical nature of man, to purify him from his imperfections in order that his heavenly and spiritual nature may become quickened, his divine qualities awakened, his perfections visible, his potential powers revealed and all the virtues of the world of humanity latent within him may come to life.[171]

The daily discipline of prayer, meditation, and reading the Creative Word nourishes the true self just as physical food sustains the body, and it keeps the focus on spiritual thoughts and actions. 'Abdu'l-Bahá says:

> The reality of man is his thought, not his material body. The thought force and the animal force are partners. Although man is part of the animal creation, he possesses a power of thought superior to all other created beings.
>
> If a man's thought is constantly aspiring toward heavenly subjects then does he become saintly; if on the other hand his thought does not soar, but is directed downwards to centre itself upon the things of this world, he grows more and more material until he arrives at a state little better than that of a mere animal.

> Thoughts may be divided into two classes: (1st) Thought that belongs to the world of thought alone; (2nd) Thought that expresses itself in action. Some men and women glory in their exalted thoughts, but if these thoughts never reach the plane of action they remain useless: the power of thought is dependent on its manifestation in deeds.[172]

Turning lofty thoughts into action often means that, after prayer and reading of the Creative Word, we meditate on any misalignment between the divine summons and our current state and take *action* to uproot these misalignments inhibiting the emergence of our higher nature. We may need to uproot habits of laziness, apathy, low self-esteem, or doubt so we can live up to our lofty thoughts. As 'Abdu'l-Bahá says:

> Holy souls are like soil which has been plowed and tilled with much earnest labor; the thorns and thistles cast aside and all weeds uprooted.[173]

Building Awareness of the Interplay between Our Higher & Lower Natures

"Earnest labor" is required to uproot the false learning implicit in unworthy habits and preoccupation with lower nature desires. Part of this earnest labor is building our awareness of, and ability to manage, the interplay between our higher and lower natures. We gain insight into this interplay from a statement by 'Abdu'l-Bahá:

> As long as man is a captive of habit, pursuing the dictates of self and desire, he is vanquished and defeated. This passionate personal ego takes the reins from his hands, crowds out the qualities of the divine ego and changes him into an animal, a creature unable to judge good from evil, or to distinguish light from darkness. He becomes blind to divine attributes, for this acquired individuality, the result of an evil routine of thought becomes the dominant note of his life.
>
> May all of you be freed from these dangers and delivered from the world of desires that you may enter into

the realm of light and become divine, radiant, merciful, Godlike.[174]

'Abdu'l-Bahá's statement illustrates how—in Compassionate Consultation or in life generally—our lower and higher natures can vie for leadership and control within our being. For example, I may have established a habit that when someone disagrees with me, and I feel my self-worth being threatened, I respond with antagonism. Or, I may experience difficulty in establishing relationships with others because my inclination is to compete with others for power or supremacy. Upon reflection, I can tell that antagonism and power-seeking are impulses from my lower nature or animal nature. In both cases, the attributes of my true self are crowded out. Worldly motivations anchor me in my lower nature rather than freeing me to reside in my true self or spiritual nature. 'Abdu'l-Bahá says:

> For attachment to the world has become the cause of the bondage of spirits, and this bondage is identical with sin…It is because of this attachment that men have been deprived of essential spirituality and exalted position.[175]

Bahá'u'lláh says:

> O My Friends!....Approach Me not with lifeless hearts, defiled with worldly desires and cravings.[176]

The Triggering of Our Lower Nature

'Abdu'l-Bahá's description in the first quotation in the preceding section suggests that habits of thought can trigger aspects of our lower nature to "take the reins from the hands" of our true self. An aspect of our lower nature be a thought, impulse, or voice inside our head—it could be an angry aspect, a fear of commitment aspect, a controlling aspect, or a biased aspect, etc.—that can trigger, drown-out the voice of the true self, and take over executive functioning from the true self.

Aspects of our lower nature that over-function in this way are driven by worldly desires that constrict our compassion and thereby inhibit our capacities for Compassionate Consultation. An angry aspect can have inordinate affection for vindication, a fear of commitment aspect for safety, a controlling aspect for the familiar and comfortable, and a biased aspect for confirmation of superiority. When aspects of our lower nature trigger in this way, we may find ourselves flooded with troubling thoughts, emotions, and desires, and responding to others with an intensity that seems inappropriate to the situation, or in other ways that are not in our or their best spiritual interests. Bahá'u'lláh exhorts us to avoid these dynamics and suggests that the true self's healthy state is to fear nothing except God:

> ...let thine heart be afraid of none except God. Obstruct not the luminous spring of thy soul with the thorns and brambles of vain and inordinate affections, and impede not the flow of the living waters that stream from the fountain of thine heart.[177]

Differentiating & Managing the Interplay between Our Higher & Lower Natures

We can learn to better manage the interplay between our true self and lower nature and progress toward the desired outcome previously expressed by 'Abdu'l-Bahá for every human being:

> When the heavenly powers are triumphant in his [man's] nature, he becomes the noblest and most superior being in the world of creation.[178]

It is beneficial to differentiate the attributes of our higher nature from those of our lower nature so that we can recognize *the source* of the thoughts, impulses, and voices when they arise within us. A partial listing of these attributes is shown in Figure 9.2. These are all drawn or extrapolated from the quotations of Bahá'u'lláh and 'Abdu'l-Bahá in this chapter and Chapter 13.

In the left-hand column are some attributes of our lower nature and in the right-hand column some corresponding attributes of our higher nature.

The Choice

Some Attributes of Our Lower Nature	Some Attributes of Our Higher Nature
1. Worldly fears	1. Fear of God only
2. Vain & inordinate affections	2. Pure & spiritual affections
3. Baseness--unable to judge good from evil	3. Nobility—attracted to virtue
4. Attraction/attachment to worldly things	4. Attraction/attachment to spiritual things
5. Constricted heart	5. Dilated heart
6. Impatience	6. Patience
7. Darkness	7. Light
8. Brutish nature	8. Heavenly nature
9. Predatory anger	9. Mercy & pity
10. Tyranny	10. Justice
11. Cunning	11. Sincerity
12. Faithlessness	12. Faithfulness
13. Ignorance	13. Knowledge-penetrates truths of existence
14. Foolhardiness	14. Wisdom
15. Un-inspired	15. Inspired, illuminated
16. Rationalization	16. Intellect
17. Circumscribed	17. Unlimited
18. Idle fancies & vain imaginings	18. Grasps the true reality of things
19. Preoccupation with transitory things	19. Occupation with eternal things
20. Subject to the power of the lusts	20. Independent of all else but God
21. Animal imperfections	21. Divine perfections
22. Wandering in the paths of delusion	22. Cleaving to the path of guidance
23. A captive of nature	23. Exaltation—rises above nature
24. Low aim, laziness, passivity	24. High aspiration

25. Resists change	25. Welcomes change
26. Change triggers fear/desire for safety	26. Change prompts courage/curiosity
27. Hatred	27. Love & Compassion
28. Rudeness, criticism	28. Kindness to all, uncritical acceptance
29. Selfishness, greed & avarice	29. Selflessness, generosity & self-sacrifice
30. The trivialities of life	30. The essence of life
31. Enmeshed in the world of desires	31. Grace—delivered from world of desires
32. Pride	32. Humility
33. Prejudice & injustice	33. Bias-free fairness
34. Covetousness	34. Detachment & contentment
35. Disputation & contest	35. Harmony & teamwork
36. Antagonism & ferocity	36. Unity & peacefulness
37. An un-spiritual education	37. A spiritual education
38. Hypocrisy	38. Authenticity & integrity
39. Revenge	39. Forgiveness
40. Competition, the struggle for existence	40. Collaboration, collective well-being
41. Jealousy & envy	41. Un-possessiveness & well-wishing
42. Self-centered focus/actions	42. Pure deeds in a spirit of humble service
43. Driven qualities	43. Guided qualities
44. Feels disconnected, separate from others	44. Feels connected, at one with others
45. Seeks liberty—free from all constraints	45. Seeks true liberty—submission to God
46. Devious, secretive	46. Trustworthy, transparent
47. Ambitious for worldly power	47. Eager for spiritual/societal advancement
48. The insistent self (the prison of self)	48. The true self (the guided self)

Figure 9.2

Given the two lists of attributes in Figure 9.2, we can begin to differentiate between the internal thoughts, impulses, and voices we experience from our lower nature and those we experience from our higher nature. Differentiating the two sets of impulses in this way is the first step toward managing the interplay between them. For example, in the midst of a calm, Consultative discussion with a colleague, I may suddenly feel at risk and have the impulse to dispute an issue with him or her. I realize that fear, disputation, and competitiveness are attributes of my lower nature and that my lower nature is trying to "take the reins" from the hands of my true self. Mindful of this, I also realize that the harmony and collaboration I had been experiencing with my colleague before I felt the impulse to disputation were attributes of my true self. I then can make a conscious choice to *turn the volume down* on the impulses from my lower nature and *turn the volume up* on the impulses from my higher nature. Consequently, rather than disputing the issue with my colleague in a spirit of contest, I pose questions to my colleague about the issue in a spirit of harmonious teamwork, which helps us both to fully explore the issue and reach a collaborative decision.

From the foregoing scenario, we can see an example of the true self's ability to "grasp the true reality of things" (right-hand column attribute #18 in Figure 9.2). Even while going through an experience (the discussion with the colleague), the true self has the capacity to stand outside the experience enough to evaluate the implications of what is being experienced (the inner conflict between the impulses of the lower and higher natures) in relation to the soul's larger journey. Left to itself, the lower nature would be inclined toward the "idle fancies and vain imaginings" (left-hand column attribute #18 in Figure 9.2) of how to compete for supremacy and win the dispute. But the true self can stand outside and observe the inner conflict generated by the lower nature's triggering, evaluate it, and, countering the impulse by an act of will, "hold onto the reins" and maintain its executive functioning.

The lower nature tends to fill us with a *driven* quality (the impulses *have us* rather than *us having* the impulses); the higher nature tends to fill us with a *mindfully guided* quality (the true self mindfully chooses the impulses it will honor based on spiritual principles). In this way, the true self can lead and coordinate the different aspects of our being with great skill, grace, and effectiveness. And it can be the master of Compassionate Consultation.

The Proper Relationship Between the True Self and the Lower Nature

Consider an analogy between your life and the theater. While your true self is intended to be the lead character in the spiritual drama of your life, aspects of the lower nature have the capacity to be either supporting characters or to steal the show. In other words, at a given moment, your true self could be at the front of the stage of your life with the lower nature standing to the rear of the stage; or one or more aspects of your lower nature could be standing at the front of the stage of your life and the true self could be standing to the rear. The former case (with the true self in the lead) is the divinely intended and optimal relationship with the lower nature; the true self is in executive function with the lower nature subordinated (e.g. you are still eating and sleeping to meet the animal needs of your body, but this is occurring in a healthy way under the leadership of the higher nature). This also represents the best internal resource alignment for Compassionate Consultation and growth-seeking. The opposite internal resource alignment (with one or more aspects of the lower nature in executive function and the true self subordinated) is typical for adversarial contest and contention and for growth-avoidance.

If you have never concentrated on differentiating your true self from your lower nature, and you have one or more over-functioning aspects of your lower nature that habitually take over executive function from your true self, you may think that your lower nature is *who you are* in that situation. However, who you *truly* are—your *true self*—has been overwhelmed or subordinated by over-functioning aspects of your lower nature. Bahá'u'lláh reminds us of who we are and the true self's primacy:

> O My servants! Could ye apprehend with what wonders of My munificence and bounty I have willed to entrust your souls, ye would, of a truth, rid yourselves of attachment to all created things, and would gain a true knowledge of your own selves—a knowledge which is the same as the comprehension of Mine own Being. Ye would find yourselves independent of all else but Me, and would perceive, with your inner and outer eye, and as manifest as the revelation of My effulgent Name, the

seas of My loving-kindness and bounty moving within you. Suffer not your idle fancies, your evil passions, your insincerity and blindness of heart to dim the luster, or stain the sanctity, of so lofty a station.[179]

PART III: MAKING COMPASSIONATE CONSULTATION DECISIONS

Introduction to Part III

Part III of this book delves into the steps of various models of Consultation, examines the role of questions during Consultation and growth-seeking, identifies decision-making patterns that show up during Consultation, and provides a variety of detailed application examples which exhibit Compassionate Consultation in action.

Our intent has been to provide enough examples so that all readers may find what they need in order for the processes to become more familiar and user-friendly. After an initial reading, one use of Part III (and the four Appendices in the free PDF available at **billandjeanharley.com/actionplan**) is as a resource to refer to when you are actually attempting to apply one of the models.

With the exception of the personal examples, all of the application examples are hybrids of a variety of individuals and groups we have worked with over the years and are not attributable to any one individual, group, or organization. Examples are organized according to the type of group using Compassionate Consultation—the individual (where the members are internal aspects of the individual), a pair, a family, and larger groups. This expansion from the intrapersonal to the interpersonal, from the small group to the larger group, and from the local to the more global requires an accompanying expansion in the capacity to manifest compassion to ever larger segments of the human family.

Chapter 10

Using the Steps of Compassionate Consultation

In this chapter we will discuss some procedural models for combining Consultation and compassion that are based on the Writings of Bahá'u'lláh, 'Abdu'l-Bahá, and Shoghi Effendi. These procedural models support the optimum *atmosphere* and expedite effective *procedures* for Compassionate Consultation. We are not suggesting that these are the *only* procedural models for combining Consultation with compassion, but Bahá'u'lláh says:

> It is incumbent upon every man of insight and understanding to strive to translate that which hath been written into reality and action.[180]

In this spirit, we submit the following models as proven methods and frameworks that have assisted individuals and groups as they endeavored to *develop skill* in the use of Compassionate Consultation.

When the spirit, atmosphere, and culture for Compassionate Consultation are right, models are transcended. However, when we are learning how to balance and pedal forward on the two-wheeler of Consultation and compassion, it helps to have a set of training wheels to lean on. Procedural models that expedite collaboration and protect us from pitfalls help us come from our true selves, gain skill, and fulfill our potential.

The models to be discussed with their step instructions are:

- The 3-Step Model of Consultation
- The 6-Step Model of Consultation
- The 6-Step Identify/Agree (I/A) Model of Consultation
- The 4-Step V x D x F Model of Consultation
- The 6-Step Reflection & Planning Model of Consultation

Further details on these models, as well as additional model versions, are included in the four Appendices in the free PDF available at **billandjeanharley.com/actionplan**. In addition, the application examples found throughout Part III also clarify model use.

The 3-Step Model of Consultation

As discussed in Chapter 2, John Kolstoe[181] infers three basic procedural steps for Consultation based on a previously referenced quote from 'Abdu'l-Bahá. These three procedural steps are contained in what we refer to as the 3-Step Model of Consultation shown in Figure 10.1.

The 3-Step Model of Consultation

1. Understanding the Situation.
2. Deciding What to Do.
3. Executing or Carrying Out the Decision.

Figure 10.1

The Steps of the 3-Step Model of Consultation

In preparing to apply the 3-Step Model (or any other Consultation model) the group should first commit to honoring the 12 Compassionate Consultation Behavioral Standards and the 7 Prime Requisites discussed in Chapters 7 and 8. The internalization of these virtues and qualities contributes more to success in Consultation than anything else.

In **Step 1**, understanding the situation, the group identifies the facts and circumstances present in the situation that is under consideration. The term "facts" is defined loosely here and includes perceptions, hunches, and feelings in addition to scientifically verifiable data. The goal is to surface and clarify all relevant aspects of the current situation.

In **Step 2**, deciding what to do, the group identifies solutions that address the situation defined in Step 1. If needed, these solutions may be sorted, ranked, and sequenced as part of Step 2, but ultimately the group decides what solutions will be carried forward.

In **Step 3**, the group lays out an execution or implementation plan that will meet its needs. This will typically include breaking the solutions down into smaller steps or paths of action and indicating what will be done by when and by whom.

These three steps align with the 3-step change process of Knowledge + Volition + Action = Attainment (see Chapter 3), and they are fundamental and effective as a general approach to Consultation. They are primarily descriptive of what we call "Rolling Compassionate Consultation Decision-Making."

Rolling Compassionate Consultation Decision-Making

Rolling Compassionate Consultation Decision-Making is often the preferred decision-making procedure for groups that meet regularly to address routine issues and/or proceed through a lengthy agenda. The group tends to "roll along" fairly smoothly through its agenda, thus giving this model of Compassionate Consultation its name. Prayers for divine assistance would be said before entering into the steps.

This procedure is ideal when the agenda items are not highly complex, controversial, or broad in scope (e.g. strategic planning issues). Typically, a group using this model is conscious of fully covering its agenda in the time available and is attempting to efficiently and effectively decide on each issue without going into great depth or detail. Usually, group members are familiar with each other and the subjects of their deliberations. This type of deliberation and decision-making can often be done without visual aids since the group can move as one body through the steps and the agenda items without the need for an augmented group memory system (as would be provided by a flipchart, white board, or sticky wall).

There is a general pattern of moving through the three steps of understanding the situation (identifying the facts), deciding what to do (agreeing on solutions), and then executing or carrying out the decision (agreeing on implementation steps and taking action). The transitions from step to step may be formally announced or informal, unannounced and apparently spontaneous. Sometimes the group may move from the facts step (understanding the situation) to the deciding what to do step and then back again until it finds its way. At times the group will seem satisfied with a very limited review of the facts in Step 1, and at other times it may be more thorough in this regard.

Occasionally, a member will raise a familiar agenda issue and make an action recommendation, and the group will agree and proceed. In these cases, the group members assume that they already have a grasp of the situation and relevant facts (Step 1). Accordingly, the group moves rapidly to the decision on solutions (Step 2) and into execution (Step 3) while Step 1 (identifying the facts) is passed over.

When done well, Rolling Compassionate Consultation Decision-Making is fluid, relaxed, and only minimally taxes the group's energy. It represents a useful and efficient procedure for fairly routine agenda items and the addressing of a range of task or policy issues that are familiar and relatively low in complexity and/or controversy for members.

Limitations with Rolling Compassionate Consultation Decision-Making

There are limitations to this procedure. Unless the group members are highly skilled in Compassionate Consultation, problems may arise when issues of greater complexity and/or controversy are encountered, or the group size exceeds nine members. In such cases, the simple 3-step procedure may prove to be too loose and unfocused to deal with the more complex and emotionally-charged issues as well as the larger quantity of data generated by the larger group size. These challenges call for a more focused set of procedural steps that allow group members to sequence, confer on, and process all of the data in an organized and unified way that will expedite reaching a decision. The 6-Step Model of Consultation offers a useful format to deal with such situations.

The 6-Step Model of Consultation

As discussed in Chapter 2, 'Abdu'l-Bahá's description of the disciples of Jesus Christ Consulting after His crucifixion can be seen as an example of the procedure that we call the 6-Step Model of Consultation. This Model is shown in Figure 10.2. Because this model provides a more defined and focused sequence to the Consultative process, it enables groups to shoulder greater complexity, controversy, and data quantity with grace.

The Option of Reversing Steps 2 & 3

The sequence of steps shown in Figure 10.2 is most appropriate for an individual or group that is in crisis and/or has just experienced a challenging event. Significantly, both circumstances were present with the disciples of Jesus Christ in 'Abdu'l-Bahá's narrative about "The most memorable instance of spiritual consultation…"[182] In such cases, the identification and agreement on the facts (Step 2) needs to precede the identification and agreement on the issue (Step 3) because the situation being faced is at first clouded and undefined. Until the group has agreed on the facts, the issue, problem, or opportunity may be too confused to articulate and agree upon.

The 6-Step Model of Consultation

1. Convening by Praying for Divine Guidance
2. Identifying & Agreeing on the Facts
3. Identifying & Agreeing on the Issue
4. Identifying & Agreeing on the Spiritual Principles Involved
5. Identifying & Agreeing on the Solutions
6. Identifying & Agreeing on Implementation Steps

Figure 10.2

However, for individuals and groups that are not in crisis or responding to a challenging event and are relatively clear about their purpose and circumstances, Steps 2 and 3 of the 6-Step Model may be reversed as shown in Figure 10.3. For family, community, and organizational groups not in crisis, the members are typically aware that a particular and loosely defined issue, problem, or opportunity has been looming and crying out to be addressed. In such cases, it is usually most helpful to define and agree on the parameters of the issue prior to identifying and agreeing on the facts as shown in Figure 10.3. In our experience, this latter format fits the *majority* of situations groups face using the 6-Step Model, and it will be the format used most often in this book.

Before describing each step of the 6-Step Model, we will address the potential need for a group memory system when using this and other models described below.

The 6-Step Model of Consultation (with *Steps 2 & 3* Reversed)

1. Convening by Praying for Divine Guidance
2. *Identifying & Agreeing on the Issue*
3. *Identifying & Agreeing on the Facts*
4. Identifying & Agreeing on the Spiritual Principles Involved
5. Identifying & Agreeing on the Solutions
6. Identifying & Agreeing on Implementation Steps

Figure 10.3

Providing for a Group Memory System

Whenever a group is undertaking a somewhat complex or challenging issue, or if the group size is larger than a few members, it works best to use some kind of group memory system. This is especially helpful in Steps 2-6 when using the 6-Step Model in the context of a couple, a family, a community, or an organizational group.

A group memory system involves the use of a flipchart (for approximately 2-10 people), a sticky wall (for 5-50 people), or an old-style overhead projector, document projector, or digital projector (for larger groups) to promptly display ideas the group is generating so that the group can see the ideas in an objective format. These tools are used to focus the attention of the group and to provide a record reflecting both the group's thought process and its memory.

The Ultimate Objective—to Orient the Group Mind

The objective of a group memory system is to orient the *group mind*. Otherwise, each person will be subject to remembering some ideas, but not others, and will fail to get the larger picture. It is the group mind (the synergistic combination of the individual minds in the group) that will reach a unanimous decision in Compassionate Consultation. The group mind will have a hard time reaching agreement on complex or challenging issues unless each member of the group sets aside his or her own selective memory system and instead makes use of the external, comprehensive, group memory system.

Additional Benefits Arising from the Use of a Group Memory System

When a designated person in the group immediately records each participant's contribution in clear view, this visual record remains on view throughout the process so that members can refer back to it as well as monitor the group's progress. Because each contribution is recorded immediately, the person presenting the idea can make sure it is written in such a way that the intended meaning is captured. Since there is no labeling to indicate who contributed each idea, each visible entry tends to decrease or eliminate the tendency to take personal ownership of ideas, assist individuals in detaching their egos from their ideas, and help all participants move along with the group. The visibility of generated ideas also assists members in avoiding repetition of ideas already recorded and contributing additional ideas when a superior idea has already been recorded.

Also, focus and concentration are expedited by being able to isolate and point to the ideas in question. The multi-sensory nature of these group memory systems (you can hear the idea, see the idea, get up and touch the idea, etc.) also tends to reduce daydreaming, engage the attention of individuals more fully, and draw members into involvement.

What Is a Sticky Wall?

Some of the Consultation models described in the chapters and the free PDF use a sticky wall as the group memory system. A sticky wall may be any size but for larger groups is typically composed of an approximately twelve feet wide by five feet high sheet of rip-stop nylon that has been hemmed on all four edges, hung on a wall (with pushpins or masking tape), sprayed with an aerosol repositionable fixative (such as Krylon® Easy-Tack Repositionable Adhesive #7020 sold in craft stores), and then used as a group memory system for group decision-making.

Because the sprayed side of the sheet of rip-stop nylon has become tacky, and the whole nylon sheet is hung on a wall, the apparatus is called a sticky wall. It allows a group to write their ideas on sheets of paper of any size using felt tip markers, place the ideas on the sticky wall, and then move the sheets of paper (and ideas) around in relation to each other so that all members can read, follow, discuss, and manipulate the ideas at once.

The Steps of the 6-Step Model of Consultation

This section will describe each step of the 6-Step Model of Consultation shown in Figure 10.4 (the steps are treated in greater detail in Appendices I and II in the free PDF).

The 6-Step Model* of Consultation

1. Convening by Praying for Divine Guidance
2. Identifying & Agreeing on the Issue
3. Identifying & Agreeing on the Facts
4. Identifying & Agreeing on the Spiritual Principles Involved
5. Identifying & Agreeing on the Solutions
6. Identifying & Agreeing on Implementation Steps

* Steps 2 and 3 may be reversed when desired by the group.

Figure 10.4

The assumption is that the participants undertaking this form of Compassionate Consultation have first committed to honoring the 12 Behavioral Standards and 7 Prime Requisites.

Step 1: Convening by Praying for Divine Guidance

In **Step 1**, the group members take turns praying aloud requesting God's guidance and assistance in their deliberations. The prayers serve the purposes of turning the members' focus inward, away from a preoccupation with the busy details of the day; helping them orient and align themselves in relation to their Creator; and softening their focus on material circumstances while sharpening their focus on spiritual reality. By humbly communing with God in this way, the members open the door to divine assistance.

Step 2: Identifying & Agreeing on the Issue

In **Step 2**, the group members come to agreement on the parameters of the issue at hand. Groups can spend entire meetings conferring unsuccessfully only to realize eventually that individual members have been focused on different issues. Step 2 is intended to prevent this by having each member articulate her or his perceptions of the issue to be addressed, recording the perceptions on a flipchart, and then editing and integrating these perceptions into an issue statement to which every member of the group can agree (see detailed examples on pages 30-31 and 85-86 in the free PDF available at **billandjeanharley.com/actionplan**).

Even though this step can be time consuming, it is fundamental in setting up the group for success in subsequent steps. As with individuals, groups also perform better when they achieve a focus. 'Abdu'l-Bahá says:

> So long as the thoughts of an individual are scattered he will achieve no results, but if his thinking be concentrated on a single point wonderful will be the fruits thereof. One cannot obtain the full force of the sunlight when it is cast on a flat mirror, but once the sun shineth upon a concave mirror, or on a lens that is convex, all its heat will be concentrated on a single point, and that one point will burn the hottest.[183]

When a group identifies and agrees on the issue, "all its heat" is concentrated on that issue, and good results tend to follow.

Step 3: Identifying & Agreeing on the Facts

In **Step 3**, the group identifies and agrees on the facts, conditions, and circumstances related to the issue being addressed. The term "facts" is defined loosely here and includes perceptions, hunches, intuitions, and feelings in addition to scientifically verifiable data. *All of these dimensions of the term "facts" are included because they are all part of the terrain that surrounds the issue.* The goal of Step 3 is to help the group members entertain and agree on all of the relevant data before they proceed into the subsequent steps. The relevant data may contain contradictory elements. This is usually not a problem and does not need to be resolved, as long as it is noticed and acknowledged by the members.

As discussed earlier, in certain situations groups may find it necessary to complete Step 3, identifying and agreeing on the facts, before Step 2, identifying and agreeing on the issue.

Step 4: Identifying & Agreeing on the Spiritual Principles Involved

In **Step 4**, group members identify the spiritual principles and human values they want to honor that are relevant to the agreed upon issue and facts.

The obvious sources for *spiritual principles* are the Holy Books of the world's revealed religions. They are the moral and ethical reservoirs which serve as touchstones to help us live in ways that will fulfill the larger purposes for which we were created. They contain spiritual principles that are eternally applicable, as well as social and administrative principles with spiritual implications that are applicable to the era in which they were revealed.

Human values tend to spring from the same original scriptural sources as do spiritual principles, but they have become so ingrained in human thinking that they are behavioral standards we just accept at face value. An example is the value of treating all human beings with dignity. While this human value may be seen as an outgrowth of the Judaic spiritual principle, "You shall love thy neighbor as thyself,"[184] it has come to be thought of as a universal value for human beings and is not necessarily associated with a specific spiritual source.

So in Step 4 of the 6-Step Consultation Model, we take time to search for, reflect upon, and agree on the spiritual principles and human values that are relevant to the issue and facts about which we are deliberating. When relevant spiritual principles are identified and agreed upon by group members in Step 4, they tend to vibrate the "truth chord" in all the members at an intuitive level. This is so because spiritual principles define the spiritual realities behind phenomenal existence—and as spiritual beings we resonate to, and are motivated by, them. When we honor these spiritual principles in our decision-making processes, we align our material circumstances with spiritual reality. This is a critically important step because honoring spiritual principles helps us rise above the limits imposed by adversarial contest and temporal expediency to honor that which has eternal value.

This means that the agreed upon eternal values will establish both the parameters for and the province of the solutions to be agreed upon in Step 5. Consequently, agreeing upon spiritual principles in Step 4 energizes the search for solutions, guides the way to inspired outcomes, and fosters spiritual and social advancement. As 'Abdu'l-Bahá says, "Progress is the expression of spirit in the world of matter."[185]

These effects of coming from spiritual principles and values in deliberative problem solving and decision-making have also been emphasized by the Universal House of Justice in its document, *The Promise of World Peace*:

> There are spiritual principles, or what some call human values, by which solutions can be found for every social problem. Any well-intentioned group can in a general sense devise practical solutions to its problems, but good intentions and practical knowledge are usually not enough. The essential merit of spiritual principle is that it not only presents a perspective which harmonizes with that which is immanent in human nature, it also induces an attitude, a dynamic, a will, an aspiration, which facilitate the discovery and implementation of practical measures. Leaders of governments and all in authority would be well served in their efforts to solve problems if they would first seek to identify the principles involved and then be guided by them.[186]

Step 5: Identifying & Agreeing on the Solutions

In **Step 5**, identifying & agreeing on the solutions, the group members create a vision of the *preferred reality* they seek that addresses the issue under discussion and aligns with the agreed upon facts and spiritual principles. The process of going through the Consultative steps up to this point and now agreeing on solutions and new vision are usually intertwined with a struggle for spiritual, intellectual, and social growth on the part of the members individually and collectively. The participants go through a winnowing process in which the true and significant have been separated from the false and irrelevant.

The fruit of this winnowing process in Compassionate Consultation is the group members' arrival at a solution or more often at a place of agreement involving several solution elements—what we call a bundle of solutions—that need to be integrated and implemented in the following step.

Step 6: Identifying & Agreeing on Implementation Steps

In **Step 6**, identifying & agreeing on implementation steps, members integrate the solution elements from Step 5 into an implementation plan. *This is a most practical step without which the solutions will never take root.* In the spirit of Muhammad's statement, "Trust in God, but tie your camel,"[187] the members make sure in Step 6 that their trust in divine guidance during Steps 1-5 leads directly into responsible, practical action. This is where "the rubber meets the road" as the group breaks the solution elements down into smaller, measurable steps, applies a timeline, and indicates who will do what by when.

Benefits of the 6-Step Model of Consultation

There are numerous benefits to using the 6-Step Consultation Model as well as the 6-Step I/A Consultation Model described in subsequent sections.

Separating Procedural Steps

One of the advantages of the 6-Step Model over the 3-Step Model is that articulating and isolating more of the procedural steps enables the group to focus on one step at a time, entertain complex or controversial data in a focused way, and move through the steps in unison. When steps are not separated, it is common for groups to experience frustration and disunity as some members concentrate on defining the issue, while others generate facts or spiritual principles, and still others offer possible solutions.

Ideal for Focused Issues, Opportunities or Problems

The 6-Step Consultation Model is especially well-suited to address complex, challenging, *focused* issues, opportunities, or problems. In this context, "focused" means a discrete or defined issue, as opposed to a more diffuse, macro-level visioning or strategic planning issue (in which case the 4-Step V x D x F Model described below may be more appropriate). An example of a focused or discrete issue in a family setting is, "How to establish and abide by a budget that will allow us to begin saving 10 percent of our income each month." An example of a focused issue for an organization is, "How to accelerate our new product development efforts so that we come out with at least six new products each year for the next four years."

Formalizing the Fulfillment of the Second Essential Requirement

Another benefit of the 6-Step Model is that the first step formalizes the fulfillment of 'Abdu'l-Bahá's second essential requirement for successfully combining Consultation and compassion—namely that the Consulting members "...turn their faces to the Kingdom on High and ask aid from the Realm of Glory."[188] Calling upon divine assistance reminds members of the sacred dimension involved in Consulting together as a group and of their responsibility to open themselves to being instruments of divine guidance.

Even More Procedural Infrastructure May Be Needed

Although the 6-Step Model clearly provides an augmented procedural infrastructure, there are circumstances when even more infrastructure may be needed. Situations commonly occur in which the rarefied spiritual environment required for Compassionate Consultation is threatened at the start by the presence of interpersonal conflict, partisan viewpoints, ideological differences, intense frustration with the complexity of the issue, or deep-seated distrust among the members. The 6-Step I/A Consultation Model is ideal for such situations.

The 6-Step Identify/Agree (I/A) Model of Consultation

Over the past thirty years, we have developed and refined a version of the 6-Step Consultation Model that provides optimum procedural infrastructure to help groups successfully work on the most complex and challenging focused issues. We call this model the 6-Step Identify/Agree

(I/A) Consultation Model. Because it provides a rhythm and discipline for the alternate *suspension* and *application* of critical judgment, it tends to constructively channel the expression of diverse viewpoints and defuse negative conflict. Most importantly, the model's procedural infrastructure actually induces, supports, and protects the honoring of the 12 Behavioral Standards and 7 Prime Requisites.

The primary difference in this model from the previous one is that Steps 2 through 6 have each been divided into two steps (A and B). As Figure 10.5 and the accompanying key indicate, the *group members* **suspend** *critical judgment during the A-lettered steps and* **apply** *critical judgment during the B-lettered steps*. Consequently, during all A Steps, group members *Identify* **(I)** ideas, while in all B Steps, members *Agree* **(A)** on ideas. As a result, we refer to this model as the 6-Step *I/A* Model.

The 6-Step Identify/Agree (I/A) Model

	1.	Convening by Praying for Divine Guidance
○	2A.	Identifying the Issue
⊕	2B.	Agreeing on the Issue
○	3A.	Identifying the Facts
⊕	3B.	Agreeing on the Facts
○	4A.	Identifying the Spiritual Principles/Values Involved
⊕	4B.	Agreeing on the Spiritual Principles/Values Involved
○	5A.	Identifying Solutions
⊕	5B.	Agreeing on Solutions
○	6A.	Identifying Implementation Steps
⊕	6B.	Agreeing on Implementation Steps

Key

○ Suspend critical judgment (A-steps)

⊕ Apply critical judgment (B-steps)

Figure 10.5

Suspending Critical Judgment Increases Idea Quality

Suspending critical judgment during all A-lettered steps means that, as in traditional brainstorming, we want to complete the generation of ideas before we judge them. In other words, if the ideas were fish, we want to throw out our nets and haul in as many fish as we possibly can before we start sorting through them to decide which fish to keep and which to throw back in the water. Research and effective practice have shown that delaying judgment and generating a larger *quantity* of ideas contributes to increased *quality* of ideas.

Suspending Critical Judgment Increases Reflection & Meditation

When we suspend critical judgment, we also encourage the power of reflection and meditation to enhance the process of Compassionate Consultation. Thought and contemplation can expand and deepen in the absence of premature critical judgment. While all the Consultation models can be enhanced by the reflection and meditation of the members, the 6-Step I/A Model actually provides structure to foster it. This is important because, as previously noted, Consultation gives man "…insight into things and enableth him to delve into questions which are unknown."[189] Part of the reason Consultation has this power may be its ability to foster reflection and meditation in its members. Regarding the importance of reflection and meditation Bahá'u'lláh says:

> The source of crafts, sciences and arts is the power of reflection. Make ye every effort that out of this ideal mine there may gleam forth such pearls of wisdom and utterance as will promote the well-being and harmony of all the kindreds of the earth.[190]

One of the signs that reflection, meditation, and contemplation are occurring during Consultation is the presence of moments of silence. 'Abdu'l-Bahá says:

> Bahá'u'lláh says there is a sign (from God) in every phenomenon: the sign of the intellect is contemplation and the sign of contemplation is silence, because it is impossible for a man to do two things at one time—he cannot both speak and meditate.[191]

Appropriately, the suspension of critical judgment during Consultation slows the members' processes of mind and heart so that unhurried contemplation during moments of silence can occur. Overall, by delaying the onset of critical judgment in each of steps 2-6 of the decision-making procedure, the 6-Step I/A Consultation Model safeguards space for the application of reflection and meditation, and this adds richness, depth, creativity, and innovation to the deliberation and decision-making process.

Nurturing Ideas

Suspending critical judgment and increasing reflection create a receptive, nurturing climate for ideas. New ideas can emerge, develop, and grow instead of being cut off by critical judgment as soon as they are brought forward. New ideas are fragile—very much like newborn infants. If they are not nurtured and kept alive, they cannot fulfill their potential. New ideas during Compassionate Consultation—however foreign they may seem—may be the result of divine guidance. So delaying judgment and increasing reflection are conducive to discovering where ideas and guidance are trying to lead us.

Finding More In-Depth Descriptions of the Steps of the 6-Step I/A Model

The preceding general description of the steps of the 6-Step I/A Consultation Model is augmented in the first two appendices in the free PDF. Appendix I provides a detailed description of using the model with a flipchart. Appendix II provides a detailed description of using the model with a sticky wall as the group memory system.

The 4-Step V x D x F Model of Consultation

We can also use the Compassionate Consultation process to make proactive improvement of a more generalized nature rather than to respond to a narrowly focused issue or problem. For example, we may want to improve the culture of a family, community, or work group, or create a comprehensive picture of how an organization, community, or relationship will look and function five years in the future. 'Abdu'l-Bahá says, "Settle all things, both great and small, by consultation."[192] He also refers to "… affairs which are general in nature and universal":

Thus consultation is acceptable in the presence of the Almighty, and hath been enjoined upon the believers, so that they may confer upon ordinary and personal matters, as well as on affairs which are general in nature and universal.

For instance, when a man hath a project to accomplish, should he consult with some of his brethren, that which is agreeable will of course be investigated and unveiled to his eyes, and the truth will be disclosed. Likewise on a higher level, should the people of a village consult one another about their affairs, the right solution will certainly be revealed. In like manner, the members of each profession, such as in industry, should consult, and those in commerce should similarly consult on business affairs. In short, consultation is desirable and acceptable in all things and on all issues.[193]

In these more generalized contexts, a 4-step Consultation model based on the D x V x F > R Model of Change & Spiritual Growth (introduced in Chapter 3) can be very useful. The concept behind this change model is that **Dissatisfaction (D)** times **Vision (V)** times **First Steps (F)** must be greater than the **Resistance to Change (R)** that exists in the individual, group, or organization if the change and growth are to be successful and lasting. The **(D)** refers to Dissatisfaction with the current situation; the **(V)** to a positive Vision or picture of the preferred future that is deemed possible; and the **(F)** to realistic, achievable First Steps that can be taken to move toward the Vision **(V)**. When the D, V, and F are robustly present, they will overpower any *resistance* to overcoming barriers and crossing the "swamp of change," which involves discomfort, messiness, and the unfamiliar. Forms of resistance are typically supported by the gravitational pull of existing habits that keep the present situation in place.

The Steps of the 4-Step V x D x F Model of Consultation[194]

When we adapt this change and growth model for use as a Consultation model, the sequence of the D and V are reversed so that they align with the actual sequence of steps used during Consultation. The steps of the 4-Step V x D x F Consultation Model shown in Figure 10.6 are based on the assumption that group members have already identified the context they want to improve. As with the other models, it is critically important that participants honor the 12 Behavioral Standards and 7 Prime Requisites.

The 4-Step V x D x F Model

1. Convening by Praying for Divine Guidance
2. Identifying & Agreeing on the Concrete Vision of the Future
3. Identifying & Agreeing on the Dissatisfying Barriers
4. Identifying & Agreeing on the First Steps

Figure 10.6

Step 1: Convening By Praying For Divine Guidance

Step 1 in this model is the same as Step 1 in the 6-Step Consultation Model described earlier in this chapter.

Step 2: Identifying & Agreeing on the Concrete Vision of the Future (V)

Vision is a thought, concept, or object formed by the imagination. It is a mode of seeing or conceiving of a potential reality which is not yet real, but that could become real in the future if the proper focus and effort were applied to creating it. The term "concrete vision" means a vision that is specific rather than vague and abstract.

Perceptible Characteristics Are Elements of the Concrete Vision

Step 2 is prompted by the question, *"What perceptible characteristics do we want to have in place by (future date)?"* The participants then identify and agree on the perceptible characteristics they envision being in place by a specific future date. Perceptible characteristics are attributes or conditions that are concretely recognizable, and they represent elements of the concrete vision of the future. By some agreed upon future date, they will be either present or absent—there is nothing vague or abstract about them. For example, a perceptible characteristic of the future agreed upon by a work group might be: "On-time project completion rates have reached 90 percent." A perceptible characteristic agreed upon by a couple or family might be: "Each night for dinner we turn off the TV and converse with each other around the dining room table." As these examples demonstrate, perceptible characteristics *are stated as though they are an accomplished reality* even though they will not be achieved until some future date. This affirmative language breathes life into the vision in the minds of the participants creating it. Collectively, these perceptible characteristics make up the Concrete Vision of the Future. A typical concrete vision would include approximately six to twelve perceptible characteristics or elements.

Vision Enhances Knowledge & Understanding

The ability to have or create a vision is a capacity conferred by God only on human beings. The value of vision is emphasized by Bahá'u'lláh when He says:

> We cherish the hope that through the loving-kindness of the All-Wise, the All-Knowing, obscuring dust may be dispelled and the power of perception enhanced, that the people may discover the purpose for which they have been called into being. In this Day whatsoever serveth to reduce blindness and to increase vision is worthy of consideration. This vision acteth as the agent and guide for true knowledge. Indeed in the estimation of men of wisdom keenness of understanding is due to keenness of vision.[195]

While these words of Bahá'u'lláh have numerous meanings and applications, it appears that one of them is the concept of "vision" as the human capacity to see a potential reality that is not yet manifest. He conveys that God's loving-kindness and compassion can enhance the human world by removing "obscuring dust," enhancing our "power of perception," and helping us "discover the purpose" of our creation; and that vision can act "as the agent or guide" to help us obtain "true knowledge." This suggests that divine assistance and the human power of vision can help us get a clearer fix on spiritual reality, the spiritual growth toward which we need to navigate, and the way we will contribute to an ever-advancing civilization ("the purpose for which" we "have been called into being"). Like Consultation itself, vision contributes to the increase in our knowledge and understanding, for Bahá'u'lláh says, "Indeed... keenness of understanding is due to keenness of vision."

The Concrete Vision of the Future (V)

When we pray for divine guidance in Step 1, we are praying to be guided (in Step 2) to a vision of a better future reality that represents both our spiritual growth goals and how we will contribute to social advancement in our family, work group, or community. In Step 2, when we identify and agree on the concrete vision of the future, we actually create this vision of spiritual growth and social advancement. We want the perceptible characteristics that make up this vision to be as specific, clear, and tangible as possible because Bahá'u'lláh tells us that "keenness of understanding is due to keenness of vision." Keenness means sharpness. In order to achieve the perceptible characteristics of our future vision we will need to *understand* them. All spiritual growth requires an increase in *understanding*. Bahá'u'lláh's statement suggests that to have a sharply defined *understanding* of our future vision, we must first have a sharply defined *vision*. In other words, the more perceptible, tangible, specific, and clearly defined our vision of the future is, the more likely we are to achieve it and make it a reality. That is why we refer to "The Concrete Vision" in Step 2. We want it to be so tangibly and clearly defined that we will know when we have achieved it *and* when we have not yet reached it. Once the concrete vision has been agreed upon, the participants move on to Step 3.

Step 3: Identifying & Agreeing On the Dissatisfying Barriers (D)

It is the presence of dissatisfaction (the D in the 4-Step V x D x F Model) which prompts the group participants to use this Compassionate Consultation model in the first place. If there *is not* a critical mass of dissatisfaction with the present situation or context, the participants will not overcome resistance to change no matter how sharply defined the concrete vision is. If there *is* a critical mass of dissatisfaction present, there is a choice to be made. On the one hand, the participants may conclude after a brief discussion that the nature of their dissatisfaction with the current state is so simple, well understood, and agreed upon that they want to omit Step 3. In such a case, they can move directly from agreeing on the concrete vision to Step 4, identifying and agreeing on the first steps (F) to achieve the vision.

On the other hand and in the majority of cases, Step 3 provides an important opportunity for the participants to deepen their understanding of the dissatisfying barriers that are blocking the path to the concrete vision of the future. Since "keenness of understanding is due to keenness of vision,"[196] the presence of the *keenly defined concrete vision* also creates the opportunity for the members to create a *keenly defined understanding of their dissatisfaction* (D).

Step 3 is prompted by the question, *"What barriers are creating dissatisfaction and blocking our path to the vision?"* This step is most effectively done when people are asked to suspend critical judgment and brainstorm at least one dissatisfying barrier for each one of the agreed upon perceptible characteristics of the concrete vision articulated in Step 2. Then when critical judgment is applied, only the most important barriers are selected and agreed upon. When the participants identify and agree on answers to the dissatisfying barriers question, it helps them name *what is present* and measure the distance between it and the concrete vision of the future.

Dissatisfying barriers are often difficult to see and articulate because they require us to summon the courage to honestly look at ourselves; we need to assess our behaviors, assumptions, relationships, beliefs, and patterns in order to recognize the barriers we ourselves have contributed to creating. Often barriers are the very walls that we need to scale and climb over to achieve new awareness as growth-seekers. Taking the time to discover and name them often helps us clearly understand our situation for the first time. An example of a dissatisfying barrier agreed upon by a work group might be, "Conflicting management goals lead to conflicting priorities." An example of a barrier agreed upon by a family might be, "Fatigue and lethargy prevent us from claiming the quality time we seek together." A typical analysis of the barriers would include approximately six to twelve agreed upon barriers, and these barriers in combination represent the dissatisfying barrier assessment.

When the participants have identified and agreed upon the dissatisfying barriers that are blocking the path to the concrete vision, they are ready to move on to Step 4.

Step 4: Identifying & Agreeing On the First Steps (F)

In Step 4, the participants identify and agree on the first action steps they will take to address the dissatisfying barriers and move forward on the path to achieving the concrete vision of the future. Assuming that the agreed upon perceptible characteristics of the future vision are to be achieved in five years, what we want in Step 4 is to define the *first set* of steps for approximately the first one to two years. When those steps have been accomplished, the surrounding terrain on the pathway to the concrete vision of the future will have changed; from that new vantage point, a *second set* of action steps can be defined more efficiently and effectively.

The question that prompts Step 4 is, *"What First Steps can we take to address the Dissatisfying Barriers and stimulate forward movement toward the Concrete Vision of the future?"* The participants need to keep one eye on the elements of the concrete vision and one eye on the barriers as they answer this question. It is useful to ask participants to suspend critical judgment and brainstorm one or more first action steps for each of the dissatisfying barriers. Then critical judgment is applied, and only the most important, effective, and sustainable first steps are agreed upon. Typically, some of the selected first steps address multiple dissatisfying barriers even though each first step was initially generated in response to only one barrier. This is beneficial because during implementation we want to get the maximum results with the minimum use of resources.

Since first action steps are really goals or objectives, the phrasing of each one needs to begin with an action verb and include specific information about what will be accomplished, by whom, and by what date. An example would be, "Schedule a one-on-one coffee date twice a week to strengthen quality time together beginning March 1 (Juan and Gretchen jointly responsible)."

When the first steps (F) have been clearly defined and agreed upon, Step 4 is complete, and the participants can go about implementing their agreement.

Further Descriptions of the Steps of the 4-Step V x D x F Model of Consultation

The preceding description of the steps of the 4-Step V x D x F Consultation Model is augmented in Appendix III in the free PDF, which provides alternative versions of the 4-Step Model for use with both a flipchart and a sticky wall as the group memory system.

The 6-Step Reflection & Planning Model of Consultation

Another Compassionate Consultation application is for reflection and planning on the part of members of neighborhoods and communities who are taking responsibility for their own spiritual, social, and material development. 'Abdu'l-Bahá says:

> Likewise on a higher level, should the people of a village consult one another about their affairs, the right solution will certainly be revealed... In short, consultation is desirable and acceptable in all things and on all issues.[197]

Groups may meet periodically to assess their progress and plan next steps and may number twenty-five to one hundred people or more. A sequence of steps is needed which includes all participants, fosters unity in diversity, and allows them to share and cross-fertilize thoughts, feelings, and inspirations regarding what they have experienced and learned and what needs to happen next. In such settings, Steps 3-6 of the 6-Step Consultation Model can be augmented with open-ended questions to form the 6-Step Reflection & Planning Consultation Model shown in Figure 10.7.

The 6-Step Reflection & Planning Model of Consultation

1. Convening by Praying for Divine Guidance
2. Identifying & Agreeing on the Issue
   How to discover & agree on what has happened in the last term of community development, what we have learned, and where we need to go in the next term.
3. Identifying & Agreeing on the Facts
   What have you/we experienced in the last term of community development? What have we learned?
4. Identifying & Agreeing on the Spiritual Principles Involved
   What spiritual principles and human values are relevant to our learning? What spiritual principles and human values need to inform our next steps?
5. Identifying & Agreeing on the Solutions
   What is the significance of where we are, and what needs to happen to move the community forward in the next term of development?
6. Identifying & Agreeing on Implementation Steps
   What will you/we commit to in the next term of development that will lock in our learning and advance our community-building process?

Figure 10.7

The model begins with prayers for guidance in Step 1 and is followed by a pre-set statement of the issue in Step 2. Next, for each of Steps 3-6, a facilitator repeatedly poses one or more open-ended questions (with a minimum fifteen second pause after each posing for input from the group) until group members seem finished with it, and then moves on to the next step's open-ended question(s) as shown in Figure 10.7. Whether capture of data is formal or informal, the steps and questions enable group members to report and process their experiences, learning, and aspirations in all their diversity, and to move as one body into the next phase of community development.

The Spirit Animating the Consultation Models

The emphasis in this chapter (and in the Appendices in the free PDF available at **billandjeanharley.com/actionplan**, which give further details) is largely on the steps and mechanics of an assortment of Consultation models that are offered as a means to assist the reader in more effectively achieving Compassionate Consultation. The models offered can be thought of as tools in the growth-seeker's tool kit. Like all tools, these tools function only as well as the craftsman using them. If we are to be true craftsmen in the use of these models, we must remind ourselves of the spirit that needs to animate them. It is the participants' internalization of the 12 Behavioral Standards and 7 Prime Requisites that provides this spirit and enables group members to come from their true selves, rise above mere consensus decision-making, and achieve Compassionate Consultation.

The participants will know they are reaching proficiency in these respects when symptoms of success begin to appear. The group will notice that it is moving from step to step within the models gracefully and almost imperceptibly; it will feel its own rhythm in moving from the suspension to the application of critical judgment; ideas will be gently generated, shared, and nurtured and then intensely, but dispassionately, debated and reconstituted; the group will manifest the apparently contradictory attributes of unity in diversity, detached caring, patient efficiency, and proactive servitude; it will increasingly experience itself as a decision-making instrument leveraging divine assistance to achieve deeper understanding, transformative decisions, and social and spiritual advancement.

Chapter 11

Harnessing the Power of Questions

One of the purposes of life is to develop the divine attributes that lie latent within each of us just waiting to be manifested through our own effort. Some of these spiritual attributes, such as generosity, humility, loving-kindness, detachment, and patience, are obvious. Some are less obvious, and one of these is the divine attribute of posing questions.[198] Posing effective, thought-provoking, growth-producing questions is spiritual behavior.

The Nature of Questions

Questions can be powerful because they cue the mind, heart, and spirit to call up information that is relevant to growth-seeking and Compassionate Consultation. Questions can lead to change, take us deeper, generate conscious reflection, and open us to what we have been unaware of and need to attend to for our growth.

Open-ended questions—questions that cannot be answered with a "yes" or a "no"—are especially powerful because they take us deeper in discussion, deeper inside ourselves, or deeper into an issue to discover ideas, thoughts, feelings, truths, aspirations, and other data that may have been out of our conscious awareness. The best lead words for open-ended questions are *What, How, Where, When*, and *Who,* and the first two of these (*What* and *How*) generate the most information.

Why is also sometimes used as a lead word in open-ended questions, but it is potentially dangerous because it carries a sense of judgment and evaluation of the other person. This raises defenses that can shut down the exploratory power of the question. To avoid that risk, one can usually substitute the word *What*. For example, instead of asking, "*Why* did you do that?" one can ask, "*What* led you to do that?"

Taking advantage of most opportunities and solving most problems and dilemmas involves being able to ask the right questions. Years ago, in a television interview, the director of the NASA space program said that the biggest challenge in planning and executing outer space travel was not resources or technology, but learning how to ask the right questions. This is because powerful questions stimulate thought, challenge our assumptions, lead us to examine and reframe our reality, deepen our awareness, and accelerate our growth. As Francis Bacon said, "A prudent question is one-half of wisdom."

Some Questions that Further Learning

Let's look at some examples of evocative, open-ended questions that people can ask themselves, and, sometimes with the simple change of a pronoun, ask in a Consultative group to further the learning. *What are some other ways to respond to this situation?* is a question that can stimulate one's thought, challenge one's assumptions, assist one to let go of old, ineffective ways of doing things, and grasp new, more effective patterns of action. Similarly, *What are some other ways this situation could be interpreted?* is a question that can help reframe our reality. A question such as *How do I think, feel, and behave when I'm in situation XYZ?* can deepen one's self-awareness in preparation for new action. The question *What was my part in the negative interaction that just occurred?* can accelerate growth in one's sense of responsibility, accountability, and inner awareness.

Some other powerfully evocative questions include the following: How can I (we) make things better? How healthy or unhealthy is this situation for me? In what ways is this situation inhibiting or advancing my spiritual growth? How can I turn this interaction around in a positive direction? What am I thinking that is causing me to feel this way? What aspect of my thinking is self-defeating? What aspect of my thinking is realistic? Such questions are valuable tools for growth-seekers and those who use Compassionate Consultation because the information, insight, and self-knowledge that come from these kinds of probing questions can help individuals and groups identify and then go over walls to new awareness.

Powerful Questions Can Be Constructive or Limiting

Not all powerful questions are *constructively* powerful. Questions can lead us to fulfillment or to disappointment, to success or failure, to unity or disunity. In many situations we may ask ourselves questions that negatively direct our mindset and pre-determine the nature of our behavior. Consider the following example. You are checking into a hotel. At the time you made the reservation two months ago, you were told by the reservations clerk that check-in time was 3:00 p.m. You arrive at 3:18 p.m. and are abruptly told your room will not be ready for at least another hour. You are upset. You had the afternoon and evening planned. You think to yourself: *How can they treat customers this way even when customers make their travel arrangements in compliance with* their *policies? How could they be so un-customer-focused? How can they be so rude and inconsiderate? Why does this have to happen to me?* These are rhetorical questions in that they are not genuinely seeking an answer. What these questions do is put one in a blaming frame of mind that generates anger, resentment, a victim mentality, and behaviors that are abrasive and alienating.

How would the situation be different if you were to come from your true self and ask sincere, open-ended questions to which you genuinely want answers such as: *How can I make the best of this? How could my waiting time be best spent? What are the sources of resistance in this situation and what is the wall I need to scale? What growth is this situation calling forth from me?* These growth-seeking questions reflect a compassionate perspective and reframe the material conditions in a spiritual context. They call for creative thinking and are likely to lead to new insights and behaviors. Questions such as these also generate further questions such as: *What is trying to happen here? What are my options? What do I really want or need?* These kinds of questions lead us toward change and growth, and they engage and spring from the true self.

Questions, then, can be useful, effectively stimulating, and growth-producing, or unanswerable and self-defeating. Psychotherapist Marilee Goldberg writes that an example of the dominant internal questions of her clients with low self-esteem is: *Why am I so unworthy?* which is a question that cannot be responded to in any useful way.[199] However, it *is* useful to consider the question: *What is preventing me from esteeming (respecting, caring for) myself?* or *How can I esteem myself?* or *What needs to change so I can esteem myself?* These questions foster growth by taking us deeper, generating creative thinking, and producing specific solution ideas that lead in a new direction. We need to ask growth-producing questions to get growth-producing answers.

The social scientist Piaget described stages of human cognitive development from birth through adulthood. In the stage he called "formal operational or second-order thinking," which is reached in adolescence, one becomes able to observe one's own thinking, behavior, and being. This requires a shift from being absorbed by a situation to having enough distance from it to be able to observe the situation and ask questions about it. With this kind of thinking we can go behind the visible to determine the inner meaning by asking ourselves questions such as: *What is really going on here? What do I want in this situation? To what extent am I being who or how I want to be?* These kinds of growth-seeking questions move us into the realm of intentional or conscious living and are constructive rather than limiting. These are also the kind of questions that can help us align our material circumstances with our spiritual circumstances.

The Role of Questions in Compassionate Consultation & Growth-Seeking

It is clear that the content or nature of a question, as well as the developmental level of the poser of the question, have the power to direct our thoughts, feelings, and behaviors toward or away from growth-seeking. They also have the power to move us toward or away from Compassionate Consultation.

In Part I of this book, we introduced the 6-Step Model of Consultation. Figure 11.1 below shows that each step of the 6-Step Consultation Model aligns with a key growth-seeking question and that the steps and the corresponding questions can inform each other. An example of growth-seeking and Consulting within one's self will illustrate how the interplay between the growth-seeking questions and the Consultation steps can work.

The 6-Step Model of Consultation:
Growth-Seeking Question for Each Corresponding Step

1. Convening by praying for divine guidance	1. How do my present circumstances relate to my ultimate life purposes?
2. Identifying & agreeing on the facts	2. What are the resistance forces in my life and where are they leading me?
3. Identifying & agreeing on the issue	3. What is the wall that I need to scale and go over?
4. Identifying & agreeing on the spiritual principles	4. What spiritual principles need to influence the pursuit of my objective?
5. Identifying & agreeing on the solutions	5. What is the objective for which I am longing?
6. Identifying & agreeing on implementation steps	6. What are the steps to the objective that align with the spiritual principles?

Figure 11.1

Let us suppose that Ed is passed over for a promotion to supervisor in his workplace even though he was the most likely candidate in the organization based on experience and seniority. The feedback from his boss is that his work peers and colleagues did not support his promotion because they felt he would be too tough on people as a boss. When Ed goes home from work that evening and commiserates with his spouse and teenage children, his spouse says, "I am sorry you were passed over, but that feedback should be familiar to you based on things I have been saying to you for years," and then leaves the room. When he asks his teenage son and daughter for their opinions, they tell him they are sorry about his being passed over, look uncomfortable, and indicate they need to do their homework.

Sitting in solitude, Ed reflects on the fact that both his spouse and children have given him feedback over several years that they feel he is constantly judging and evaluating them. He realizes that his own family has left the room, and it reminds him of similar experiences in the workplace when his peers and colleagues have left the room after he has stated his opinions. Suddenly, it hits him that this situation is a growth-seeking situation.

Ed poses the first growth-seeking question to himself: *How do my present circumstances relate to my ultimate life purposes?* Initially, his mind whirls, and no ideas come to him, so he decides to use the first step of Consultation: *Convening by Praying for Divine Guidance.* He prays for divine assistance, and as he prays he feels himself relaxing and his heart dilating. After praying, the growth-seeking question about how his present circumstances relate to his ultimate life purposes has the desired effect on him. He realizes that everything he knows and believes about the purposes of life suggests he should be loving and compassionate toward others, but he finds himself being hard on others. Clearly, there is something to which he needs to attend.

Ed realizes that his mind is already starting to *identify and agree on the facts* of his situation (the second step of Consultation) in terms of the patterns he has noticed at home and the workplace in which he judges and evaluates others. To extend his understanding of the facts he poses the second growth-seeking question, *What are the resistance forces in my life and where are they leading me?* He realizes that his boss, his work colleagues, his spouse, and his children are all resistance forces in his life, and they are leading him to face the fact that he is judgmental and "hard" on people.

Having reached this awareness, Ed's mind naturally wonders what the real issue is (Consultation Step #3). He poses the third growth-seeking question to himself, *What is the wall I need to scale and go over?* His first thought is that he needs to stop judging and evaluating others all the time, but he realizes that this is stating the issue in the negative. He wonders how he can state it in the positive. After some meditation and reflection, it occurs to him that the opposite of judging and evaluating others is feeling compassion for others. Instantly, he realizes that the wall he is facing, and the issue he needs to address is, *how can I unblock and release my capacity for expressing compassion for others?*

The fourth growth-seeking question and the fourth Consultation step are both about identifying the spiritual principles involved. The growth-seeking question is, *what spiritual principles need to influence the pursuit of my objective?* At this point, Ed is not sure what the objective is that he is seeking, but the first relevant spiritual principle that comes to his mind is to "love thy neighbor as thyself." As he meditates on this spiritual principle, he thinks about loving and treating his neighbors (at work and in his home) the same way he treats himself. He is startled to realize that he is already doing that. In fact, this is part of the problem. He realizes that he is sitting in judgment of himself in the same way he is sitting in judgment of others. In other words, the harshness that characterizes his interactions with others is a reflection of the harshness that characterizes his interactions with himself.

Ed continues to meditate on spiritual principles that need to influence the pursuit of his objective and that are relevant to his issue. One that comes to mind is the following injunction from Bahá'u'lláh:

> All men have been created to carry forward an ever-advancing civilization. The Almighty beareth Me witness: To act like the beasts of the field is unworthy of man. Those virtues that befit his dignity are forbearance, mercy, compassion and loving-kindness toward all the peoples and kindreds of the earth.[200]

As he meditates on this quotation, it occurs to him that he is also one of the "peoples and kindreds of the earth" and that he must treat himself with "forbearance, mercy, compassion, and loving-kindness" so that he can, in turn, treat others the same way.

Ed now turns to identifying the fifth growth-seeking question, *What is the objective for which I am longing*? As he meditates on this question, he feels his throat constrict and is filled with emotion. Scanning the demanding and unforgiving internal emotional terrain he has occupied for most of his life, he realizes that the objective for which he is longing is self-acceptance and the freedom to experience love and compassion for, and from, others. His eyes well up as he comes to this recognition.

While meditating on this fifth growth-seeking question, Ed also considers Consultation Step 5 which is *identifying and agreeing on the solutions*. He thinks of a range of possible solutions, but settles on having a number of discussions with his spouse and children about his new-found awareness and searching for a coach or counselor who can assist him in making progress to scale and go over the wall to achieve his objective.

Finally, Ed works at *identifying and agreeing on implementation steps* (Consultation Step 6) and the corresponding growth-seeking question, *What are the steps to the objective that align with the spiritual principles?* He looks at his calendar and pencils in two evening dinners with his family in the coming week to share and discuss his new awareness and also makes a note to call a friend who is capable of guiding him to an appropriate counselor or coach. He also makes a note to meet with his work colleagues, at a later point, to discuss his newfound awareness and to share the personal changes he will be working to implement in the future. He checks to make sure these implementation steps align with the two spiritual principles he has identified and is satisfied that they do.

Questions & Meditation Feed Compassionate Consultation & Growth-Seeking

In the foregoing scenario of Consulting and growth-seeking with the self, both meditation and questions play powerful roles. 'Abdu'l-Bahá describes the true nature of meditation and the role that questions play for human beings:

> It is an axiomatic fact that while you meditate you are speaking with your own spirit. In that state of mind, you put certain questions to your spirit and the spirit answers: the light breaks forth and the reality is revealed. You cannot apply the name 'man' to any being void of this faculty of meditation; without it he would be a mere animal, lower than the beasts. Through the faculty of meditation man attains to eternal life; through it he receives the breath of the Holy Spirit—the bestowal of the Spirit is given in reflection and meditation. The spirit of man is itself informed and strengthened during meditation; through it affairs of which man knew nothing are unfolded before his view. Through it he receives Divine inspiration, through it he receives heavenly food.[201]

It is apparent that questions and meditation should be inseparable parts of both Compassionate Consultation and growth-seeking. In both individual and group settings, questions, followed by pauses that enable participants to meditate on the questions, are crucial aspects of successful practice. When being done within the individual, pauses may sometimes need to extend for hours or days. In group settings, if talking is continuous, there is either no room for meditation, or participants must stop listening to the talk in order to meditate. Either of these two latter scenarios creates an inhibition to optimum Consultation and growth-seeking.

The Primary Questions That Drive Each Consultation Step

There are primary questions that drive each step of the 6-Step Consultation Model, and they can be compared to the primary growth-seeking questions that correspond to each Consultation Step as shown in Figure 11.2.

In both Consultation and growth-seeking the objective is to deal with issues immediately at hand without losing sight of the larger purposes of life and the spiritual principles involved. These primary questions direct our focus inward or deeper to engage our spirits in meditation, to get behind or under the visible, and to help us understand what is happening and what needs to happen at the spiritual level first, and at the material level second.

Additional Questions that Drive Consultation & Growth-Seeking

In addition to the primary questions for the 6 steps of Consultation and for growth-seeking in Figure 11.2, there are a host of other questions that can also be used. For each of the primary questions there are a variety of supporting questions that can deepen and expand exploration and growth in groups and individuals.

THE 6-STEP MODEL OF CONSULTATION WITH PRIMARY QUESTIONS FOR EACH STEP	PRIMARY GROWTH-SEEKING QUESTION FOR EACH CORRESPONDING STEP
1. Convening by praying for divine guidance	1. How do my present circumstances relate to my ultimate life purposes?
Question: How can I/we open myself/ourselves to receive divine assistance in this situation?	
2. Identifying & agreeing on the facts	2. What are the resistance forces in my life and where are they leading me?

Question: What are the current conditions I/we need to consider?	
3. Identifying & agreeing on the issue	3. What is the wall that I need to scale and go over?
Question: What is the specific issue that needs to be addressed?	
4. Identifying & agreeing on the spiritual principles	4. What spiritual principles need to influence the pursuit of my objective?
Question: What relevant spiritual principles or values do I/we want to honor in my/our search for solutions?	
5. Identifying & agreeing on the solutions	5. What is the objective for which I am longing?
Question: What solutions address the issue while aligning with and honoring my/our spiritual principles and values?	
6. Identifying & agreeing on implementation steps	6. What are the steps to the objective that align with the spiritual principles?
Question: What are the steps that will implement the solution(s) and align with my/our spiritual principles and values, and who will do what by when?	

Figure 11.2

Some of these questions are organized below, according to each Consultation step, into two categories as follows:

1. Consultation Questions.
2. Growth-Seeking Questions.

Some questions are appropriate for both categories.

The 6 Consultation Steps with Supporting Consultation and Growth-Seeking Questions:

Consultation Step 1: Convening by Praying for Divine Guidance

A. Consultation Questions:

- How can I open myself to receive divine assistance on this issue?
- How can I feel compassion for myself and for other individuals in the group?
- How can I feel genuine concern for the situation the group is considering?
- How can I be alert, focused, and accepting of every contribution that is made?
- How can I be aware of my prejudices and set them aside?
- What spiritual qualities do I need to manifest for Consultation to be effective?

B. Growth-Seeking Questions:

- How do my present circumstances relate to my ultimate life purposes?
- How much compassion am I feeling for myself and for others?
- How can I be open to perspectives different than I commonly hold?
- How can I reframe the situation I am facing in spiritual terms?

Consultation Step 2: Identifying & Agreeing on the Facts

A. Consultation Questions:

- What are the current conditions I/we need to address?
- What are the facts?
- What happened?
- What perceptions, feelings, hunches, and scientifically verifiable data do I/we have about this situation?
- How relevant is this fact to the apparent situation I am/we are addressing?
- What other facts bear on this situation?
- What does this situation look/feel/sound/smell like?
- What other angles can I/we think of?
- What more is there about this?
- What led up to this situation?

- What are the causes of this situation?
- What am I feeling about this?
- What am I thinking about this?
- What body sensations am I experiencing about this?
- What is the condition of my heart?
- What are my/our needs and wants regarding this situation?
- How miserable am I/are we in the current situation?
- How ready am I/are we to make a change?
- How motivated am I/are we to make a change?
- What other information do I/we need?

B. *Growth-Seeking Questions:*

- What are the resistance forces in my life, and where are they leading me?
- What am I feeling about this?
- What am I thinking about this?
- What body sensations am I experiencing about this?
- What is the condition of my heart?
- What is the true longing behind my wants?
- Who or what are the resistance forces in my life right now?
- Where or to what do the resistance forces seem to be guiding me?
- How miserable am I in the current situation?
- How ready am I to make a change?
- How motivated am I to make a change?
- How ready am I to scale a wall and throw myself into new terrain?

Consultation Step 3: Identifying & Agreeing on the Issue

A. *Consultation Questions:*

- What is the specific issue that needs to be addressed?
- What do I/we make of it all?
- How would I/we summarize the situation?
- What seems to be the trouble?
- How would I/we describe this situation?
- What is the picture I/we have right now?
- How can I/we pull this all together?
- What does this all amount to?
- What is stopping me/us?

- What is trying to happen?
- What seems to be the main obstacle?
- What concerns me/us most about this situation?
- Frame the issue statement: How to……..? (For example, "How to keep relationships strong and the sense of family important when individual family members are busy and have conflicting schedules.")

B. Growth-Seeking Questions:

- What is the wall in my life that I need to scale and go over?
- Where is the wall in my life that I need to scale and go over?
- What is trying to happen in my life that would represent spiritual growth for me?

Consultation Step 4: Identifying & Agreeing on the Spiritual Principles

A. Consultation Questions:

- What relevant spiritual principles or values do I/we want to honor in my/our search for solutions?
- What is the principle involved here?
- How do these facts fit with our plans/values/ways of life?
- In the bigger scheme of things, how important is this?
- What spiritual principles or values do I/we need to keep in mind in order to stay focused on achieving my/our life purposes and growing spiritually?
- How relevant is this spiritual principle or value to the issue and facts I am/we are addressing?

B. Growth-Seeking Questions:

- What spiritual principles need to influence the pursuit of my objective?
- What spiritual principles or values do I need to keep in mind in order to stay focused on achieving my life purposes and growing spiritually?

Consultation Step 5: Identifying & Agreeing on the Solutions

A. Consultation Questions:

- What solutions address the issue while aligning with and honoring my/our spiritual principles and values?
- What solutions are the spiritual principles drawing me/us toward?
- What do I/we want?
- How can I/we make things better?
- How do I/we want it to be?
- What are the possibilities?
- What is one more possibility?
- What is my/our desired outcome?
- What are the possible solutions?
- How can I/we improve the situation?
- How else could this be handled?
- What part of the solution is already here?
- What parts of the solution are missing?
- To what degree is the solution right in front of me/us and I am not/we are not seeing it?
- What solutions would remove or address the obstacles?
- What have I/we tried so far?
- What other ideas do I/we have about this?
- If I/we could do anything I/we wanted, what would I/we do?
- What is the thing I/we want to attain?
- What is the situation I/we want to attain?
- What is the person/couple/family/organization I/we want to be?
- How relevant is this solution to the facts, issue, and spiritual principles or values I am/we are addressing?
- If I/we implemented this solution, what are the probable outcomes?
- What do the forces of life seem to be moving me/us toward?
- How can I/we make this happen?
- What will move me/us forward?
- What else do I/we need to take into account?
- What other solution angles can I/we think of?
- What are the probable outcomes and ramifications of this solution?
- How does this solution impact the big picture?
- What are the chances of success?
- What accomplishments do I/we want to achieve?
- What key tasks or actions need to occur?

B. *Growth-Seeking Questions:*

- What is the objective for which I am longing?
- How will I engage with the resistance forces?
- What would make me ready to scale a wall and throw myself into new terrain?
- What form, shape, or character is the objective I seek taking?
- What part of the objective is already here?
- To what degree is the objective right in front of me, and I am not seeing it?
- What objective would remove or address the obstacle?
- What is the thing I want to attain?
- What is the situation I want to attain?
- Who is the person I want to become?
- What do the forces of life seem to be moving me toward?
- How can I make this happen?
- What will move me forward?
- What is the first step?
- What are the key steps?

Consultation Step 6: Identifying & Agreeing on Implementation Steps

A. *Consultation Questions:*

- What are the steps that will implement the solution(s) and align with my/our spiritual principles and values, and who will do what by when?
- What will I/we need to do to get the solution(s) in place?
- What is the plan I/we need to create?
- Where do I/we go from here?
- What will I/we do?
- When will I/we do it by?
- What will move me/us forward?
- What is my/our game plan?
- What support do I/we need to accomplish these implementation steps?
- What is the first step?
- What is the next step?
- What smaller steps can I/we identify?

- How effectively have I/we sequenced the steps?
- How measurable is each step?
- What is the timetable for these steps?
- How realistic is the timetable?
- Who will own each step?
- What are the chances of success?
- What is my/our back-up plan?

B. *Growth-Seeking Questions:*

- What are the steps to the objective that align with the spiritual principles?
- How will I attain the objective?
- What will move me forward?
- What behaviors and actions do I need to manifest in order to approach the objective?
- How and when will I practice the new behaviors and actions?
- How will I assess progress?
- What is the first step?
- What is the next step?
- What smaller steps can I identify?
- How effectively have I sequenced the steps?
- What is the timetable for these steps?
- How realistic is the timetable?
- What steps will I own?
- Later: Now that I have assimilated the last round of change and spiritual growth, what is next for me? What other resistance forces/walls do I see?

Question-Driven Steps Keep Us on the Spiritual Path

There is great benefit in the fact that both the Consultation procedure and the growth-seeking process break down decision-making, problem-solving, and growth acceleration into a series of logical steps that are *question-driven*. These questions keep us spiritually alert so that we can make decisions that are in our and other people's best spiritual interests. If we are not using questions in this way, we are at great risk of being swayed on the *inside* by insistent voices of our lower nature and on the *outside* by materially-focused culture, family, friends, co-workers, bosses, institutions, and media that cue us about what we "should" think, "should" believe, and "should" do. With all of these influences acting on us, there is a threat of being pulled off course.

Thought-provoking questions drive us back to mindfulness and consideration of the true purposes of life by asking us how we are doing, what we are doing, where we are going, and what we are becoming. They call forth our true selves, refocus our perspective on the big picture of our lives, and connect us to our aspiration for ultimate meaning and purpose.

In the next chapter we will explore recognizable *decision-making patterns* that show up in Compassionate Consultation. Awareness of these patterns can help Consulting members deepen their understanding and appreciation of the Consultative process, reorient themselves in the midst of the process, and stimulate their perseverance as growth-seekers when the pathway gets difficult.

Chapter 12

Seeing Decision-Making Patterns in Compassionate Consultation

When people use Compassionate Consultation to address an issue, they are often trying to navigate through a confusing mess of some kind to a breakthrough decision that constructively addresses the issue. Along the way, the members of the group exchange ideas, thoughts, opinions, and emotions while also trying to be attuned to what divine assistance may make apparent to them. This is a complex process that is often non-linear and may tax our patience.

In this chapter we will explore some ways of better understanding and recognizing decision-making *patterns* in Compassionate Consultation. Anticipating and recognizing these patterns can reduce our frustrations and enhance our patience with, and confidence in, letting the Consultation process unfold.

Mature Practice & Linear Patterns

It seems that when the growth-seeking and Compassionate Consultation resources referred to in Parts I and II are brought to bear by highly experienced, *mature practitioners* of Compassionate Consultation, the members can often move with great speed and effectiveness to deepened understanding, solutions, and decisions. Such a process may be experienced by members as *a gracefully <u>linear</u> movement through the steps of Consultation to the desired outcome with minimal growth-seeking struggle*. This graceful pattern can also sometimes be experienced by members (highly experienced or not) who are highly inspired. In these situations, the "muscles" of both growth-seeking and Compassionate Consultation appear to have been so effectively applied by the members that they are able to move expeditiously as one body to a robust decision.

Immature Practice & Non-Linear Patterns

But more typically, Compassionate Consultation members are less experienced, *immature practitioners* of Compassionate Consultation and growth-seeking, and the process entails struggle, stretching, and hard work. Compassionate Consultation is often hard work for most of us. This appears to be true for two primary reasons. First, during Compassionate Consultation we are trying to be attuned to divine assistance in the midst of our imperfect efforts to manifest compassion, the 7 Prime Requisites, and the 12 Behavioral Standards. Naturally, this imperfect practice can cause interference that complicates and slows the process of Compassionate Consultation.

Secondly, individuals tend to bring their own issues to the table, and growth-seeking (or at least the opportunity for spiritual, social, and intellectual growth) of some kind is usually occurring individually and collectively during every step of Compassionate Consultation. This is significant because growth and difficulties are inseparable in this world. These personal and collective struggles can also make the process of Consultation slower and bumpier.

Even those who might qualify as experienced, *mature practitioners* of Compassionate Consultation in some situations may find their skills being taxed when the issue being addressed is exceptionally complex, the issue is one which is unrelated to their life experiences, or the Consulting group is unusually diverse and/or numerically large.

Any and all of these factors and conditions operating among the Consulting members can inhibit receptivity to the flow of divine assistance and slow the process of Compassionate Consultation. Consequently, the process may be experienced as *a relatively <u>non-linear</u> movement through the steps of Consultation to the desired outcome with a considerable amount of growth-seeking struggle.* In effect, the "muscles" of both growth-seeking and Compassionate Consultation have been under-developed by one or more of the members. This interferes with the ability of the group to move as one body directly to a robust decision. This interference does not reflect an inability of the members to access divine assistance, but simply causes a delay in their ability to sense and align with it.

The Bird of the Human Heart

Bahá'u'lláh associates the human heart with a bird when He says:

> The bird seeketh its nest; the nightingale the charm of the rose; whilst those birds, the hearts of men, content with transient dust, have strayed far from their eternal nest, and with eyes turned toward the slough of heedlessness are bereft of the glory of the divine presence. Alas! How strange and pitiful; for a mere cupful, they have turned away from the billowing seas of the Most High, and remained far from the most effulgent horizon.[202]

Bahá'u'lláh likens the human heart to a bird that can *choose* what it will become attracted and attached to. In Compassionate Consultation, our hearts need to choose to be in a conscious spiritual state of *detachment from the temporal*, and *attraction to the divine* (see Prime Requisites 3 and 4). This heart state maintains an open channel for the assistance that will guide the birds of human hearts to alight on the best solutions, decisions, knowledge, or deepened understanding. Like autumn leaves being carried along by the wind, the members' hearts can move freely in response to the breezes of God's guidance. This heart state is the opposite of one where a member may be attached to a particular outcome, engaged in a competitive ego battle with another member, or striving for a partisan objective.

Bahá'u'lláh makes clear that it is the human heart that is the first recipient of divine guidance, knowledge, and understanding, and only afterwards does the brain grasp and absorb it. In this connection, Bahá'u'lláh confirms and reiterates a statement from Islam when He says:

> Knowledge is a light which God casteth into the heart of whomsoever He willeth.[203]

Bahá'u'lláh expands upon this statement saying:

> Wherefore, a man should make ready his heart that it be worthy of the descent of heavenly grace, and that the bounteous Cup-Bearer may give him to drink of the wine of bestowal from the merciful vessel.[204]

And 'Abdu'l-Bahá says:

> The more pure and sanctified the heart of man becomes, the nearer it draws to God, and the light of the Sun of Reality is revealed within it. This light sets hearts aglow with the fire of the love of God, opens in them the doors of knowledge and unseals the divine mysteries so that spiritual discoveries are made possible.[205]

The Movement of Human Hearts & the Flocking Patterns of Birds

Bahá'u'lláh often refers to "the birds of human hearts," and 'Abdu'l-Bahá says that "…the material world corresponds to the spiritual world."[206] With these ideas in mind, we studied the flight patterns of birds to see what we could learn about human heart patterns during Consultation. We studied the take-off, flight, and landing patterns of flocking birds as they foraged for food and migrated. Often very large flocks of birds would take-off, rise up into the air, move together in one direction, then reverse direction, split apart, and move together again in a new direction all the while holding very close proximity with one another. In this organic, airborne dance, the individual birds were components of a larger organism, the flock, and the flock moved as one. It made us think of Bahá'u'lláh's admonition to human beings that we should be, "…as one soul and one body."[207]

Eventually, we realized that the various flocking patterns of the birds—ranging from the simple to the complex—mirrored the movements of human hearts during different agreement and decision-making patterns we observed in Compassionate Consultation. We recognized the correspondences between flocking birds and moving human hearts as both tried to move together into new terrain that would be more suited to their collective needs. Their journeys, and their decisions along the way, were navigated in reference to the source of illumination—the sun for the birds, the Creator for the hearts of Compassionate Consultation members. Recognizing these patterns helped us to better understand, persevere, and be patient in the process of Compassionate Consultation.

Specific Patterns of Decision-Making in Compassionate Consultation

The parallels between the movements of human hearts and the takeoff, flight, and landing patterns[208] of flocking birds remind us that there are numerous ways to reach a desired destination as a unified group. Let us look at some common patterns we have observed (and acknowledge that there are probably many more not defined here).

1. Direct Flight & Alight Decision-Making Pattern (Linear)

In the Direct Flight & Alight Pattern (see Figure 12.1), as the Consulting members address an issue, their hearts and minds rise up in one unified vector from Point A and move together as one in a single sweeping motion to a new place of agreement at Point B.

Direct Flight & Alight Decision-Making Pattern

Figure 12.1:

The movement is linear, clear, and unambiguous, and it typically reflects a mature (or highly inspired) practice of Compassionate Consultation and growth-seeking in which the members move gracefully as one body to a robust decision. As thoughts and opinions are shared, the hearts of the members promptly resonate to the articulated ideas and move directly and unitedly to an agreement. 'Abdu'l-Bahá's description of the meeting of the disciples of Jesus Christ on the mountain after Christ's ascension (see Chapter 2) represents a clear example of a series of agreements and decisions that are in the Direct Flight & Alight Pattern.

2. Divergence Followed by Convergence Decision-Making Pattern (Non-Linear)

In this pattern, the hearts of members rise up from a starting Point A and almost immediately divide or diverge in two (or more) directions (toward Points B and C respectively). Then, after moving away from each other for a time, and without landing, the two sub-groups of diverging hearts turn back toward each other (like flocking birds) converging into a single group and alighting in agreement at a new location (Point D). This pattern is shown in Figure 12.2.

Divergence Followed by Convergence Decision-Making Pattern

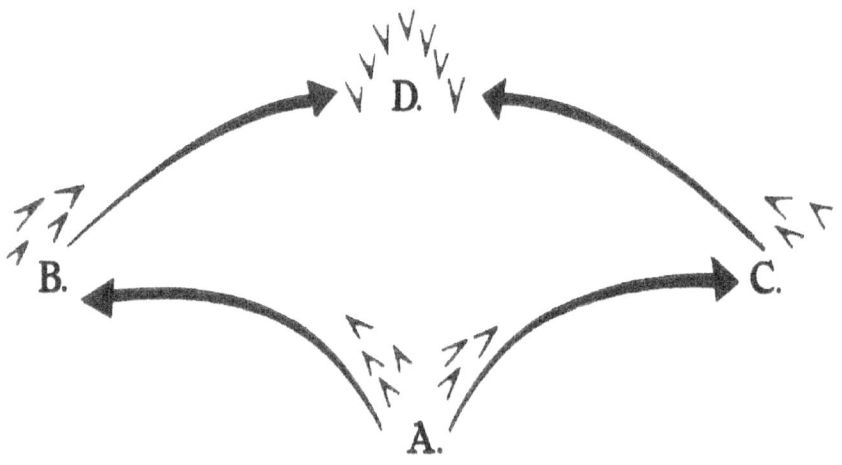

Figure 12.2:

In practice, this pattern tends to occur when two separate but apparently competing ideas divide the allegiance of group members. Individual members struggle to align their hearts as they work through Compassionate Consultation and/or growth-seeking blocks; there is a period of intellectually conferring upon and gaining insight regarding the merits and shortcomings of the two perspectives; the sub-groups begin to converge by integrating the perspectives, and the whole group then moves as one to a new agreement.

This pattern is more non-linear and typically more time-consuming than the first pattern. Both patience (Prime Requisite 6) and trusting the group as an instrument for receiving divine guidance (Behavioral Standard 5) are needed by members to allow this decision-making pattern to complete itself.

3. Divergence, Then Convergence, Then Direct Flight & Alight Decision-Making Pattern (Non-Linear)

This pattern starts off just like the previous pattern (Divergence Followed By Convergence Pattern), but after the initial convergence of opinion and tentative agreement at Point D the group further expands or develops the agreed upon ideas bringing the group to a new agreement at Point E. This decision-making pattern is shown in Figure 12.3 and is a combination of Patterns 2 and 1 above.

Divergence, Then Convergence, Then Direct Flight & Alight Decision-Making Pattern

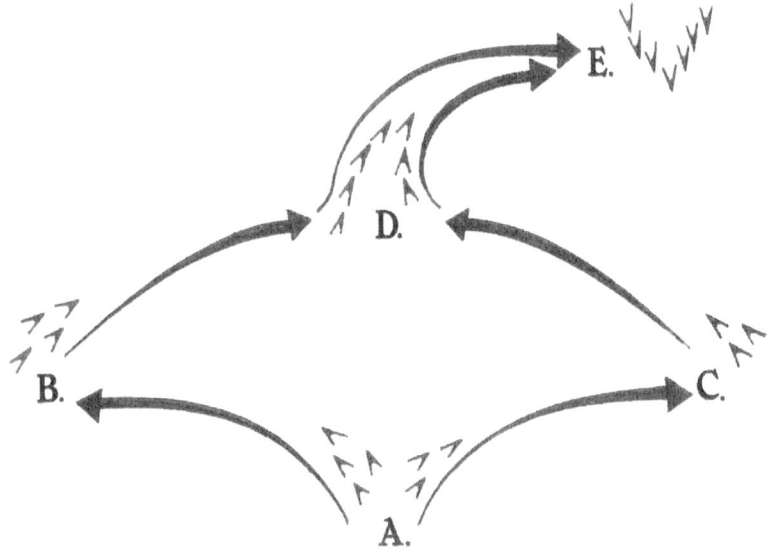

Figure 12.3:

The hearts of the consulting members (and the flocking birds in nature) diverge, then converge in a tentative agreement, and finally advance and move as one to a new position where they alight in final agreement. For members experiencing this deliberation and decision-making pattern there is often a sense of energy emerging from the initial convergence that propels the group further forward to an even more refined or deepened level of understanding and agreement.

4. Direct Flight with Boomerang Double-Back to Alight Decision-Making Pattern (Non-Linear)

This decision-making pattern is illustrated in Figure 12.4. The hearts of the members initially start out from the same Point A and move in unity toward a solution idea at B, reject it, then move in a long or short circular boomerang pattern away from, and then back to, the idea previously rejected, and accept it at Bz. Sometimes the idea accepted in the end is exactly the idea that was rejected earlier, and sometimes the idea accepted in the end has slight modifications.

Direct Flight with Boomerang Double-Back to Alight Decision-Making Pattern

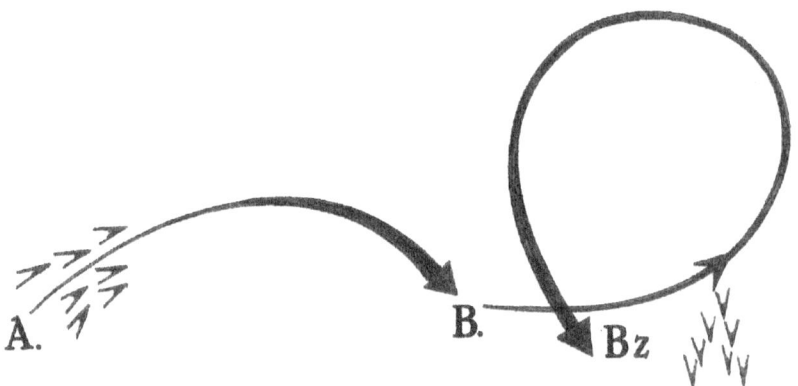

Figure 12.4

It is common for the group member who initially articulated the rejected idea that was later accepted to say or feel at the end, "This idea we just agreed upon is the same idea I articulated twenty minutes ago, but everyone rejected it—what a waste of time!" However, the initial rejection of, and circling away from and then back to, the idea was a necessary journey for the group. The initial articulation of the idea was premature in terms of *agreement,* but a timely service in terms of *process* in that it created an initial push-off point for the group from which the circular boomerang exploration pattern could both begin and complete.

5. Narrowing Gyre Decision-Making Pattern (Non-Linear)

In this pattern, the birds of human hearts rise up from a common Point A and move together into a high and wide circular motion that gradually begins to narrow into the form of a gyre (or funnel) down to a specific point of agreement at Point B as shown in Figure 12.5. The general pattern here is that of a gradual, funnel-shaped movement from a broad, and possibly superficial, exploration of a potential solution or decision territory down to a much deeper understanding of a solution or decision. This pattern usually occurs when a group is getting to the bottom of an issue or working its way down to the root cause of a situation.

Narrowing Gyre Decision-Making Pattern

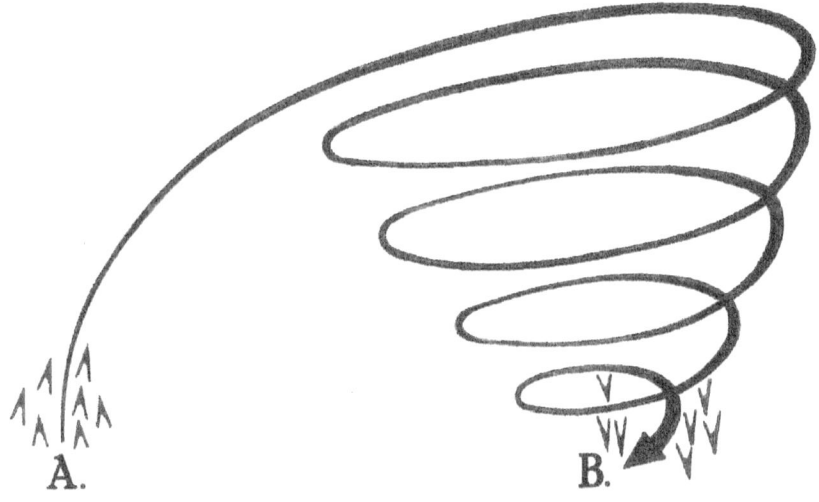

Figure 12.5:

In the midst of this decision-making pattern, discerning members may experience a sense of both moving in circles and of penetrating deeper into a subject each time a circle is completed. Less discerning members may only notice the circular pattern, which can lead to frustration that needs to be countered by *recognizing* that this is a decision-making pattern and cleaving to the 7 Prime Requisites and the 12 Behavioral Standards.

6. Widening Gyre Decision-Making Pattern (Non-Linear)

This pattern is the reverse of the previous one. In this pattern, the birds of human hearts initially rise up from Point A in a compressed and tight circular pattern and gradually widen into a gyre-shaped circular pattern that moves to an agreement at Point B as shown in Figure 12.6. The general pattern is that of a funnel which moves upward and outward from the micro to the macro, from the local to the global in terms of perspective. This pattern typically appears when a group is addressing a micro issue that has significant macro implications, trying to agree on a big picture view of things or create a comprehensive vision of a future state toward which it wants to move.

Widening Gyre Decision-Making Pattern

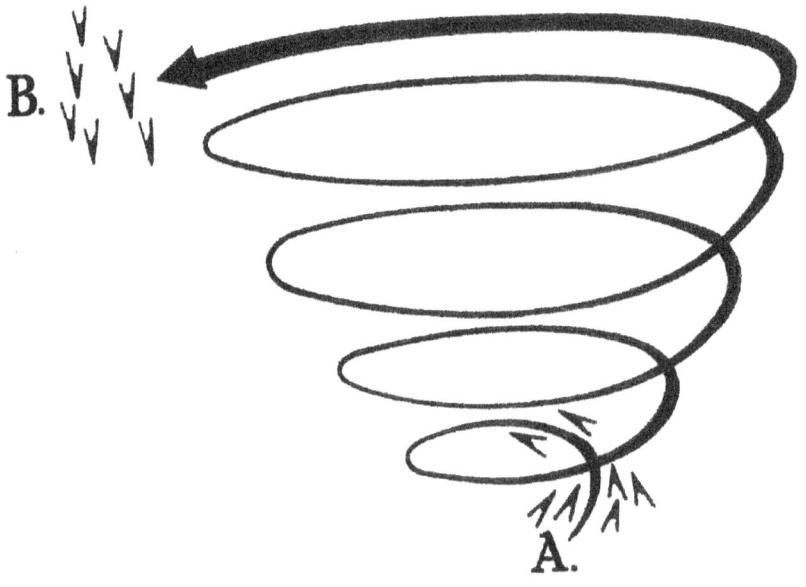

Figure 12.6:

Both similarly and in *contrast* to the previous pattern, members will often have a sense of both moving in circles and of *expanding* their awareness or vision each time a circle is completed.

7. Serpentine Decision-Making Pattern (Non-Linear)

This pattern appears to be the most aimless and can be the most frustrating for group members. As shown in Figure 12.7, the birds of human hearts start off from a common Point A, then move in one direction to Point B, then move in a different direction to Point C, then move in a different direction to Point D, and so on (for a medium or lengthy time) leading to ultimate agreement and alighting on Point G. The pattern moves like a serpent and can look and feel so aimless to participants that they conclude agreement is being frustrated at every turn.

Nevertheless, if members, a chairperson, or a facilitator do an effective job of articulating and summarizing what perspectives, elements of agreement, and elements of disagreement have been identified at each point, the group will see that there is a progression underway and that the pattern will result in an agreement in the end.

Serpentine Decision-Making Pattern

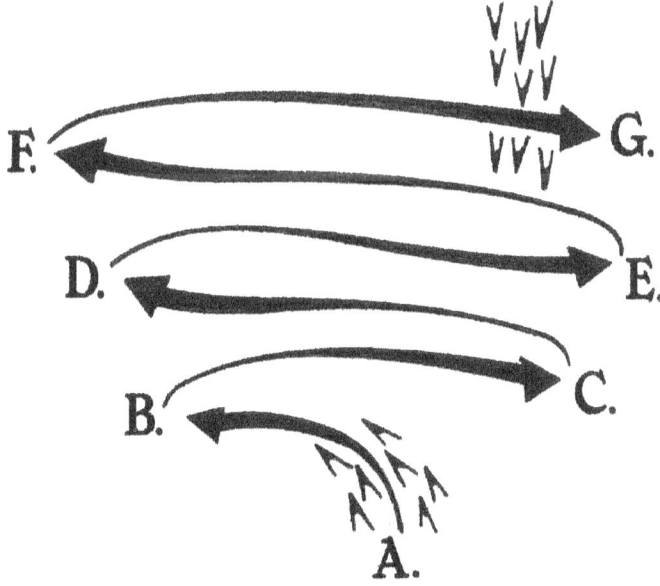

Figure 12.7

Seeing the Beauty & Complexity in Decision-Making Patterns

Except for the Direct Flight & Alight Pattern, all of the deliberation and decision-making patterns described above are non-linear. They take longer to unfold than a linear pattern, and they require greater trust in, and patience with, the Compassionate Consultation process. Rather than becoming impatient with, and distrustful of, non-linear patterns, we can take a lesson from nature. Just as migrating and foraging birds do not usually move in a straight line from point A to point B, neither do the birds of human hearts. And just as the patterns of migrating birds may sometimes divide members of the flock and have them moving at variance with each other, the birds always come back together in unity at the end of the pattern. Knowing this can help us appreciate the beauty and complexity in these patterns and recognize them as ways in which we go about honoring Bahá'u'lláh's admonition to, "Be united in counsel, be one in thought."[209]

Chapter 13

Making Transformative Decisions within the Individual

Complex or challenging issues in life often activate conflicting voices and impulses *within* us. At this personal level, the Compassionate Consultation process involves engaging with the true self and other aspects of one's being in a growth-seeking spirit to gather and organize relevant information, to consider different internal perspectives about a situation, to identify relevant spiritual principles, to gain deeper understanding, to find a solution, to make a decision, and to take action in alignment with the spiritual principles and decisions. In addition, it involves doing all of this in an atmosphere of compassion where the 7 Prime Requisites and 12 Behavioral Standards are being honored *intra*personally.

'Abdu'l-Bahá is reported to have said that "when one thinks, it is like consulting with oneself."[210] So, at its simplest level, combining Consultation with compassion within one's self is thinking—thinking about, and through, an issue to reach deeper understanding and possibly a conclusion that leads to action. To be true Consultation, it must begin with prayer and be accompanied by compassion for self and others; but beyond that, it involves having an internal discussion. In describing such a scenario, 'Abdu'l-Bahá says:

> As in a dream one talks with a friend while the mouth is silent, so is it in the conversation of the spirit. A man may converse with the ego within him saying: "May I do this? Would it be advisable for me to do this work?"

Such as this is conversation with the higher self.[211]

In the most straightforward scenarios of life then, I pose questions to myself, my true self answers with new perspectives that arrive in the form of new ideas entering my heart and mind, and I arrive at a decision that informs my actions.

Using Compassionate Consultation within the Individual on Simple Issues

On a daily basis, *most* situations in which we can use Compassionate Consultation within ourselves involve choices that do not cause significant degrees of internal distress. For example, you may have numerous errands you need to do after work that require you to drive to several different places. Some of the errands are urgent, and some are less so, but all are in the same vicinity, and because gas prices are high and are putting a strain on your budget, you want to do all of them at one time in order to drive as few miles as possible. However, you are meeting a friend at a play that night, and you will not have time to eat dinner before going to the play if you do all the errands. In addition, trying to do all the errands could lead you to be late to the play and upset your friend in the process. Because this situation is relatively simple and straight-forward, you decide to use the 3-Step Consultation Model (introduced in Chapter 2) in the following way.

Example of Compassionate Consultation within the Individual—the 3-Step Model

- Say a prayer for divine guidance.
- Make sure I am feeling compassion for my friend, for myself, and for others I may encounter—that is, make sure my true self is engaged.

1. Understanding the situation

- I have five errands to get done that are in close proximity to each other.
- Should I skip dinner and do all the errands?
- Shall I grab a burger at a drive-thru restaurant as well as doing all the errands and arrive at the play exhausted and possibly late?

- Shall I postpone some of the errands to another day even though I will be using more gas—so I can eat dinner before the play and still get there on time?
- I want to save gas to economize and do all the errands in one trip.
- If I do all five of the errands at once, I will be rushed, worn out, and probably go without dinner because the start time of the play is fixed.
- If I do all the errands, I could be late to the play and upset my friend.
- I want to be at the play by 7:15 p.m. so as not to keep my friend waiting.
- I need to have dinner before I arrive at the play in order to be alert and enjoy the play.
- I have a tendency to over-estimate how much I can get done in a span of time.
- I am trying to have my life be less frenetic and more tranquil.

2. *Deciding what to do*

- I'll do the two most pressing errands—one that needs to be done by today and one that needs to be done by tomorrow, and the others can wait until next week.
- By next week I may have something else I need to do in that geographical area so that I can fold the new errands into the same trip with the remaining errands and still be efficient with gas and time.
- This approach will leave me time to go into a fast-food restaurant, sit down, and relax as I eat so that I'll be refreshed for the play and my life will be less frenetic.
- This approach will assure me of getting to the play on time and allow me to honor my relationship with my friend

3. *Executing or carrying out the decision*

- Schedule my departure time from work.
- Map out the most efficient route to the errands.
- Select a restaurant on the route to the theater.
- Carry out the decision.

This kind of thinking and internal deliberation process is probably somewhat familiar to most of us as we move through daily life. Probably unfamiliar to most of us are the use of a prayer for guidance, the conscious accessing of compassion, and the formal use of the three Consultation steps. These added dimensions turn what could have been a random, arbitrary, and impulse-driven decision-making process into one that deepens self-understanding of the significance of, and the personal values involved in, the issue. This process fosters a more peaceful state of mind and is more likely to generate spiritual growth.

Using Compassionate Consultation within the Individual on More Complex Issues

At a more complex level, however, Consulting with one's self entails thinking about different and more intensely conflicting internal perspectives and emotions. This sort of thinking, too, is probably familiar to most of us. It is not unusual to hear a human being say, "I'm torn about this issue—one part of me thinks this way, while another part of me thinks that way." The internal "parts" referred to may be encouraging us to act from our higher nature or from our lower nature. In a given situation, while the true self may be inclined toward a middle path, other aspects of our being may be lazy or impatient, overly cautious or impetuous, antagonistic or excessively compliant, overly careful or careless, and over-confident or timid. These other aspects may challenge each other and the true self for "the reins" of our being and contribute complicating perspectives and intense emotions to our internal dialogues and deliberations. 'Abdu'l-Bahá calls upon us to struggle "against the insistent self,"[212] which he associates with the promptings of the lower nature in the human heart.

Committing & Preparing Ourselves to Do Our Inner Work

Facing and dealing with intense internal conflict requires courage and perseverance. Among the attributes that Shoghi Effendi associated with mature and effective human beings was the ability to "fight their own spiritual battles."[213] One foundational resource for doing this important inner work is prayer because it feeds and invigorates our soul or true self just as physical food feeds the body. 'Abdu'l-Bahá describes prayer as "conversation with God."[214] Another important resource for doing our inner work is meditation and inner contemplation. We need to use our God-given intellect, a faculty of our rational soul, to make wise, growth-producing decisions. 'Abdu'l-Bahá tells us:

Bahá'u'lláh says there is a sign (from God) in every phenomenon: the sign of the intellect is contemplation and the sign of contemplation is silence, because it is impossible for a man to do two things at one time—he cannot both speak and meditate. It is an axiomatic fact that while you meditate you are speaking with your own spirit. In that state of mind you put certain questions to your spirit and the spirit answers: the light breaks forth and the reality is revealed.

You cannot apply the name 'man' to any being void of this faculty of meditation; without it he would be a mere animal, lower than the beasts. Through the faculty of meditation man attains to eternal life; through it he receives the breath of the Holy Spirit—the bestowal of the Spirit is given in reflection and meditation.[215]

Compassionate Consultation within the individual is a form of contemplation, reflection, and meditation in which we confer with our own spirit in an effort to hear, differentiate, understand, and align the inner voices of our lower and higher nature. This process allows us to mindfully determine how we will act in alignment with our spiritual values.

Bringing Our Inner Members to the Compassionate Consultation Table

To free ourselves to Consult internally, our true self needs to bring all of our inner voices to the Consultation table. Our true self does this by creating a compassionate internal environment within which we can differentiate, unify, and integrate our lower nature's voices under the guidance of our true self. Our true self needs to function as a wise, compassionate facilitator or chairperson during this process. The lower nature voices need to be heard, acknowledged, and understood, but trained to trust and rely on the true self's vision and spiritual leadership.

Before we can change and grow, we must acknowledge the pulls that are working on us internally. Once we do, we can determine which inner voices conduce to our spiritual advancement, which to our detriment, and which to heed. Doing this inner work regularly enables us to honor Bahá'u'lláh's admonition that:

...man should know his own self, and recognize that which leadeth unto loftiness or lowliness, glory or abasement, wealth or poverty.[216]

An Introductory Example of Consultation within the Individual—the 6-Step Model

To do this inner work in more complex and emotionally charged situations, the 6-Step Consultation Model shown in Figure 13.1 (and introduced in Chapter 2) may prove most helpful.

The 6-Step Consultation Model

1. Convening by Praying for Divine Guidance
2. Identifying & Agreeing on the Issue
3. Identifying & Agreeing on the Facts
4. Identifying & Agreeing on the Spiritual Principles
5. Identifying & Agreeing on the Solutions
6. Identifying & Agreeing on Implementation Steps

Figure 13.1

Let's look at an example of how this works. Suppose you learn that someone in your work group has strongly criticized you to colleagues. You instantly notice feelings of hurt and anger surging within you. Because you have been consistently doing your inner work, your true self already knows your cast of internal characters: the anxious part that expresses fear that you will be abandoned or rejected if someone is not pleased with you; the sad part that conveys depressive thoughts about not being able to do anything right; the angry part that wants to scream and counter-attack; and the withdrawing part that thinks you should shut down, fade into the woodwork, and not be noticed.

Coming from your true self, you decide to: take a break; say a prayer for divine assistance; compassionately hear, acknowledge, and calm the diverse voices within you; and align your inner resources around the issue of how to respond to the criticism of your co-worker. Your true self reviews the facts raised by the internal voices, identifies relevant spiritual principles, and then begins considering possibilities with the other parts of your being. You say, "Given the facts and spiritual principles we have reviewed, there is a whole range of options we can consider. For example, we could clearly express our thoughts and feelings directly to the co-worker; we might write a memo to the co-worker; we could talk to our supervisor if that would be appropriate; we may decide that no response is the best response; we might look to see if there is a kernel of truth behind the criticism; or we might start looking for another job."

Acting as a wise and trusted chairperson of your internal being, your true self follows the Consultative steps, confers with the aspects of your lower nature, soothes them with compassion, trains them with spiritual principles, and arrives at a decision with them. The process flows relatively easily because you "recognize that which leadeth unto loftiness or lowliness, glory or abasement, wealth or poverty" in your inner life as a result of having regularly done your inner work.

If this inner work is not done, aspects of our lower nature may subtly control our life, inhibit our growth-seeking, impair our ability to fulfill the three purposes of life, and relegate us to spiritual immaturity.

A Note to the Reader: Many of the Consultation examples in Part III are highly detailed. Users of the models need not be this detailed in their own practice. Detail is provided here in order to clearly demonstrate the application of the models and tools. Although the detail may suggest use of the models is time-consuming in practice, using all of the steps (or even some of them) can be seen as an investment which results in dramatically improved decision quality, relationships, growth-seeking habits, and Compassionate Consultation skills. In the end, this saves time.

The Example of Eric—Thorough Consultation within the Individual—6-Step Model

Let us look at a more complete example of how to apply Consultation within ourselves on a challenging issue. Eric had a battle going on inside him. He had been suspecting for some time that he needed a new career path. He had been doing the same work for over ten years, had lost his excitement about it, did not feel like he was growing anymore, and wanted more challenge from his work. For about two years he had been mentally dancing away from the issue each time it came to his mind because it made him anxious to think about making such a huge change in his life—a change that might affect the well-being of his family. Having resolved to become a growth-seeker, he decided to face the issue squarely.

Eric decided to use the 6-Step Model of Compassionate Consultation. He also decided to consider the *Growth-Seeking Questions* that align with each of the steps in the 6-Step Consultation Model that were introduced in Chapter 11 and the more *issue-focused questions* introduced below, as tools to facilitate his meditation, contemplation, and reflection during each of the six steps. Eric's process follows.

1. Convening By Praying For Divine Guidance

Prompting Growth-Seeker Question: How do my present circumstances relate to my ultimate life purpose?

Prompting Issue-Focused Question: What is the general nature of the divine guidance and assistance I need to pray for?

Eric thought about his belief that work delivered in a spirit of service to others is one form of worshiping God. He felt this was part of the purpose of life. He realized that his growing disenchantment with his work was making it increasingly difficult for him to do his work in a spirit of service. He wanted to change this situation so that he could express worship through his work again. He prayed for divine guidance to find this work.

2. Identifying & Agreeing On The Issue*

*Steps 2 and 3 may be reversed in sequence depending upon preference.

Prompting Growth-Seeker Question: What is the wall that I need to go over?

Prompting Issue-Focused Question: What is the issue I need to resolve?

- I have held the same job for ten years.
- I am getting bored and finding it hard to do my work in a spirit of service. Discontent with my work is an obstruction guiding me to change & grow.

- I have been thinking for some time that I want to find a job with more responsibility. I want a job with more growth opportunities, both personally and professionally.
- My circumstances require that I find a job with a salary that is comparable to or higher than what I am earning in my present position.
- Despite these thoughts and feelings, I don't seem to do anything about it.
- I have come to an internal wall, and I need to figure out how to scale it.
- The years keep going by, and I don't make a career change.
- The issue is: how to break out of my passive inaction and go over the wall into proactive action regarding my career path.

3. Identifying & Agreeing On The Facts*

*Steps 2 and 3 may be reversed in sequence depending upon preference.

<u>Prompting Growth-Seeker Question</u>: What are the resistance forces in my life, and where are they leading me?

<u>Prompting Issue-Focused Question</u>: As I face this issue or problem, what am I aware of in terms of what has been going on with me, and what is currently going on with me?

- I think about this issue at least once a day.
- There are voices in my head that are creating internal obstacles.
- A critical voice says I am not talented enough to get a job with more responsibility and that no one will hire me.
- A scolding voice is criticizing me for not moving forward on this sooner.
- My true self is excited about the prospect of change and growth.
- A cautious voice tells me that everything is going fine, I know the current job, and why rock the boat?
- A nay-sayer voice is telling me that there will be many other applicants who will be more qualified than I am.
- I believe that there is more in me that I can offer the world.
- A fearful voice is afraid to launch out into the world on this new pathway.
- While some of my voices are working hard to prevent change, the voice of my true self says that, if I put in the effort, God will guide me to the right thing.

4. Identifying & Agreeing on the Spiritual Principles

Prompting Growth-Seeker Question: What spiritual principles and values need to influence the resolution of my issue?

Prompting Issue-Focused Question: What spiritual principles or values can I think of that are relevant to this problem/issue and to these facts?

- We should strive for excellence in all things.
- Work done in the spirit of service is worship.
- Life is constant struggle; we grow through tests and challenges.
- We should use our God-given capacities and talents as fully as we can.
- Bahá'u'lláh says, "While placing thy whole trust in God, engage in some profession."[217]
- Before God can help me, I need to take some steps toward my goal.

5. Identifying & Agreeing on the Solutions

Prompting Growth-Seeker Question: What is the objective for which I am longing?

Prompting Issue-Focused Question: Considering these spiritual principles and values, what solutions can I think of that are relevant to this problem/issue and to these facts?

- Start seeing inner voices that are critical and fearful as aspects of my lower nature which constitute internal walls I need to go over in order to move on and grow.
- Visualize myself in a new job that inspires me to serve others, challenges me, and fosters my growth (this is the objective I am seeking).
- Pray for the ability to place my "whole trust in God."
- Pray for courage, for insight, for confidence, for assistance, and guidance—for the strengthening of my higher nature.
- Meditate on the Scriptures that talk about a human being's station, capacities, and nobility.
- Start moving toward the new job and career path even though it isn't clear yet what they are.
- Stay in movement on this.
- Assess my strengths and transferable skills.
- Redesign my resumé to merchandise these strengths and transferable skills.

- Identify the fields and types of jobs in which I am interested.
- Redesign my resumé again to focus on these new jobs and career fields.
- Start to look at job postings online and in newspapers.
- Make a list of possible people with whom to network. Follow up by making lunch or coffee dates with them to discuss my direction.
- Talk to a career counselor or coach.
- Think of this whole process as a learning opportunity—if I'm turned down for a job, I will ask what changes would be needed for me to have gotten the job.
- Whenever a door closes, look to see what door has opened.

6. Identifying & Agreeing on the Implementation Steps

<u>Prompting Growth-Seeker Question</u>: What are the steps to the objective that align with the spiritual principles?

<u>Prompting Issue-Focused Question</u>: Which solutions do I feel the most energy around, and what sequenced implementation steps can I break those down into so that I can make at least one forward step this coming week in alignment with the spiritual principles?

1. Pray for the ability to place my "whole trust in God."
    a. Memorize the quotation from Bahá'u'lláh, "While placing thy whole trust in God, engage in some profession"[218] (do by Monday noon).
    b. Make it my mantra, repeating it at least five times per day (start by Tuesday).
2. Pray for courage, insight, confidence, assistance, and guidance.
    a. Make praying about this issue a part of my morning and evening prayers (start tonight).
3. Assess my strengths and transferable skills.
    a. Make a preliminary list by myself (by bedtime Wednesday).
    b. Confer with my spouse and trusted colleagues to augment and refine the list (by the following Monday).
    c. Narrow the list down to my top six key transferable skills (by following Tuesday).
4. Identify the fields and types of jobs in which I am interested.
    a. Based on my six key transferable skills and my favorite subject areas, make a list of the fields and types of jobs in

which I am interested (by the following Monday—after completion of 3c).
  b. Confer with my spouse and trusted colleagues to refine the list (by following Friday).
  c. Redesign my resumé around my six key transferable skills and the new list of fields and jobs I want to pursue (by the following Sunday at noon).
  d. Begin combing job postings online and in newspapers (start by the same Sunday as in 4c).
  e. Schedule a minimum of two people per week to have coffee with from my network of contacts to discuss my job goals and extend my network (start by the week following the Sunday in 4c).
5. Whenever a door closes, look to see what door has opened.
  a. When meditating after my morning prayers each day, make a list of at least two doors that have opened for every door that has closed—focus on opportunities, not limitations (start by the Sunday described in 4c).

Debriefing Eric's Compassionate Consultation Process

Let us step back and review Eric's process:
- Eric's process has not yet accomplished the goal of finding a new job and establishing a new career path, but it has made him clear about his issue, his objective, the forces of resistance, and the wall to be scaled. It has also moved him into proactive action;
- Overall Eric came from his true self, but was open to, noticed, and acknowledged the voices of his lower nature. His true self was like a compassionate chairperson who led the process and was open to diverse input;
- In Step 2, Identifying & Agreeing on the Issue, Eric did not differentiate between the voices of his true self and aspects of his lower nature. He just referred to "I" as in the phrase, "The years keep going by, and I don't make career changes." While there was nothing to prevent him from differentiating in Step 2, he chose to keep the issue identification process simple by postponing differentiation between his true self and aspects of his lower nature until Step 3;

- In Step 3, Identifying & Agreeing on the Facts, Eric did differentiate between his true self and lower nature. He wanted to go into more depth and detail in Step 3 to get at underlying factors. He simply described the voiced messages and perspectives of his lower nature and also the voiced perspectives and messages of his true self;
- Step 4, Identifying & Agreeing on the Spiritual Principles, was led by his true self because aspects of the lower nature tend to be defensively or aggressively focused on this world and without insight into eternal spiritual principles. Spiritual principles need to be taught to the lower nature by the true self. Helping voices from the lower nature align with spiritual principles can be seen as one aspect of training and disciplining the lower nature to be subordinated to, and guided by, the true self. One of the benefits of using the 6-Step Model is that it expedites this process;
- In Step 5, the solution ideas came largely from his true self and seemed conducive to further energizing the true self and having the cautioning aspects of the lower nature step back. This is true partly because when we search for solutions we are asking, "How can we make it better?" and posing this question engages the true self rather than the lower nature. In addition, the previous Step 4, Identifying & Agreeing on the Spiritual Principles, has already had the effect of calming, de-energizing, and quieting the lower nature while vitalizing the true self;
- This momentum from Steps 4 and 5 carried over into Step 6 where the selected Implementation Steps further energized the true self's ability to stay in executive function and effectively lead the transformation process within the individual.

The Example of Deborah--Inner Consultation to Improve Relationships

Deborah was not happy with her relationships; they did not give her comfort or happiness. She would ask people about themselves, but no one seemed to want to know anything about her. In fact, people seemed to take advantage of her good nature. They would call her when they needed something, but wouldn't call her to just spend time together. Deborah realized she had played a part in creating these unsatisfactory relationship patterns and resolved to Consult within herself about them.

She began by reflecting on her true self's attributes (using the list shown in Figure 9.2 in Chapter 9) to make sure she was coming from her higher nature and then prayed, meditated, and reflected about her relationship issues. As she did this she realized that she was constantly trying to please others and gradually recognized that she believed she would not be accepted by others if they truly knew her because they would see that she was incompetent and defective. She wondered where she got these ideas.

After much reflection, Deborah realized that her low self-esteem resulted at least in part from her father's constant criticism of her as she grew up. She recognized that, as a result, she had critical, self-sabotaging inner voices that had been over-powering the aspirational, mature, realistic, compassionate, and encouraging voice of her true self. Further meditation resulted in Deborah's realization that her assumption that she was defective had led her to create a false self which minimized herself and over-estimated others. She was reminded of 'Abdu'l-Bahá's reference to an "acquired individuality" which is "the result of an evil routine of thought" in the lower nature that "becomes the dominant note" of a person's life.[219]

This new understanding yielded the insight that she was not coming from her true self (her authentic self) in her relationships, which prevented her from truly connecting with others. She decided to use Compassionate Consultation within herself to clarify how she could strengthen her true self and forge nutritious relationships in which she was an equal partner. She used the 6-Step Model and recorded her steps as follows.

1. Convening by Praying for Divine Guidance

2. Identifying & Agreeing on the Issue:

How to develop and come from my true self to build nutritious and authentic relationships with others.

3. Identifying & Agreeing on the Facts:

- Inner voices have me being afraid to let people know who I am.
- Inner voices have me being afraid to let myself know who I am.
- Growing up, my father was highly critical of me, and it made me feel defective.
- This pattern of thinking began early in my life.
- I am lonely and want more human connection in my life.

- I often terminate relationships because I get worn out trying to be acceptable.
- Relationships that haven't worked for me are resistance forces guiding me toward recognizing the wall(s) I need to go over.
- Aspects of my lower nature think I will always be alone.
- Inner voices have me trying too hard to people please.
- These inner voices are preventing me from finding relationship fulfillment.
- I am not accustomed to coming from my true self because I'm so busy trying to protect myself from rejection and to please others.
- I'm not sure about who I am—I know I have a true self, but I am not clear on what I value, what energizes me, and what specifically I want in life and relationships.

4. **Identifying & Agreeing on the Spiritual Principles:**

    - I need to pray, meditate, and read the Creative Word daily to stay focused on this important work because prayer is nutrition for the spirit just as food is nutrition for the body.
    - Praying, meditating, and reading the Creative Word daily will clarify who I am.
    - Human beings are created noble.
    - Every human being is precious to God.
    - There is a purpose for my life here on earth, and that purpose relates to authentically connecting with others.
    - I have a unique set of capacities and talents that I need to manifest in my life.
    - I need to know myself so that I can develop, use, and be thankful for my gifts.
    - One grows and builds healthy relationships by learning to work in cooperation with others, not by subjugating one's self to others.
    - One must know one's own self and "recognize that which leadeth unto loftiness or lowliness, glory or abasement, wealth or poverty."[220]

5. **Identifying & Agreeing on the Solutions:**

    - Pray, meditate, and read the Creative Word daily—thirty minutes in the morning and twenty minutes in the evening. Pray specifically for guidance/assistance on this issue.

- Identify some simple activities that center me and are nutritious for me (i.e., having tea, reading, walking). Do at least two of them daily to nurture myself.
- Journal around what I enjoyed doing as a child and how it relates to me presently.
- Make a list of the hobbies, subjects, or areas of interest I have ever been drawn to.
- Based on these interests, identify clubs, associations, or groups I may be interested in joining.
- Check into the schedules of these groups and try some of them out as a means of nurturing those interests and learning to build authentic relationships as well.
- Identify the people in my life I don't have to work hard to be with; invite them to coffee or to other social venues.
- Reflect on, and make a list of, what I care about in life—what I truly value.
- Decide what I can do that will put my energy and action into living those values.

6. *Identifying & Agreeing on the Implementation Steps:*

- Pray, meditate and read the Creative Word daily—thirty minutes in the morning, twenty minutes in the evening, and at noon for a few minutes when alone. Pray specifically for guidance and assistance on this issue. Begin today.
- Study the attributes of the true self each morning and envision how I will live my day from my true self. Begin tomorrow.
- Build and maintain a twenty-five-item (or more) list of simple, nutritious activities; schedule in at least two per day. Begin Monday.
- Create a ranked list of subjects and areas of interest I am drawn to and select two that I will invest time and energy in. Complete by next Friday.
- Identify clubs or associations that focus in these interest areas and begin consistently participating in them to build my interests and relationships—come from my true self. Create a schedule of what I will attend by next weekend.
- Take a community education watercolor painting class to honor my interest in painting. Start next month.

- Identify four people with whom I feel the most comfortable (including at least one male) and invite one of the four out each week for coffee. Share some things about myself with them as well as being interested in them. Start next week.
- Journal for fifteen minutes per day right after dinner on events and experiences in my life that day that were nutritious, toxic, or neutral in terms of spiritual growth. Do this as a way to get to know my true self better. Start by the end of two weeks.
- Keep a journal list of qualities I value that I would like to bring out in myself (i.e., compassion for myself and others, generosity, honesty, etc.). Work on manifesting one per week. Make an entry each day about how I was able to use that attribute. Buy myself a small gift if I have used that quality every day that week. Start in two weeks.

Debriefing Thoughts on Deborah's Compassionate Consultation Process

Deborah's process illustrates the fact that the purpose of looking into our past to understand thoughts and feelings that are preventing us from fulfilling our potential is not to place blame on our parents or other caregivers. They were probably doing their best, and their behaviors were likely rooted in how they were raised. The purpose is to get clarity and understanding about any dysfunctional dynamics in our inner life, turn down the voice volume on those dynamics, and turn up the voice volume on our true self.

The Example of John--Using Consultation to Reframe a Difficult Situation

Not all Compassionate Consultation sessions within the individual need to be done in the framework of the true self and the voices of the lower nature. While the following example could have been done within this framework, the individual involved chose not to.

Thirty-nine-year-old John realized that he was not experiencing fulfillment in his life. Everything he tried to do required a huge act of willpower—he had to "drive" himself in order to keep going. He was not coping well with even the smallest tasks of daily life, and he did not feel good about himself, others, or his future. A friend told him that his symptoms sounded like depression, and John decided he needed to do something about it.

He began by researching information about depression and discovered that one definition of the condition is "learned helplessness." This condition involves a belief that one does not have choices, and it leads to viewing life through a filter of negativity and pessimism. As John thought about this, he became aware that he was feeling dissatisfied at work, but he also noticed that he was fighting those feelings by telling himself that he should be satisfied because of his excellent salary, benefits, and job location. He had the surprising realization that he had been silently struggling with and repressing this inner conflict about his work situation for many months and that he felt helpless to do anything about it.

This awareness motivated him to discover what other thoughts and feelings were out of his conscious awareness. Gradually, he identified resentment he was carrying toward his boss. He was feeling hurt and anger—and more specifically, disregarded, unimportant, and not valued—because of the way his boss treated him. John acknowledged to himself that the hurt and angry feelings evoked by his boss's behavior were unhealthy for him and that he needed to make changes to recover his emotional health. He concluded that he actually did have choices. He could find a new job, he could learn to think differently about the boss's behavior so that he would not have the anger and hurt which were causing depressive symptoms, or he could talk to the boss about the boss's disrespectful treatment of him.

John prayed, meditated, and read the Creative Word over the next several days to help him understand his situation better. Then he realized that the primary reason he had left his last two jobs was insensitive treatment from his bosses. Considering that his co-workers in the current and previous jobs did not seem overly concerned about the bosses' behavior, he wondered whether he was being overly sensitive and whether he could learn to be less sensitive.

John remembered reading in his research on depression that changing the way you think about something also changes the way you feel about it. John said to himself, "Maybe I could reframe the way I look at my boss's rudeness and inconsideration so I will be less negatively impacted by that behavior." This idea had a powerful impact on John, and he intuitively sensed that it represented a wall he needed to scale. From a growth-seeking perspective he considered the idea that his current boss and his previous two bosses could be resistance forces guiding him to an area of growth he needed to address. He decided to use the 6-Step Compassionate Consultation Model to deepen his understanding and forge a plan of action. John recorded his Consultation steps as follows:

1. Convening By Praying for Divine Guidance

2. Identifying & Agreeing on the Issue:

How to reframe what I perceive to be my negative work situation into one in which I continue to grow and develop, feel peace and contentment rather than depression, effectively serve my customers, and slough off my boss's insensitive behavior.

3. Identifying & Agreeing on the Facts:
- I am depressed (feeling sad, hopeless, having difficulty sleeping and eating, experiencing decreased motivation, and isolating myself).
- I feel the worst when I am at work.
- I feel disrespected, unimportant, and not valued by my boss.
- My boss treats others with disrespect also.
- Most of my other colleagues seem less bothered than me by the boss's behavior.
- I like the rest of my colleagues very much.
- The work is meaningful and the benefits, salary, and location are excellent.
- I have previously left two jobs because of my bosses' behavior toward me.
- If I changed jobs locally, I could end up with a lower salary and may have to get a place to live with lower rent and possibly forego travel vacations.
- I feel good about life (and less depressed) when I am around people who are accepting and respectful.
- Since I was a child I have known that I am a very sensitive person.
- I am becoming more passive.
- My spirit feels like it is shrinking.
- My work is challenging, it keeps me engaged, and I am normally able to do it in a spirit of service to others.
- I have done good work until lately; I am having trouble concentrating now.

- My boss could be an obstruction force guiding me to leave this job.
- My boss could be an obstruction force guiding me to stay and grow in some way.
- My colleagues and the parts of this job I really like could be obstruction forces guiding me to stay and grow in some way.
- The wall to scale could be me learning to reside more fully in my true self.

4. Identifying & Agreeing on the Spiritual Principles:

- I am responsible for my own spiritual condition.
- One of the primary purposes of life is to grow spiritually.
- It is important to be in environments in which one can grow and develop.
- Tests and difficulties are conducive to spiritual growth and development.
- If we fail to pass a spiritual growth test, our Creator often keeps giving us the same test again until we pass it.
- While some kinds of adversity can be toxic, others can foster growth and development.
- It is important to unfold and use all your capacities, talents, and gifts.
- My well-being and value are not dependent on the views of others, but upon the view of my Creator and my own view of myself.

5. Identifying & Agreeing on the Solutions:

- Ask for God's assistance on this issue through daily prayer.
- Pray, read scripture, and meditate daily to learn to be peaceful and content in spite of adversity.
- Learn to detach myself from worldly conditions and rely on God more fully.
- Try not to let my boss's behavior feel so personal; interpret it as him having problems or issues of his own, and try to have compassion for him.
- Learn to accept my own value and make my self-worth less conditioned by the attitudes/actions of others—this seems to be the objective for which I am longing.

- Start seeing my boss as a resistance force that is guiding me toward a wall I need to go over.
- Consider being a resistance force for my boss by expressing to him that I don't feel valued by him.
- Consider asking my boss if there is something he wants me to be doing differently.
- Put my focus on the good work I do and the service I provide to others.
- Focus on the positive attributes I am able to use each day.
- If after doing the above I decide I need to get another job, ask for God's assistance, and use Consultation to formulate a plan—possibly asking trusted friends to Consult with me.

Identifying & Agreeing on the Implementation Steps:

- Starting this weekend, establish a habit of doing morning and evening devotions (to include fifteen minutes of prayers, scriptural readings, and meditation) with the goals of asking for God's assistance in my life, detaching myself from worldly conditions, learning to be more peaceful and content despite adversity, and relying more fully on God.
- About the previous item, select ahead of time scriptural readings that are inspiring to me about the worthiness and potential of every soul. Accomplish this before going to bed Friday night.
- In everything I do, establish the habit of having compassion for myself and others. Start monitoring how I am doing in this by recording how much compassion I had for myself and for others each day on a zero to ten scale beginning this weekend.
- Identify and then begin recognizing and acknowledging the spiritual attributes I value in myself each day—e.g., patience, persistence, cooperation, and a motive of service. Record these qualities each day in my journal starting tomorrow.
- Write three affirmation scripts that I can rotate each day to give myself healthy doses of encouraging self-talk—before, during, and after work. Write the scripts this weekend and begin using them daily on Monday.
- Give myself silent "kudos" when I accomplish or do something significant in my work. Begin recording these items in my journal

starting tomorrow and feed these items back into my expanding affirmation scripts (see previous item).
- When I feel criticized, ask myself whether my intentions were pure and if I was doing my best per my understanding of the situation. If so, feel good about myself. If not, make appropriate changes in my thinking and/or doing. Begin establishing this habit today.
- Start recording in my journal (by the weekend after next) events in my life history that strengthen my sense of self-worth. Continue to record and accumulate these events on a weekly basis and feed them back into my affirmation scripts (see above).
- When I feel criticized or not appreciated, journal about it. Try to clearly put my feelings into words so that I am not ignoring and storing up my feelings. Begin next Wednesday.
- Over the next thirty days, observe my boss's behavior with other people; notice when he acts disrespectfully to others and how they handle it. Identify my colleagues who handle it best and use them as role models to stimulate my growth.
- For the next sixty days, consider whether it would be safe and constructive for me to clearly, unemotionally, and compassionately state my feelings to my boss and whether it is likely to create positive change in his behavior. If so, do it. If not, rely solely on my other implementation steps. I reserve the right to have him be a resistance force for me, but for me not to be a resistance force for him.

Debriefing John's Process

As John's process illustrates, when we are feeling helpless in our lives, making no progress, or going down one path after another similar path only to be blocked by similar obstructing forces in similar ways, it is time to take an inner inventory. When we use Compassionate Consultation within ourselves for this purpose, it can lead to dramatic growth because it causes us to access divine assistance, identify the specific issue that is causing a problem, truly see the range of facts involved, determine the spiritual dimensions of the situation, and come up with tailored ways to make the situation better that motivate us to act. As a result, we deepen our understanding, reframe our situation, realign ourselves around the ultimate purposes of life, and advance on the growth path.

The Example of Tanya--Using Compassionate Consultation to Change a Life Filter

Following is another example of how Compassionate Consultation can be used—this time to change a filter through which one is experiencing life, thereby fostering major life changes that accelerate spiritual growth.

Tanya was thirty-four years old and painfully lonely. She believed that everyone, including her family, thought that she was "odd" because she had not married and felt awkward in social situations. She also thought that people avoided her or only made brief, superficial comments to her because they did not know what to talk to her about, and they did not care enough to find out. Her perceptions had created a filter which took in any evidence suggesting she was odd, unlikable, and unlovable; it filtered out any evidence to the contrary.

Consequently, Tanya sought counseling, during which she discovered she was angry with family members and friends because they did not care about her. She also realized that she did not believe she was likeable or lovable, and she expected to be rejected. Gradually, Tanya was able to accept that her self-image caused her to act in ways that made it difficult for others to get close to her; she was defensive, projected underlying anger, avoided eye contact, and did not reach out to others. She recognized that she was not coming from her true self in social situations.

Having obtained some objectivity about her situation and realizing she was playing a part in the creation of her own misery, Tanya decided to use Compassionate Consultation within herself to change the filter through which she was seeing life and to redesign her thoughts, feelings, and behaviors as they related to connecting and building relationships with others. She chose the 6-Step Model to further deepen her understanding and craft a plan of action. Because the exact issue she wanted to address was still not fully clear to her, she chose the option of placing "Identifying & Agreeing on the Facts" as Step 2 and "Identifying & Agreeing on the Issue" as Step 3. She recorded her Consultation steps as follows:

1. *Convening by Praying for Divine Guidance*

2. *Identifying & Agreeing on the Facts:*
    - I feel lonely and unhappy.
    - I think I am not likeable.

- I think I will always be alone.
- I don't think I can trust anyone, because they may hurt me or not care about me.
- I am uncomfortable going to social events alone.
- I am hesitant to date because dating situations have caused me pain in the past.
- In social gatherings, people don't talk to me as much as they talk to other people.
- In social situations, I have a hard time initiating and sustaining conversations.
- I always had a few friends when I was going through school, but in recent years I am more disconnected than I have ever been.
- I want to have friends.
- I want people to enjoy talking with me.
- I have been self-absorbed.
- I have not been focusing on how I can be friendlier, but rather on using my energy to blame others for not making me feel better.
- I am so preoccupied with my aloneness that I resist or don't notice people's attempts to connect with me.
- I have been choosing isolation rather than connection with others.
- I have not been coming from my true self in social situations.
- My world view (my life filter) seems to be perfectly designed to keep me lonely and insensitive to opportunities for connecting with people.
- My thought patterns about connecting and building relationships with others are self-deprecating and self-defeating.
- All of the foregoing factors are resistance forces making my life so miserable that I must make a change.
- My connecting and relationship building skills are under-developed and rusty.
- My true self has the inherent qualities of compassion, uncritical acceptance, a dilated heart, curiosity, spiritual perspective, and guided confidence.

3. *Identifying & Agreeing on the Issue*:

How to interact with people in a way that will enable me to make and sustain authentic friendships.

4. Identifying & Agreeing on the Spiritual Principles:

- I have been created with talents and capacities that the world needs.
- There is a unique purpose for me in the world.
- There are people in the world who need to be touched by me.
- The scriptures describe human beings as "holy, noble, having a shining self, as a lamp of God's light."
- The scriptures convey that everyone is valuable and worthy.
- To grow in life, we must arise and struggle to overcome our weaknesses.
- The "golden rule" is that I must do unto others as I would have them do unto me.
- We should quickly replace a feeling of hate with a feeling of love.
- We should bring ourselves to account each day in terms of learning and growth.
- Humankind is one family.
- We need to care for, and attempt to meet the needs of, our fellow human beings.
- We need to see ourselves as connected to all the members of the human family.
- True happiness comes from spiritual thoughts, feelings, and actions.
- My true self has the inherent qualities of compassion, uncritical acceptance, a dilated heart, curiosity, spiritual perspective, and guided confidence.

5. Identifying & Agreeing on the Solutions:

In addressing Step #5, Tanya asked herself, "What do I know about people who are good at friendships—what do they do, and how do they behave?" She defined her solutions as the vision created by the items below:

- They act in ways that draw people toward them rather than push people away.
- They get out of themselves and have curiosity about the other person.
- They accept people as they are.
- They are non-judgmental about others.
- They are caring and compassionate.
- They ask the other person questions.

- They truly listen to others.
- They make the other person feel comfortable—not self-conscious.
- They are friendly—they reach out to others.
- They smile at others.
- They talk about things that they have in common with others.
- They are responsive to others.
- They look at the other when the other is speaking, and they respond appropriately.
- They encourage others.

6. *Identifying & Agreeing on the Implementation Steps:*

1. Visualize my true self emerging each morning when I do my prayers and scriptural readings and move through the day coming from my true self. Begin tomorrow morning.
2. Visualize myself being interested in others and interacting with others in an open, friendly, and accepting way (see the bulleted items in Step #5 above) for ten minutes in the morning and ten minutes in the evening every day, starting today.
3. Come from curiosity, and practice asking people open-ended questions about themselves—do this with five people per day starting Monday.
4. Prepare the questions I will use in #3 by the end of the day Sunday.
5. Practice active listening; ask clarifying follow-up questions if I'm not sure what someone means. Add an inventory of follow-up questions to the list of questions in #4 by next Wednesday night.
6. Silently say "STOP!" to myself when I find myself judging another person. Realize immediately that I have slipped out of coming from my true self, and promptly look for a positive quality about the person to replace the critical thought (this should help me reconnect with my true self). Start this tomorrow, and count and track the number of STOPs I need to say each day.
7. When I am with others, focus on them and stop thinking about myself. Place a small sticker on my watch face to remind me to do this whenever I look at my watch—apply the sticker by tomorrow night.
8. Identify automatic, negative thoughts from my old life filter and

quickly replace them with positive thoughts. Record my positive replacement thoughts, and use these as affirmations each morning and evening when I do #2. Start tomorrow.
9. By next Friday, buy and start using a book that will guide me to practice deep breathing and progressive relaxation daily to make me feel less anxious. Make this part of my regimen in #1.
10. Bring myself to account each day around how I am doing in my effort to become more caring, accepting, and compassionate. Measure myself daily on a zero to ten scale and maintain a trend line so that I can monitor my progress. Start by Friday of next week.
11. Ask God to help me achieve the purposes for which I was created, to develop spiritual attributes, and to express my talents and capacities as part of my regimen in #1. Begin tomorrow morning.

Consultation within the Individual—a Source of Welfare & Well-Being

The foregoing examples illustrate the transformative power that can come from using Compassionate Consultation within ourselves. Bahá'u'lláh's admonition that "No welfare and no well-being can be attained except through consultation"[221] indicates that we cannot flourish individually or collectively unless we process, work through, and resolve our issues in this way. If we are not using Compassionate Consultation to go over our walls and grow, we are inhibiting our welfare and our well-being.

By not dealing with our personal issues, we deaden our *intra*personal and *inter*personal relationships by loading them down with the burden of accumulated, unaddressed, and unresolved issues. It has been said, "There is nothing heavier than the weight of an undone task," and when we do not take on the task of dealing with issues in ourselves, the weight can become heavy indeed.

Chapter 14

Making Transformative Decisions with Twos

When we move from using Compassionate Consultation within the individual to using it with a pair of individuals (or larger group), we gain access to the power 'Abdu'l-Bahá describes when he says:

> The purpose of consultation is to show that the views of several individuals are assuredly preferable to one man, even as the power of a number of men is of course greater than the power of one man.[222]

Compassionate Consultation with Twos Increases Power & Complexity

Consequently, when we use Compassionate Consultation as a pair—which might be marriage partners, business partners, a parent and child, siblings, roommates, friends, or co-workers—we access greater potential and power on the one hand, and a greater complexity of issues being carried by each individual on the other hand. Each person will be at a different stage in their personal growth-seeking journey, will be dealing with their own set of resistance forces, and will be seeking their own desired outcome in the moment.

The Compassionate Consultation path through this complexity will be made smoother to the degree that the two parties have strengthened their capacity to maintain a compassionate perspective and come consistently from their true selves. One of the primary benefits of constantly reminding ourselves of the 12 Behavioral Standards and 7 Prime Requisites is that they de-energize our lower natures and invigorate our true selves.

Compassionate Consultation for Twos—Application Examples

Let us turn to some application examples below using several different Consultation Models including the 3-Step Model, the 6-Step Model, and the 4-Step V x D x F Model (used for visioning the future of a relationship). We will also look at some additional tools to support couples in using Compassionate Consultation successfully.

Using Compassionate Consultation on Your Issue with Your Partner as a Resource

Sometimes one partner in a relationship asks the other partner to assist him or her with an issue in order to achieve deeper understanding, change, and/or growth. In Chapter 6, we examined the case of Gina and David. Gina was feeling grumpy and did not understand why. We saw David begin the Compassionate Consultation process with her by creating a compassionate atmosphere, not having an agenda for Gina, reflecting back the feelings Gina was expressing, and asking questions to bring focus to what Gina was experiencing. She then used the compassionate space David had created to apply self-compassion, to courageously look more deeply at her feelings and experience, and to begin to understand how she wanted to transcend her cultural learning.

The obstacles and triggers in Gina's growth-seeking journey were the burdensome amount of work she had at the office, the co-worker who had given her an additional task at work, the children's relentless needs, the agitating thoughts generated by her cultural learning, and David's probing questions to understand why Gina was so grumpy. By having the courage to step into the compassionate space available to her rather than shifting attention away from her feelings by changing the subject, Gina was beginning to see a wall that she needed to scale which separated her from a more authentic way of being. Together, Gina and David had articulated the following statement of Gina's issue: *How to achieve balance of my body, mind, and spirit (get my needs met) while meeting my office and home responsibilities.*

The Example of Gina & David Continued—the 6-Step Consultation Model

The next step was for Gina and David to continue their process more formally to determine what specific changes she needed to make in order to be able to manifest the personal attributes and virtues she valued so highly. She and David resolved to use the 6-Step Model to address the issue. Here is Gina's record of their process:

1. Convening by Praying for Divine Guidance:

We prayed to be compassionate toward ourselves and each other and for divine assistance in achieving spiritual growth and transformation.

2. Identifying & Agreeing on the Issue:

We agreed that the issue statement we had previously identified was still valid: how to achieve balance of my body, mind, and spirit (get my needs met) while meeting my office and home responsibilities.

3. Identifying & Agreeing on the Facts:

- Gina is feeling irritable.
- She is feeling resentful toward her family.
- She is feeling resentful toward co-workers at her office.
- She feels like she needs to get away—to take a vacation by herself.
- She feels angry that some of her friends don't have to work as hard as she does.
- She feels depressed more and more of the time.
- Nothing seems to be as much fun as it once seemed.
- Although Gina is "doing" a lot, she is not happy with who she is "being."
- Gina does most of the indoor chores in the household—cooking, food shopping, buying gifts, cleaning, and straightening up.
- The kids do some chores but have to be supervised.
- David does the outdoor chores.
- The kids usually ask Gina when they need help with homework.
- David will do additional chores if Gina asks him to, but he does them on his own time and at his own pace—so Gina usually ends up doing the chores herself.
- Gina doesn't have time to spend with her best friend Gail or any of her other friends.
- Gina is feeling like a martyr and is angry with herself for feeling that way.
- Gina loves her husband, her family, has a good job, and she feels guilty for not being happy.

4. Identifying & Agreeing on the Spiritual Principles:

- The education and spiritual development of children is a primary responsibility of parents.
- A unified and healthy family is the basic building block of a unified and healthy society.
- We have all been created with talents and capacities that the world needs and should use them to contribute to the world's progress.
- Taking and fulfilling one's responsibilities is an important virtue.
- We should be selfless in our service to others.
- We should strive for excellence in all things.
- Justice and equity are twin guardians that watch over humanity.
- The body of humankind needs to be adorned with the mantle of justice and wisdom.
- One who cleaves to justice must not transgress the limits of moderation.

5. Identifying & Agreeing on the Solutions:

As we began Step 5, we discovered that the first five Spiritual Principles in Step 4 tended to confirm my current behavioral patterns, while the last four tended to challenge my current behavioral patterns. We realized that my current patterns were not allowing me to achieve excellence in my "being" qualities and that my anger was at least partly due to justice, equity, and fairness issues. My own needs were going unmet as I struggled to fulfill tasks at home and at work. The resulting resentment I felt was inhibiting my ability to feel loving. These insights fed the following solution-finding process.

- Have a family meeting with the children and David to share my feelings and ask for help from family members to:
    - Try to be more considerate of me in specific ways such as asking how my day was and how I'm feeling.
    - Ask me when it would be convenient to talk with me about something they want or need my help with.
    - Show appreciation for my help.
    - Give me some extra hugs.
    - Respect my need for personal alone time: fifteen minutes each morning for prayers and a half hour each evening—to go for a walk, to meditate, reflect, pray, read, take a long

bath, etc.
- o Give me more assistance with some household chores; I need to be specific about the time period (e.g. indefinite or just for the next three weeks until the project at the office has been completed and my work load is back to normal); be specific about who needs to do what and by when.
- Ask for additional help at the office or an extension on the deadline of the project.
- Plan outside activities that are relaxing, such as seeing Gail or going to a movie.
- Increase exercise to relieve stress.
- Eat healthier, more nutritious foods—fruits for snacks.
- Get more rest—go to bed a half hour earlier.
- Slow down whenever possible and make lunch the night before to avoid having to rush as much in the morning.

6. *Identifying & Agreeing on the Implementation Steps:*

After completing Step 5, we reviewed the bundle of agreed upon solution ideas and David asked me which ones I felt the most energy around. Based on my response, we crafted the following implementation steps:

- Schedule a family meeting for next Saturday morning with mandatory attendance by all family members.
- Start the meeting by saying that I have not known what I have needed, that now I realize that I do have some needs, and that this is going to require some changes from everyone in the family. Explain that since change is hard, this is going to require some conscious effort on everyone's part.
- Then surface my needs to have more time for myself, and to have family members pay attention to my needs as I hopefully pay attention to theirs.
- Ask each person to think of some ways they might make me feel more important, like I am loved and cared about. Record and post these ideas (I may add to their ideas—i.e., thank me for my help, ask how my day was, ask if I need some help, give me extra hugs). Challenge the family members to start applying these ideas immediately.
- Announce that I need to have my private time respected. I will go

to bed by ten p.m. (no one should disturb me after that time); I will have a prayer/meditation time for fifteen minutes in the a.m. (when the den door is closed, do not disturb me); after dinner I will take a half hour of personal time (7:30-8:00 p.m.). Start this program on Sunday.
- Announce that when I need to have extra help with chores I will post a list on the refrigerator with assignments for each family member and a deadline for completion. Start Monday of next week.
- Schedule a meeting with my supervisor and co-worker to discuss a distribution of responsibilities that I can handle and do well. Make a list before the meeting that outlines what would be viable for me. Schedule the future meeting on Monday.
- Start monitoring daily on a zero to ten scale the degree to which I am feeling happy, loving, enthusiastic, excited, peaceful, and joyful at home and at work. Manage the trend line by using Compassionate Consultation further with David and/or the children to make any necessary adjustments in my plan to enhance progress.

Debriefing the Gina & David Compassionate Consultation Example

Gina and David's process is a striking illustration of how powerful compassion for the other and compassion for self can be. First, David opened the way for Gina to explore what was going on inside herself by applying compassion. Next she applied self-compassion by acknowledging and looking more deeply at her uncomfortable feelings. Compassion can shift us away from a useless preoccupation with who and what to blame for our uncomfortable feelings and move us toward a deepened understanding that will help us become the person we want to be.

Technically, *a feeling* is a physiological response, and *emotion* is the name we put to the feeling. Whether we call them feelings or emotions, they can get us into trouble *or* guide us to the fulfillment of our life purposes; they can literally make us sick *or* be a source of great joy. They have tremendous power because, whether we know it or not, feelings and emotions influence our every moment. Because they have so much power, it behooves us to use Compassionate Consultation to understand them like Gina did and practice making them our allies rather than annoyances we try to hide.

Primary pair relationships like this one are often the most rewarding *and* difficult contexts for doing change and spiritual growth work. They touch us the most and can cause us the most joy *or* distress. While Bahá'u'lláh calls the institution of marriage "...a fortress for well-being and salvation,"[223] He also says, speaking generally, that "No welfare and no well-being can be attained except through consultation."[224] The implication of the two quotations combined seems to be that marriage can be a fortress for well-being *if* the partners effectively use Consultation and compassion to struggle over walls, make decisions, and solve problems together.

Being Open to Learning about Feelings & Emotions

A significant part of the work we do in counseling and coaching—whether involving individuals, pairs, or larger groups—has to do with learning about feelings because even though feelings constantly influence us, most people are not aware of their own feelings. Some of the most common myths people have about feelings and emotions include:

- If you don't pay attention to them, they will go away.
- Only weak people have emotions.
- Emotions may be acceptable for girls, but not for boys.
- I don't have any feelings (emotions).
- Emotions aren't important and should be ignored.
- There are good emotions and bad emotions.
- We should never have "negative" emotions.
- Being emotional means being out of control.
- It is weak to let others know you feel hurt or sad.
- Emotions happen for no reason.
- If you have painful emotions, it is because you have a bad attitude.
- You can't be depressed if you have a nice spouse, a good job, a house, are thin, have a fortune, or (fill in the blank).

We have observed clients in coaching or counseling sessions sitting rigidly upright, tightening their hands into fists, and saying through clenched teeth, "I'm not a bit angry." Although the client's anger is clear to us, the client truly believes he or she is not angry. To some extent we all deny, resist, suppress, or repress uncomfortable feelings—feelings we don't think we should have—in countless creative ways. And while that may work for the moment, we usually are still carrying the feelings inside. It is often said that uncomfortable, painful feelings *flourish in the dark* and *perish in the light*. What is meant by this is that as long as we keep pushing feelings out of our conscious awareness, they will grow in power. However, when we allow ourselves to experience and process unwanted feelings with an attitude of compassion as Gina and David did, the feelings will lose their power. What is more, the act of processing these feelings using Compassionate Consultation gives us important information we need in order to deepen our understanding, discover and go over walls, and make decisions that are aligned with our spiritual purposes. From the standpoint of the growth-seeker, *the light that makes uncomfortable and painful feelings perish is compassion—for self and for others.*

Resolving Joint Issues—Marriage, Conflict, and Compassion

The example of Gina and David illustrates a situation where one partner has an issue and requests the other partner to use Compassionate Consultation with her to deepen her understanding and make a change. More often, there are situations in which *both* parties have an issue together and they need to *jointly* resolve it.

At least one popular theory says that we often fall in love with someone who makes up for what is missing in us;[225] that a person pairs up "with an incompatible partner to create the chemistry for growth."[226] If this is true, the potential for conflict is high. Psychologist John Gottman's empirical marital research indicates that because of the many differences that the two parties bring to the marriage relationship, 69 percent of all marital issues are *perpetual* in nature.[227] This means that an issue a couple argues about while getting to know each other may still be causing some level of conflict on their fiftieth wedding anniversary. These perpetual issues cannot be permanently resolved, but they can be effectively managed through dialogue and Compassionate Consultation.

When we add to these findings the fact that marriage partners live in close proximity, that whatever either partner says or does in life impacts the other partner's life, and that there is incredible power in even a subtle facial expression by a partner, it becomes clear that marriage, despite the many blessings it provides, is also a very challenging institution. It requires a great deal of persistence, patience, and compassion from the partners. In fact, *marriage is the ideal spiritual growth accelerator for growth-seekers.* Where else can we find an environment where the primary loved one is also the regular source of triggering resistance or obstruction that prompts us to grow? Indeed, one role of each spouse is to ask for their partner's assistance in helping them scale their walls and to compassionately help their partner discover walls that partner needs to scale. When both of these roles are being played *compassionately*, marriage optimally facilitates and accelerates spiritual growth.

Consultation Examples & Additional Tools for Marriage Relationships

For all these reasons, and because unified couples are the cornerstone of unified families and unified families the cornerstone for unified societies, every couple has a need for resources and tools to help them address issues, resolve conflicts, solve problems, and make decisions that generate spiritual, social, and intellectual growth. While the structures, tools, and Consultation examples in the remainder of this chapter pertain especially to the marriage relationship, they are also useful in other relationships.

The Consultation Climate Safety Scale Tool

Compassion is the attribute that creates an environment in which it feels safe to explore concerns, fears, hopes, needs, and wants—all the things that directly impact the making of a decision. In our work with couples, we have found that the Consultation Climate Safety Scale (see Figure 14.1) can be a helpful tool to determine when it is, or is not, an appropriate time to use Consultation. The Safety Scale can be useful for other twosomes and larger groups as well. To use the Safety Scale, each person rates on the zero to ten scale how safe it feels to open up with the other and share thoughts and feelings in the given moment. When compassion is low in either person, attempting to become vulnerable and open up can lead to *increased* distress. It has been our experience that the assessed measure on the Safety Scale should be at least seven for both parties before Consultation is advisable. Compassionate Consultation may be unavailable to us unless a substantial amount of compassion is in the environment.

Consultation Climate Safety Scale

Extremely Dangerous To Share My Thoughts & Feelings
0 1 2 3 4 5 6 7 8 9 10
Extremely Safe To Share My Thoughts & Feelings

Figure 14.1

It may be possible for the parties to raise the Safety Scale number to an acceptable level in a short time by taking a break, going for a walk, drinking a glass of water, meditating, or praying together longer and with more intensity in the first step of Consultation. Regular use of the Safety Scale helps each person build the "compassion muscle" (see Chapter 4) by noticing the *choice point* where compassion needs to be generated and then *flipping the switch* that allows one to apply it in a given situation. If more time is needed before the Safety Scale number is at an acceptable level, both parties can simply record what the "presenting issue" is and schedule another time to come together and begin again.

Stopping Power Struggles with the 5-Step Change-The-Game Procedure

A time when it is *not* safe to Consult on an issue is when the parties are in a verbal attack-and-defend mode. This typically means a power struggle is underway. *While all couples will have differences, it is how they talk about their differences that determines whether they will stay together or separate.* Gottman's empirical research has shown that the four behaviors that consistently cause the deterioration of a marriage relationship and predict divorce are criticism, contempt, defensiveness, and stonewalling.[228] *These four behavioral predictors are the antithesis of compassion* as each behavior conveys no interest in understanding the other person's feelings or alleviating his or her suffering. Not only are these behaviors toxic for all relationships, but they are disqualifiers for participation in Compassionate Consultation. The 7 Prime Requisites and 12 Behavioral Standards by definition prohibit their use.

The 5-Step Change-The-Game Procedure is a simple tool to stop power struggles and the criticism, contempt, defensiveness, and stonewalling that accompany them. It involves the following steps:

The 5-Step Change-The-Game Procedure

1. Prior to the next power struggle, the partners agree on a signal that means "stop." When either one realizes a power struggle has begun or witnesses criticism, contempt, defensiveness, or stonewalling, he or she gives the "stop" signal.

2. Both people stop immediately when the signal is given.
3. Both partners take a cool-down period if necessary.
4. After the cool-down or when the partners have reestablished equanimity, both partners write down a brief description of the conflictual issue while it is fresh in their minds.
5. Whenever the Consultation Climate Safety Scale numbers for both parties are at seven or more, the two parties come together, share their notes from Step 4, ask themselves, *"How can we make it better?"* and forge a consensus description of the issue beginning with the words "How to…………" so that it is in a form suitable for Consultation. Now the parties begin at Step 1 (Convening by Praying for Divine Guidance) of the Consultation Process.

Slipping into a Power Struggle—The Example of June & Bob

Following is an example of the kind of mundane issues that often plague couples and over time lead to accumulating resentment and anger. These seemingly small issues cry out for the use of the 5-Step Change-The-Game Procedure. June and Bob are a married couple who slip into a power struggle in the following dialogue.

Bob: June, what happened to the movie section of the newspaper that is supposed to be on the shelf under the table in the den?

June: I threw that away when I was cleaning the den for the meeting you had in there yesterday.

Bob: When you were at work last night, I wanted to go to a movie, and I didn't have the newspaper to check the movie listings. I couldn't find out where a movie I wanted to see was playing.

June: Oh… But, that was Thursday and I always think that if it's not the weekend, we won't need the movie section because we get a new one on Friday for the weekend. And that's when we usually go to the movies—on the weekend.

Bob: Darn it! I like to save that section in case I want to go to a movie during the week—like I wanted to do last night. You're *always* throwing things away too soon. By the way, where is that flyer from Target with the sale ad for the lawn chairs? I suppose you threw that out too?

June: Yes, I threw that away because we know the lawn chairs are on sale, and we know we're going to go and buy them.

Bob: Yes, but I wanted to keep the ad as a reminder—so I wouldn't forget to go and buy the chairs while they're on sale. It's really frustrating—if things aren't nailed down around here, you throw them away without a second thought!

June: That's ridiculous! If you weren't so absentminded, you wouldn't need things like that lying around. If I didn't keep throwing things away, our house would get too full to walk through. Unlike you, I can't stand living in a pig-pen!

Countering the Power Struggle—The Example of June & Bob

It is apparent from the dialogue above that June and Bob have moved into a power struggle and that both are now in an attack-and-defend mode. Bob is the first to realize that he has moved into the power struggle mode, and he immediately starts the 5-Step Change-The-Game Procedure as follows:

1. Bob looks at June, clears his voice, and then silently puts his index finger alongside his nose (the "stop" signal they have previously agreed upon).
2. June looks at Bob, and both of them stop talking immediately.
3. They agree to sit down together and take a three-minute cool-down period.
4. After the cool-down period, both June and Bob write down a brief description of the conflictual issue while it is fresh in their minds. June writes: It's a conflict over household mess versus neatness. Bob writes: June wants the house all tidy. I want papers that are important to me left in place.
5. With the nature of the power struggle recorded by each party in Step 4, June and Bob agree to come together at 4:00 PM over coffee to have Compassionate Consultation together in order to resolve the issue. When they meet for coffee, they each recite a prayer for guidance and assistance. Then they check their Safety Scale numbers and both of them give the Consultation climate an eight. They acknowledge that they are both approaching the issue with compassion for themselves and for each other. They then share their notes from Step #4 with each other and ask themselves, "How can we make it better?" Then they work on forging a consensus description of the issue beginning with the words "How

to…" so that it is in a form suitable for Consultation. They arrive at the phrase, *"How to keep the house neat enough for June to feel comfortable while keeping important papers accessible to Bob."* Because the issue seems quite straightforward to them, they decide to use the 3-Step Consultation Model.

The Compassionate Consultation Example of June & Bob— the 3-Step Model

1. Understanding The Situation

With the power struggle behind them and with their compassion and true selves engaged, June and Bob find themselves ready to identify the facts of their situation without criticism, contempt, or defensiveness. Consequently, they can arrive at a more objective understanding of their issue and the related facts as follows:

- Bob is more comfortable with disorder than June.
- An orderly environment contributes to June's sense of well-being.
- Bob appreciates the lack of clutter that June maintains—it contributes to his sense of well-being too—as long as he can find his things.
- Bob likes to hold onto things—because "you never know when something will be needed."
- Bob's "things" tend to spread out on the surfaces of counters and tables.
- June's "things" tend to be contained, put away, or thrown away.
- Keeping things that need to get attended to visible in the environment helps Bob to stay on top of them—he says that if something is out of his sight, it's out of his mind.
- Since June is the main housekeeper and she likes things neat, she feels that her work isn't done when there is clutter around; she can't rest completely.
- Bob doesn't want any of his things thrown away by anyone but him.
- June wishes Bob would write himself "to do" notes rather than keep materials all around him.
- Bob acknowledges that there is validity to June's perspective on the issue.

- June acknowledges that there is validity to Bob's perspective.
- Both June and Bob realize that this is one of those perpetual issues in their relationship that can't be eliminated but can be better managed by them.

2. Deciding What To Do

- Both June and Bob want the house to be uncluttered and orderly.
- Both June and Bob agree that Bob needs to have some spaces in the house where he can keep his materials without fear that June will move them or throw them away.
- They decide that the materials Bob wants around, but doesn't need to keep on display so that he won't forget them (e.g. the movie section of the newspaper), will be kept in either of the two cabinets in the family room. June will not straighten up the contents of the two cabinets—that will be Bob's responsibility when he chooses to do it.
- They decide that any of Bob's materials that he wants to keep out on display so that he won't forget them (e.g. the sale ad from Target) will be kept in Bob's home office. June will not move or throw away materials in Bob's office.
- They decide that any of Bob's materials left in other parts of the house will be subject to June's judgments about what should be kept or thrown out.

3. Implementing & Carrying Out The Decision

- Bob will move all of his cluttering materials to either his office or the cabinets in the family room by the end of the day tomorrow.
- When June begins her tidying up the following day, she will show Bob anything she is planning to throw out in case he missed something in his sweep through the house in the action item above.
- Beginning on the third day, June is free to tidy up anywhere except the family room cabinets and Bob's office without notifying Bob of her decisions on what to throw away.

Debriefing the June & Bob Compassionate Consultation Example

By using the 5-Step Change-The-Game Procedure to counter their power struggle, by delaying their Consultation until they had replaced their resentiments with compassion for themselves and each other, by using prayer to detach from the need to control the situation, and by using the 3-Step Model, June and Bob achieved true Compassionate Consultation and some other things as well. They deepened their understanding of some of the differences and similarities in their personality styles; they more fully understood their issue; they both went over a wall, which enabled them to better flex their preferred behaviors for the benefit of their relationship; they arrived at a robust, long-term solution to a perpetual issue that was bedeviling their relationship, and they strengthened both their relationship and their confidence in their ability to resolve future issues with Compassionate Consultation.

No One Is an Island

In his often-quoted "Meditation XVII," Poet John Donne says, "No man is an island entire of himself; every man is a piece of the continent, a part of the main."[229] In the metaphor, the islands in the sea seem totally separated at sea level, but if one goes deep under the water to the ocean floor, one sees that the islands are really only high points of a single land mass. They are all one. A similar phenomenon occurs when we go deep beneath the parties' positions in a particular conflict to their underlying concerns and then articulate and address the issue or problem at this deeper level. As with June and Bob, we usually find that the parties are not as separated and disconnected as we had feared. At a deeper level, like June and Bob, they are one. This is important learning to incorporate in the use of Compassionate Consultation with any sized group, but especially with couples.

Going deeper beneath the parties' positions to underlying interests and concerns *requires the use of compassion* and *is expedited through the use of open-ended questions.*

Using the Deep 8 Open-Ended Questions Technique to Assess Facts & Concerns

Rather than allowing themselves to move toward argumentation and a power struggle in reaction to an issue, couples (and larger groups) can use a simple, open-ended questioning technique that can be of great assistance in getting a deeper grasp on both the facts and the underlying interests and concerns. While we are calling this a technique, it is a form of Consultation because it deepens understanding, which is one of the purposes of using Consultation. The technique involves each party asking the other the following series of eight open-ended questions from a place of true compassion and curiosity:

The Deep 8 Open-Ended Questions

1. What is happening now in connection with this situation?
2. What do you want in connection with this situation?
3. What else do you want?
4. What would that look like if you had it in place?
5. What will that get you?
6. How important is this for you?
7. What gets in the way of your having what you want?
8. What is that like for you?

The Example of Dane & Ellen Revisited—Using the Deep 8 Technique

In Chapter 3, we used the case of Dane and Ellen to illustrate how the application of compassion could dramatically deepen understanding. Now, we want to demonstrate how Dane and Ellen used the Deep 8 Open-Ended Questions Technique to get that result.

The disagreement between Dane and Ellen was about "money" according to Dane and about "Dane being inconsiderate" according to Ellen. Ellen wanted a new dining room set and believed that Dane was disregarding her feelings and being "inconsiderate and stingy." Dane believed they needed to be saving their money and that Ellen was being extravagant, disregarding his feelings, and wanting to "aggravate" him.

They decided to take a time out, said prayers for divine assistance, checked to make sure their Safety Scale numbers were at seven or higher, and then began again. Ellen offered to go first, made sure she was coming from sincere compassion and curiosity, then asked Dane the Deep Eight Questions and recorded his responses as follows:

1. What is happening now in connection with this situation?

- I am trying my best to hold the line on expenditures and save money.
- You are persistently coming at me about getting a new dining room set.

- I'm trying to come up with creative ways of saying "no," but I am running out of ideas.
- I've never seen you so tenacious about anything before.

2. **What do you want in this situation?**

    - I want to put money away for the future.
    - My parents always struggled to have enough money to live on, and I don't want to replicate that. So I'm always working toward financial security.
    - I don't want to spend money on a new dining room set—we can't afford it, and the kitchen set we have is all we need.

3. **What else do you want?**

    - I feel like it's my responsibility to assure the financial well-being of this family. We have to save for the children's education and for our own retirement. Any expenditure that can be postponed should be.
    - I want to earn more money so that we have more discretionary funds, but that seems to be slow in coming.

4. **What would that look like if you had it in place?**

    - Our mortgage would be paid off, we would live totally within our budget and have positive cash flow every month, and we would have no debts.
    - We would have savings accounts for all our future expenditures such as education, vacations, the dining room set, retirement, rainy day fund, etc.

5. **What will that get you?**

    - A great sense of security and well-being, and the feeling that I have done well for my family.

6. **How important is this for you?**

    - Very important. It's a big part of what determines whether I will see myself as having been a success or a failure in life.

7. What gets in the way of your having what you want?

- A constant flow of unexpected or unnecessary expenses.

8. What is that like for you?

- It's really frustrating. Often I feel like I am spinning my wheels in terms of getting ahead financially.

When Dane had finished, Ellen said, "For the first time, I feel like I understand why you have such steely determination about saving for the future. Thanks for sharing that."

Then Dane, making sure he was coming from sincere compassion and curiosity, asked Ellen the same questions and recorded her responses as follows.

1. What is happening now in this situation?

- I am trying my best to persuade you that getting a new dining room set is important.
- I cut out pictures of dining room sets from ads and put them on the kitchen counter for you to see so you'll realize how important this purchase is to me.
- I continually drop hints to you about dining room furniture sales.

2. What do you want in this situation?

- I want a new dining room set with a round table and a sideboard, a place for family and friends to congregate.

3. What else do you want?

- (Ellen's eyes filled with tears as she began to speak.) When I was growing up in my family, the dining room was the heart of the home, the place where everyone gathered. I want to have a place like that in our home.
- The kitchen feels cramped and isn't a place where people relax and just hang out after a meal. My family spent hours around the dining room table during and after meals. We shared special times there. We played games there, did our homework there—it was a place where we would all be together.
- The way it is now, family members and friends scatter to different rooms and we don't have that sense of togetherness and unity.

4. What would that look like if you had it in place?

- I can picture our dining room as a very warm, inviting space with a round table that everyone gathers around. It would mean "home" to all of us and would be the center of our family and social life.
- I would feel that I had created the kind of environment in which everyone could connect and be close.

5. What will that get you?

- It will get me a magnet space where our family's unity is nurtured and protected and where we welcome our friends as an even larger family. It's a place where we have important conversations and really tune into, and focus on, each other.
- This will make me feel happy and contented.

6. How important is this for you?

- It's extremely important to me—I feel like I need that kind of space to fulfill my dream for the family I have always hoped to create.

7. What gets in the way of your having what you want?

- Your relentless focus on putting money away for the future.
- Not valuing the present—now is the time we need to be making memories, and environment plays a big part in creating those memories.

8. What is that like for you?

- Very frustrating. I am not an extravagant person, but I think you think I am. I want us to save too, but some aspects of life shouldn't be postponed. I can't reconcile myself to postponing the creation of the space that is the heart of our home.

When she finished speaking, Dane said he had not understood before *how much* the dining room set meant to her and *why* it meant so much.

Debriefing the Ellen & Dane Application Example

Since the primary goals in using the Deep 8 Questions are to discover *what* is important to each party, *why* it is important, and *how* important it is, Ellen and Dane were able to use the questions to deepen their understanding of each other and the issue. They then leveraged their deepened understanding to move forward with additional Consultative steps and agreed on a program for putting a certain amount of money into savings each month, with a certain percentage of that amount earmarked for purchasing the dining room set. Their process clarified a second issue for later Consultation, which was: *how to create a warm, friendly atmosphere in our home and have it become a place where family and friends regularly gather.*

Ellen and Dane's disagreement about the dining room set had caused anger and resentment for a long time while they were locked into their "positions." When they used the Deep 8 Questions Technique to discover "underlying concerns," the disagreement was transformed into a vehicle that strengthened their understanding of each other and deepened their bond. They went deeper—which is needed to strengthen any relationship—and when they did, they found common ground and agreement. At a deeper level, they were not islands—they were one.

Combining 5-Step Change-the-Game, the Deep 8 Questions & Consultation Steps

The 5-Step Change-The-Game Procedure, the Deep 8 Open-Ended Questions Technique and the Consultation Steps can be used independently, together, or in various combinations. When they are used together in sequence they create a seamless Compassionate Consultation flow to deeper understanding, agreement, and transformative decision-making.

When used together with the 6-Step Model, the couple (or larger group) starts with Step 1: Convening By Praying for Divine Guidance; then the 5-Step Change-the-Game Procedure fills the role of Step 2: Identifying and Agreeing on the Issue; then the Deep 8 Open-Ended Questions Technique fills *all or part* of the role of Step 3: Identifying and Agreeing On the Facts; and then the 6-Step Model continues with Step 4: Identifying & Agreeing on the Spiritual Principles, Step 5: Identifying & Agreeing on the Solutions, and Step 6: Identifying & Agreeing on the Implementation Steps.

Following the Whole Consultative Sequence—The Example of Joan & Mike

Let's follow this whole sequence with another example. Joan and Mike are a couple having a difference of opinion. They get into a verbal attack-and-defend pattern almost immediately; the discussion escalates into blaming, and there is no movement toward resolution. It begins with the following exchange.

Mike: It's time for us to get an underground sprinkling system for the yard.

Joan: That costs too much money. It's a luxury.

Mike: This argument between us has been going on for twenty years. When we had our house built, I had pre-piping installed in the house so it would cost less when we could afford it. We're never going to feel like we can afford it. We should just go ahead and do it.

Joan: It doesn't matter how long this discussion has gone on—we can't afford it—it's too much of a stretch.

Mike: Look. I'm trying to run a business out of my home office, and I don't have time to run outside and adjust the sprinklers every half-hour.

Joan: The lawn looks fine to me.

Mike: That's because I'm spending so much time taking care of the watering!

Joan: Can't we all help? There are four of us in this house!

Mike: We have talked about this again and again. Nobody is there to help when the need arises!

Joan: Well, we could make a schedule.

Mike: We're the only ones on the cul-de-sac who don't have an underground sprinkling system.

Joan: Is this about keeping up with other people?

Mike: No. I'm trying to tell you that it's commonplace to have an underground sprinkling system—it's not a luxury.

Joan: So what? We can't afford it.

Mike: We couldn't afford redecorating your living room either, but we just finished doing that. Now, it's my turn.

Joan: The living room was for everybody.

Mike: So is the lawn.

Joan: It's outdoors, so we don't see it much.

Mike: I see it every day.

Joan: The living room is something we all see every day. The lawn is only a problem a few months each year.

Mike: I can't believe you are so insensitive!
Joan: I can't believe you are such a spender!

It is clear that verbal attack-and-defend behaviors are causing resentment in both Joan and Mike, weakening the attachment bond, and decreasing intimacy in the relationship. Fortunately, Joan suddenly realizes what's happening and asks, "How's your Aunt Martha?"

The 5-Step Change-The-Game Procedure—Joan & Mike

Step 1

Joan's and Mike's previously agreed upon "stop" signal to begin the 5-Step Change the Game Procedure is, "How's your Aunt Martha?"

Step 2

Both Joan and Mike stop talking immediately.

Step 3

They agree to sit down together and take a three-minute cool-down period.

Step 4

After the cool-down period, both Joan and Mike write down a brief description of the conflictual issue while it is fresh in their minds. Mike writes: I want an underground sprinkling system. Joan writes: I want to hold to the budget.

Step 5

With the nature of the power struggle recorded by each party in Step 4, Joan and Mike decide to move directly into Compassionate Consultation. They have been practicing "shifting gears" out of attack-and-defend mode into true selves with compassion mode and want to do just that. They want to use the **6-Step Consultation Model** and decide to use Consultation Step 1: Convening by Praying for Divine Guidance to help them shift gears. After saying several prayers for assistance and guidance together, they check their Consultation Climate Safety Scale numbers and both of them give the climate an eight. They acknowledge that they are both approaching the issue with compassion for themselves and for each other.

They then share their notes from Step 4 with each other and ask themselves, "How can we make it better?" They work on **Consultation Step 2: Identifying & Agreeing on the Issue** by forging a consensus description of the issue beginning with the words "How to…" so that it is in a form suitable for Consultation. They arrive at the phrase, *"How to work toward getting an underground sprinkling system without breaking the budget."* Now Joan and Mike continue their Consultation session by working on Consultation Step 3: Identifying & Agreeing on the Facts through the use of the Deep 8 Open-Ended Questions Technique.

Using the Deep 8 Questions for Identifying & Agreeing on the Facts—Joan & Mike

Having completed Step 1: Convening by Praying for Divine Guidance and Step 2: Identifying & Agreeing on the Issue (using the 5-Step Change-The-Game Procedure), Joan and Mike now proceed to use the Deep 8 Open-Ended Questions Technique as a means of working through Step 3: Identifying & Agreeing on the Facts. Joan comes from compassion and curiosity, asks the eight questions of Mike first and records his answers. The dialogue proceeds as follows:

Joan: What is happening now in connection with this situation?

Mike: Every day that it doesn't rain, which is almost every day during the spring, summer, and fall, I am leaving my office downstairs and spending a large share of my discretionary time during the work day moving hoses and sprinklers around the lawn trying to keep it adequately watered. On most days when you get home from work, I complain that we need an underground sprinkling system, and you reject the idea without hesitation.

Joan: What do you want in connection with the issue on which we are Consulting?

Mike: An automatic sprinkling system that will keep the lawn looking nice—for us, our neighbors, and my clients who come here—without taking my time and energy.

Joan: What else do you want?

Mike: I want peace of mind for the six to seven months of the year that the lawn needs care. I don't want to have to keep monitoring the condition of the lawn, sweating as I run outside in my business clothes and drag the sprinklers into position, getting sprayed with

	water, while frantically calculating whether my time with clients will allow me to be back in time to shut off or move the sprinklers and not waste water. I don't want that burden.
Joan:	What would that look like to have the underground sprinkling system in place?
Mike:	The lawn would automatically be watered every other day in zones on a timer and I could put away the hoses, use water more efficiently, and let go of the daily responsibility to deal with it—it would be a huge relief—much less worry and struggle. In addition, the lawn would look nice for my clients, our family, and neighbors. The climate is hot and often dry here so the watering isn't optional if we want the lawn to look nice.
Joan:	What will that get you?
Mike:	A professional, in-control appearance for the site of my business, more time to focus on my business and the needs of my clients, and much less stress and strain. I would even feel more excited about each day because of this reduced burden. I think the investment would quickly pay for itself in terms of my increased productivity during the work day and more efficient use of water. It's not uncommon for the sprinklers to run way too long in one section of the yard because I am tied up with a client.
Joan:	How important is this for you?
Mike:	Very important. My business requires focus on my clients and concentration all the time. The lawn care is a big distraction during the warm months. In addition, you are off-site at work all day during the week and the kids are at school or at other activities—I'm the only one here to handle this, and it's too much.
Joan:	What gets in your way?
Mike:	You—because you don't think it is a high priority.
Joan:	What is that like for you?
Mike:	Very frustrating. It seems like you aren't listening to me—like you don't understand what I'm experiencing.

These open-ended questions help Mike express his thoughts, feelings, needs, and wants clearly, and his answers give Joan additional insight into Mike's perspective and experiences. She begins to have a deeper understanding of, and greater compassion for, his daily struggle with the lawn care.

Now they reverse their roles and Mike comes from compassion and curiosity, asks Joan the same eight questions, and records her answers. The dialogue continues as follows:

Mike: What is happening now in connection with this situation?

Joan: You seem relentless about wanting an underground sprinkler system, and I feel like I have to resist you and hold the line so that we save enough money to address needs that are looming in the future. It seems like we are battling over needs versus wants.

Mike: What do you want in connection with the issue on which we are Consulting?

Joan: I want to have money put away for our daughters' weddings, for our family pilgrimage to Israel, for graduate school for Tara (just as we paid for Adriana's graduate school), and for our retirement.

Mike: What else do you want?

Joan: Peace of mind and security—a sense that we will be financially ready when the time comes for each of these needs. When I was growing up, my parents never used a credit card and never bought anything unless they had enough in their checking account for the expense, which gave me the impression that they always planned ahead so they would be ready when the expense came. There was always a sense of being careful and conservative about money. That learning is deeply rooted in me.

Mike: What would that look like?

Joan: We would have a budget with specific amounts for each need, a savings fund for each need, and would be putting enough into each fund each month that the targets would seem within reach. I'd know where we stand and that we were moving effectively toward those goals.

Mike: What will that get you?

Joan: A sense that our family's financial needs were going to be met and that each significant expenditure we make wasn't putting that at risk. I would feel like things were under control financially and that would give me a real sense of contentment.

Mike: How important is this for you?

Joan: Very important. As you know, I'm not a last-minute person. I like security, consistency, and having everything in place.

Mike: What gets in your way?

Joan: Your priorities seem to be different than mine in this regard. You're more spontaneous about financial matters. I know you are thinking ahead about retirement. You manage the finances, and I try not to think about it. So far, everything has worked out, but we spend on our credit cards and don't talk about our goals regularly, so I'm not sure what you're thinking or doing about these goals and whether we even share them.

Mike: What is that like for you?

Joan: I've gotten used to it. I just don't ask, and I assume it will work out because it always has in the past. But, I worry about it and feel I always have to put on the financial brakes because I'm not sure where we stand.

When Joan finished expressing her thoughts, feelings, needs, and wants in response to Mike's eight questions, Mike said, "I have a lot more insight into your perspective on all of this." As Joan looked into his eyes, she could see and feel that he had a much deeper understanding of, and compassion for, her resistance to spending money on lawn care.

Then they discussed whether they felt that they had identified and agreed upon enough facts about their issue of *"How to work toward getting an underground sprinkling system without breaking the budget."* They realized there were some additional facts they needed that the Deep 8 Questions had not turned up.

Augmented Step 3 Fact Generation after Using the Deep 8 Open-Ended Questions

To satisfactorily complete *Step 3: Identifying & Agreeing on the Facts*, Joan and Mike continued to generate and agree upon the facts as follows.

- Mike has established a single all-purpose savings account for education, pilgrimage, weddings, and retirement (exclusive of tax-advantaged retirement accounts).
- The cost to complete the installation of the underground sprinkler system is $2,100 based on the pre-plumbing having been done when the house was built.
- Based on the balance in the all-purpose savings account, the projected additional savings needed for the pilgrimage to Israel for the four family members is $4,000.
- The projected additional savings needed for Adriana's and Tara's future weddings is $5,000 each for a total of $10,000.

- The projected additional savings needed for Tara's graduate school tuition and books is $3,000.
- The projected additional savings needed for retirement (exclusive of tax-advantaged retirement accounts) is $300 per month for the next ten years.
- The current balance in the all-purpose savings account indicates that Joan and Mike are currently on schedule to reach all of their savings goals.
- Mike has $600 per month automatically going into this savings account from his paycheck.
- Of the $600, $300 per month goes toward retirement, and $100 per month each goes toward the pilgrimage, the weddings, and Tara's graduate school tuition.

Step 4: Identifying & Agreeing on the Spiritual Principles

Next, Joan and Mike addressed the spiritual principles that related to their issue and the foregoing facts (both the augmented facts and those identified by the Deep 8 Questions). They arrived at the following.
- We should strive for excellence in all things.
- Parents are responsible before God for the spiritual and intellectual education of their children.
- It is important to be unified as a family.
- One of the purposes of life is to carry forward an ever-advancing civilization.
- Work done in the spirit of service to others is worship.
- The purpose of material progress should be to enhance spiritual progress and service to others.
- We should observe moderation in all things.
- The husband and wife "are two helpmates, two intimate friends, who should be concerned about the welfare of each other."[230]
- Do unto others as you would have them do unto you.

Step 5: Identifying & Agreeing on Solutions

Next, Joan and Mike generated and agreed on solutions to their issue that aligned with the facts and the spiritual principles they had identified. They arrived at the following.

- We need to start discussing financial matters together regularly so that we can have harmony and unity of purpose instead of conflict around financial issues.
- We need to have a joint plan that can be jointly monitored regarding how we are going to meet all our financial goals.
- The plan needs to be organized in such a way that Joan can understand it and monitor it.
- Since we are currently on schedule in terms of meeting our financial goals, we don't have a crisis.
- Given the appearance issues for the lawn, the goal of improvement of our property, the economical use of water, and Mike being distracted from focusing on, and serving, his clients' needs in order to address lawn care needs, it makes sense that the underground sprinkling system needs to be installed.
- Since it is now the beginning of September, it doesn't make sense to install the system now—we should target the spring of next year.
- We can't delay our savings toward retirement.
- Since the due dates are well off in the future for weddings, pilgrimage, and graduate school tuition, we could temporarily delay the savings toward these goals to make the installation of the sprinkler system possible.

Step 6: Identifying & Agreeing on the Implementation Steps:

Next, Joan and Mike identified and agreed on implementation steps that would make their solutions actionable, resolve their issue, and align with the facts and spiritual principles they had agreed upon. They arrived at the following.
- To expedite discussion, joint tracking of progress and a greater sense of security for Joan, open a separate savings account for each of the five areas: underground sprinkler system, weddings, pilgrimage, graduate school, and retirement (separate from the other tax-advantaged retirement accounts). Discuss account statements and monitor our progress toward the goals together. Mike will open the separate accounts by the end of this week.
- Begin to regularly discuss financial matters and financial planning together so that we have unity of purpose in this area of our married life. Have these discussions starting with the arrival of our

next monthly statements and monthly thereafter. Joan will be the convener for the monthly meetings.
- Starting this month (September), continue to put $300 per month into the retirement account, but stop putting the $100 per month each into the weddings, pilgrimage, and graduate school accounts. Mike will implement by the end of this week.
- For the next seven months, put the $300 per month saved from the previous implementation step into the new underground sprinkler system account. If we do this from September through March (7 months), we will have $2,100 saved and can order the underground sprinkler system to be installed in April at the beginning of the next lawn watering season to relieve Mike of this duty. Mike will implement the savings flow into the sprinkler account by the end of this week and will order and schedule the sprinkler system installation in March.
- Starting in April next year, reroute the $300 per month no longer needed for the sprinkler system back into the weddings, pilgrimage, and graduate school accounts at the previous rate of $100 per month each. Mike will implement in April, and Joan and Mike will monitor the change together in their monthly meetings.

Debriefing the Joan & Mike Compassionate Consultation Application Example

Joan and Mike successfully combined the 5-Step Change-the-Game Procedure, the Deep 8 Open-Ended Questions Technique, and the 6-Step Consultation Model to identify and address their issue. Although at first it may seem that this process is complicated and time-consuming, it takes significantly less time the more it is practiced. The time and energy spent are *small* when compared with the time and energy expended over a long period with an unresolved issue that continues to rear its head, cause repeated conflicts, and generate resentment. Such time and effort expended in a couple's use of Compassionate Consultation should be seen as an *investment* in the enrichment of the relationship and in the spiritual growth of the parties. We have found that whenever the process is used, the wisdom of the decisions made and the improvement in the relationships fostered between those who participate make the investment of time and energy well worth it.

In the case of Joan and Mike, Mike noticed that after they used the Compassionate Consultation process to resolve the issue, the angry impatience he had felt about getting the underground sprinkler system entirely disappeared. Instead, he felt satisfied that he and Joan were moving over time toward the goal of a sprinkler system, but equally satisfied that they were collaborating to create separate budgets for the anticipated expenses that had been bothering Joan. He also realized that clarifying and agreeing on the spiritual principles involved (Step 4) had inspired a search for, and agreement on, solutions and implementation steps that were different from, and more growth-producing than, what they would have been without reference to spiritual values. In essence, the complex and interpenetrating array of spiritual principles they had agreed upon had fostered a movement away from "either/or" thinking to "yes/and" thinking and agreement. Most of all, both Joan and Mike experienced a new level of understanding about themselves, each other, and the situation. One is reminded of Bahá'u'lláh's assertion that "The heaven of divine wisdom is illumined with the two luminaries of consultation and compassion."[231]

Ultimately, Mike found himself with a deeper understanding and sympathy toward Joan's financial concerns and became a greater champion for saving the necessary money and discussing the progress with Joan. On her part, Joan found herself with a new sympathy and understanding for Mike's needs and began to engage in and champion the goal of getting the underground sprinkling system. They both realized that the compassion each demonstrated for the other during the Compassionate Consultation process had cleared up the emotional fog they had been experiencing on this issue and increased the tenderness in their relationship.

What Does the Living System Need?

The participants in Compassionate Consultation must learn to acknowledge and serve a living system. Just as the internal Consulting group within the individual (the true self and aspects of the lower nature) is obviously a living system, so a Consulting group composed of two or more people is also a living system. Dissonance is partly about *each party* having different needs and wants; but it is even more importantly about the *living system* having needs and wants. Dissonance in relationships is always at least partly about the living system—the relationship—trying to grow, transform itself as it moves to the next level, and get its own emerging needs met. Effective parties to relationships and Compassionate Consultation establish the habit of asking, *what is trying to happen in the living system? What does the living system need from the parties in order to get its needs met and grow in capacity?*

In the case of Joan and Mike, the initial needs of *each party* appeared to be simple—Mike wanted the sprinkler system now, and Joan wanted uninterrupted saving for future needs. However, the dissonance in the *living system*—the *relationship* of Joan and Mike—revealed through Compassionate Consultation that it was trying to move to the next level. The *living system* needed Joan and Mike to learn to confer together about financial issues, develop higher levels of compassion, intimacy, and understanding, and achieve unity of purpose. In other words, the living system wanted spiritual growth and transformation for the relationship, and Compassionate Consultation was the vehicle which fostered this growth and transformation. As Bahá'u'lláh says, "…consultation is the lamp of guidance which leadeth the way, and is the bestower of understanding."[232]

Consultation for Twos Using the 4-Step V x D x F Consultation Model

Many of the situations couples encounter in which Compassionate Consultation can be helpful involve narrowly focused, micro-level issues, problems, challenges, or opportunities that arise in the course of daily life. An example would be the underground sprinkler vs. saving-for-the-future issue Mike and Joan resolved.

At other times in a couple's life together, they may want to address big picture, strategic, or macro-level issues or opportunities such as the direction they want their lives to take. Compassionate Consultation processes can be very helpful here as well. Whereas addressing narrowly focused or micro-level issues tends to be a *reactive* process (the issue arises, and *then* the couple addresses it), addressing the macro-level or big-picture issues (i.e., visions, plans, and goals) tends to be a *proactive* process. It is often found that the more micro-level issues a couple has *reactively* and effectively resolved, the more space it creates for macro-level issues that the couple can *proactively* address. Conversely, the more a twosome *proactively* addresses their big picture or macro-level issues, the fewer the micro-level issues that will cause *reactive* conflict between them.

Reviewing the Steps of the 4-Step V x D x F Consultation Model

In the 4-Step V x D x F Consultation Model (previously described in Chapter 3 and further described in Appendix III in the free PDF), the **V** stands for a **V**ision or picture of a preferred future state that the partners deem to be possible. The **D** stands for **D**issatisfaction with the present state in terms of barriers that block the path to the Vision. The **F** stands for **F**irst Steps that are designed to start movement toward the Vision. There must be a critical mass of energy vested in each of the elements in order to overcome the status quo.

This model makes the assumption that the group members have *already* identified what they want to improve. For example, they may already know they want to create and achieve a new vision for their relationship, for their family, for their organization, or for their work group; or they may want to agree on the guiding principles and values they want to inform their interactions as a couple, family, organization, or work group. The basic steps are shown in Figure 14.2.

The 4-Step V x D x F Model of Consultation

1. Convening by Praying for Divine Guidance
2. Identifying & Agreeing on the Concrete Vision of the Future
3. Identifying & Agreeing on the Dissatisfying Barriers (an optional step)
4. Identifying & Agreeing on the First Steps toward the Vision

Figure 14.2

Some Benefits of Using the 4-Step V x D x F Model of Consultation

This model can be used when a couple wants to agree on a desired future for their lives together. When an individual, twosome, family, or group describes a detailed picture of a preferred future, we call this a concrete vision of the future. The value in doing this is that if we can articulate and agree on a *concrete, specific,* and *clear* picture of the future we want, the likelihood that we can achieve it is greatly increased. In other words, if we have a concrete, specific, and clear *outcome* in mind, we will have a clearer sense of what decisions and actions we need to take to get us there and more motivation to actually accomplish it.

One of the most powerful ways to unify a couple (or larger group) is for the members to create something together, and the 4-Step V x D x F Model of Consultation allows a couple to create something together at two levels. First, the couple becomes more unified as they go through the process of creating the concrete vision of the future. Second, the couple becomes still more unified as they implement the vision of the future—that is, they use the concrete vision of the future as a navigational tool to make choices and decisions in their individual and collective lives that draw them ever closer to making the concrete vision a reality.

Detailed steps and formats for using the 4-Step V x D x F Model can be found in Appendix III of the free PDF. Also included there is a detailed example of the authors forging a 7-Year Vision of the Future for their relationship.

A New Type of Recreation

The root meaning of the word "re-creation" is to be created anew. In this sense, the transformative power of a decision made by combining Consultation and compassion *re-creates* a couple's relationship. It enables them to grow spiritually—both individually and in relationship, it deepens the awareness and understanding they have about themselves and each other, and it dramatically increases their sense of unity. In these ways it renews, revitalizes, and re-creates the individual and the relationship. When couples gain skill in the Compassionate Consultation process, they start looking forward to dealing with issues together because of their *confidence* that they can reach deeper understanding and agreement together. While this process certainly takes both detachment and effort, the payoff is enormous. Growth-seekers see relevance in the following words of 'Abdu'l-Bahá: "For a man who has love, effort is a rest."[233]

Chapter 15

Making Transformative Decisions with Families

Just as a unified couple is the cornerstone of a unified family, so a unified family is the cornerstone of a unified society, nation, and world at large. 'Abdu'l-Bahá says:

> If love and agreement are manifest in a single family, that family will advance, become illumined and spiritual; but if enmity and hatred exist within it destruction and dispersion are inevitable. This is likewise true of a city. If those who dwell within it manifest a spirit of accord and fellowship it will progress steadily and human conditions become brighter… In the same way the people of a nation develop and advance toward civilization and enlightenment through love and accord, and are disintegrated by war and strife. Finally, this is true of humanity itself in the aggregate. When love is realized and the ideal spiritual bonds unite the hearts of men, the whole human race will be uplifted, the world will continually grow more spiritual and radiant and the happiness and tranquility of mankind be immeasurably increased.[234]

The family unit should provide an environment of safety and security which encourages the healthy and holistic growth of each member.

When Consultation and compassion are combined regularly in a family, it fosters the development of positive attributes such as respect, openness to diverse perspectives, the attitude of an investigator of truth, reliance on God, and detachment from ego. As a result, family members are enabled to grow spiritually, intellectually, and socially, and to move forward together. Although people often use Compassionate Consultation in families to *find answers or solutions* to deal with situation-specific issues or problems, the *process and the interactive patterns* it calls forth are as important as the solutions themselves. Compassionate Consultation promotes a sense of well-being in each family member by providing a process through which he or she can be heard and understood, and it provides a forum in which participants can practice listening to and understanding those closest to them. It creates an arena that fosters compassion, which is the most important ingredient in healthy relationships. The deep understanding that comes from applying compassion can mitigate resentment, hostility, and frustration, which disrupt and can eventually destroy intimacy in families.

What impacts one person in a family impacts everyone, or put another way, in a family one person's problem is everyone's problem. Working together to create a safe, respectful environment in which each person's beliefs, desires, needs, and goals are heard, understood, and addressed benefits the entire family and fosters unity. When these patterns are learned in the family, it empowers the family members to extend them into the world at large with the family of humankind.

Creating a Compassionate Consultation Culture in the Family

Guiding principles and values are the foundation of any culture. These values and principles—whether spoken or unspoken—dictate behaviors and rules and become deeply embedded in the culture. If a family culture operates in dysfunctional ways, there are certain explicit or implicit guiding principles, values, and rules that are keeping that dysfunction in place. For example, a family may have an unspoken but implicit rule that children should be seen and not heard, a rule that disenfranchises certain members of the group. In contrast, if a family culture is operating in highly effective ways, there are also certain explicit or implicit guiding principles and values that are keeping that effectiveness in place. For example, a family may have an unspoken but implicit value that the members do not go to bed at night until all relationship conflicts in the family are constructively resolved.

One of the most powerful ways for a family to strengthen its culture is to discuss and agree on the guiding principles and values the members want to honor as they address issues and interact together. While the family could just post and refer to the 12 Behavioral Standards and 7 Prime Requisites, crafting family-derived principles and values articulated in the members' own language can create an important bridge to the loftier Requisites and Standards. Such an agreement represents the family's collective vision of the deliberation and decision-making culture they choose to co-create.

The Example of the Alt Family—Forging Consultation Guiding Principles & Values

The Alt family is composed of two adults, two teenagers, and one nine-year-old. The family members are dissatisfied with the way they deal with family issues and decide they want to consistently use Compassionate Consultation to resolve family issues together. They decide to *loosely apply* the first two steps of the 4-Step V x D x F Model (in a sticky wall format) to agree on the guiding principles and values that will inform and transform their family deliberation and decision-making culture.

The basic steps of the 4-Step V x D x F Consultation Model are shown in Figure 15.1 (more detailed information on the 4-Step Model is included in Chapters 3 and 14 of this book and in Appendices III and IV in the free PDF). Realizing that the agreement on Guiding Principles and

The 4-Step V x D x F Model of Consultation

1. Convening by Praying for Divine Guidance
2. Identifying & Agreeing on the Concrete Vision of the Future
3. Identifying & Agreeing on the Dissatisfying Barriers (an optional step)
4. Identifying & Agreeing on the First Steps toward the Vision

Figure 15.1

Values for using Compassionate Consultation in their family would be one form of a Concrete Vision of the Future, the Alt family decides to use only Steps 1 and 2 and then skip Steps 3 and 4 of the model. They also decide to use an abbreviated, sticky wall version of the model shown in Figure 15.2; they intend to complete Step 1 and Steps 2A, 2B and 2C formally and then complete Step 2D loosely. Consequently, they begin with Step 1 (Note: a more detailed description of the Alt family's process is included in Appendix IV in the free PDF):

1. Convening By Praying For Divine Guidance

After praying for guidance, the family does a Consultation Climate Safety Scale check to make sure their compassion for themselves and each other is engaged. When they have satisfied themselves that the climate is right, they proceed with Step 2.

The 4-Step V x D x F Consultation Model — *Abbreviated Sticky Wall Version*:

    1.   Convening by Praying for Divine Guidance

○   2A.   Identifying the Vision—*individual*

○   2B.   Identifying the Vision—*family*

⊕   2C.   Agreeing on the Vision—Affinity Only—*family*

⊕   2D.   Agreeing on the Vision—*family*

Figure 15.2

2. Identifying & Agreeing on the Vision in Sub-Steps A-D (*Loose Approach*)

The family first decides that they do not need to agree on how many years into the future they want to project their vision of the future because, unlike a future vision in which perceptible characteristics are trying to be achieved over time, guiding principles and values can be claimed in the present moment and are not time-limited.

    The family also decides that they want to follow Step 2 *loosely* rather than formally. They do not want to unduly wordsmith the agreed upon principles and values, and they want the actual language of the individual family members to be reflected in the final document. To accomplish Step 2 in this looser fashion, they go through sub-steps A through D as follows:

2A. The family poses the following question to themselves: *What guiding principles and values do we want to honor in our interactions together as we address family issues using Compassionate Consultation?* Then, working alone, each family member suspends critical judgment, brainstorms his or her own answers to this question, writes each answer idea on a large (8½"x 5½") Post-It® note using felt-tipped markers, and uses one sheet per idea.

2B. Now the family members sit side-by-side in front of a wall that they can use to post their notes. With critical judgment still suspended and each family member holding his or her own stack of Post-it® notes, each takes his or her turn placing one sheet on the wall randomly and reading it to the other family members. When the Alt family finishes this process, the ideas on the wall, reading from left to right and top to bottom, are as follows:

- No one gets stifled.
- Each person sees things differently.
- Trying to win or get our own way is counter to our process.
- We can confer again after the fact if a decision seems not to be working.
- We all want the best for each other.
- We learn from our differences.
- Each person's beliefs, goals, needs, and desires will be heard.
- We continuously build our skills at Consultation.
- Passively withholding support is not acceptable.
- The rights of other family members will be respected.
- We keep discussing until we reach a decision with which everyone agrees.
- We work to find a solution that respects each family member.
- We respect individual differences.
- All contributions are valid.
- We develop compassion for each other.

- We will all help to follow through on our decisions/solutions.
- We create a safe, respectful environment in which every family member grows.
- We will come up with several solutions/ideas.
- A decision/solution must be within the budget, safety, and health limits set by parents.
- No one way is good or bad, worse or better.
- We work toward what is in the best interest of everyone.
- We do not use power or control to get our way.
- Each person has the right to come up with solutions.
- Each person has the right to be heard and feel understood.
- We help each member achieve his or her full potential.
- Each person is important and valuable.

2C. Next, the family members apply critical judgment to discuss and identify how all of the sheets can be combined into affinity groups based on the similarity of the guiding principle and value being described. When the Alt family finishes this process, the affinity groups (with provisional symbols as titles), reading from left to right on the wall, are as follows.

- We work to find a solution that respects each family member.
- We create a safe, respectful environment in which every family member grows.
- We help each member achieve his or her full potential.
- We work toward what is in the best interest of everyone.
- We develop compassion for each other.
- We build our skills at Consultation.

- Each person is important and valuable.
- Each person has the right to be heard and feel understood.
- All contributions are valid.
- Each person's beliefs, goals, needs, and desires will be heard.
- No one gets stifled.

$

- Each person sees things differently.
- No one way is good or bad, worse or better.
- We respect individual differences.
- We learn from our differences.

%

- Each person has a right to come up with solutions.
- A decision/solution must be within the budget, safety, and health limits set by parents.
- We keep discussing until we reach a decision with which everyone agrees.

&

- We do not use power or control to get our way.
- We will come up with several solutions/ideas.
- The rights of other family members will be respected.
- We all want the best for each other.
- Trying to win or get our own way is counter to our process.

- We will all help to follow through on our decisions/solutions.
- Passively withholding support is not acceptable.
- We can confer again after the fact if a decision seems not to be working.

2D. The family members now apply critical judgment, look at the ideas in each affinity group, and ask whether anyone is uncomfortable with any of the ideas. They quickly acknowledge and agree that all the ideas have merit with one exception. The parents say that while the spirit of affinity group 5 is clear, they would prefer that the idea, "We will not use power or control to get our way," be deleted because they can envision potential situations in which they may need to assert their power or control as responsible parents for the welfare of the family. The other members of the family accept the parents' concerns, and the idea is deleted. Now, to complete their process, they look at each affinity column one at a time and fairly quickly agree on what that column is about so that they can add a subject heading at the top of each column. This is done not with the intent of superseding the ideas below the subject headings (as in some of the descriptions given in earlier chapters or the examples in Appendix III in the free PDF), but with the intent of including both the subject headings and the list of supporting guiding principles and values in the final product. When all of the subject headings are complete, the Alt family's completed Compassionate Consultation Guiding Principles & Values agreement reads as follows.

Alt Family Guiding Principles & Values for Compassionate Consultation

1.) *We have goals for using Compassionate Consultation in the family:*

- We work to find a solution that respects each family member.
- We create a safe, respectful environment in which every family member grows.
- We help each member achieve his or her full potential.
- We work toward what is in the best interest of everyone.
- We develop compassion for each other.
- We build our skills at Consultation.

2.) *We acknowledge each person's inherent value:*

- Each person is important and valuable.
- Each person has the right to be heard and feel understood.
- All contributions are valid.
- Each person's beliefs, goals, needs, and desires will be heard.
- No one gets stifled.

3.) *We value diversity:*

- Each person sees things differently.
- No one way is good or bad, worse or better.
- We respect individual differences.
- We learn from our differences.

4.) We make decisions:

- Each person has a right to come up with solutions.
- A decision/solution must be within the budget, safety, and health limits set by parents.
- We keep discussing until we reach a decision with which everyone agrees.

5.) We separate our egos from our ideas:

- We will come up with several solutions/ideas.
- The rights of other family members will be respected.
- We all want the best for each other.
- Trying to win or get our own way is counter to our process.

6.) We implement decisions/solutions:

- We will all help to follow through on our decisions/solutions.
- Passively withholding support is not acceptable.
- We can confer again after the fact if a decision seems not to be working.

Having completed their "Family Guiding Principles & Values for Compassionate Consultation," the Alt family members agree that whenever a family member believes any of these principles and values are being violated during future Consultation sessions, he or she should bring that to the family's attention and corrective action will be taken.

The Lopez Family Example—Equitably Dividing Household Tasks

Families are more than a group of relatives; they are also work groups, and many challenges can arise in relation to getting the family's work done. The Lopez family members (composed of two parents and three children ages eleven, thirteen, and sixteen years) were experiencing frustration and conflict over the distribution and execution of household tasks. After numerous, only moderately successful command decisions by the parents and a variety of disputes between individual family members, everyone agreed to address the issue through Compassionate Consultation. Because of the contention this issue had generated in the family, the parents proposed using the flipchart version of the 6-Step Identify/Agree (I/A) Model shown in Figure 15.3 (see Chapter 10 of this book and Appendix I in the free PDF for more information) so that ideas could be generated with critical judgment *suspended* prior to ideas being agreed upon with critical judgment *applied* (Note: more detailed steps of the Lopez family process are included in Appendix IV in the free PDF).

The 6-Step Identify/Agree (I/A) Consultation Model
Flipchart Version:

	1.	Convening by Praying for Divine Guidance
○	2A.	Identifying the Issue
⊕	2B.	Agreeing on the Issue
○	3A.	Identifying the Facts
⊕	3B.	Agreeing on the Facts
○	4A.	Identifying the Spiritual Principles/Values Involved
⊕	4B.	Agreeing on the Spiritual Principles/Values Involved
○	5A.	Identifying Solutions
⊕	5B.	Agreeing on Solutions
○	6A.	Identifying Implementation Steps
⊕	6B.	Agreeing on Implementation Steps

KEY

○ Suspend critical judgment (A-steps)
⊕ Apply critical judgment (B-steps)

Figure 15.3

Step 1: Convening by Praying for Divine Guidance

After using the Consultation Climate Safety Scale to make sure everyone felt the climate was at a seven level or better, the family members reviewed the 12 Behavioral Standards and 7 Prime Requisites. Then they began the process by completing Step 1: Convening by Praying for Divine Guidance. The members then proceeded to Step 2.

Step 2: Identifying & Agreeing on the Issue

The family members began Step 2 by suspending critical judgment and brainstorming the question, *"What is the issue we need to address?"* When the brainstorming was complete, the ideas on the flipchart pages read as follows.

How to:

- deal with the fact that the kids aren't doing enough housework and the parents are doing too much.
- get family members to care more about pressures on each other.
- get my parents off my back about chores.
- have the children do what they say.
- figure out why some of us think there is a problem.
- leave things alone.
- make all family members realize there is a dilemma.
- allow family members to have time to do things they want to do.
- understand family priorities.
- act on family priorities.
- equitably divide the household tasks.

Now the family members applied critical judgment, discussed the eleven phrases, and agreed on the distilled issue statement as follows (for more details on this distillation process see pages 85-86 of the free PDF available at **billandjeanharley.com/actionplan**):

Issue Statement: How to equitably divide the household tasks to allow family members to have the time to do what they want while assuring that everyone follows through on their commitments and all of the tasks get done.

They then proceeded to Step 3.

Step 3: Identifying & Agreeing on the Facts

The family members began by suspending critical judgment and brainstorming the question, *"What are the facts that are relevant to the issue we are addressing?"* When the generation of facts was complete, they applied critical judgment to the facts and agreed on the wording and relevance of each fact. When finished, their agreed upon fact list was as follows:

- Mom and Dad are feeling overwhelmed with household chores.
- The children feel like they are being nagged most of the time about attending to chores.
- Mom is tired of asking people to do things over and over.
- After school and homework, the children want to relax.
- Used dishes are left on the kitchen counter or in the sink.
- Used glasses are left in the children's bedrooms.
- Used glasses and dishes are left in the family and living rooms.
- Bathrooms are not cleaned often enough.
- When company comes over, there is too much to do to make the house ready.
- Resentments and anger about these things are building up and spilling over.
- The house belongs to the whole family, but each family member is not doing his/her fair share of household tasks.
- Some of us tolerate more mess than others.

They then proceeded to Step 4.

Step 4: Identifying & Agreeing on the Spiritual Principles/Values Involved

The family members began by suspending critical judgment and brainstorming the question, *"What are the spiritual principles and values we want to live by that are relevant to the agreed upon issue and facts we are addressing?"* When the brainstorming was complete, they applied critical judgment and agreed on the wording and relevance of each spiritual principle and value as follows:

- Unity, peace, and harmony in the family are the cornerstone to unity, peace, and harmony in society.
- Children should show respect to their parents, and parents should show respect to their children.
- Having compassion is a spiritual attribute we should be developing, and it means having empathy for the stress and suffering of others and desiring to alleviate it.

- Work done with a motive of service to others is accepted by God as worship.
- Becoming mature means everyone takes responsibility (age appropriately).
- Honoring justice and fairness means that no one is over-burdened or under-burdened.
- Kindness is a virtue we should be developing and expressing to each other.
- Cleanliness is a spiritual quality we should be developing and expressing to each other.
- Good health is a desirable attribute that is an outcome of cleanliness.

Now the family turned to Step 5.

Step 5: Identifying & Agreeing on Solutions

The family members began Step 5 by suspending critical judgment and brainstorming the question, *"What are the solutions to this issue that align with the agreed upon facts and spiritual principles and values?"* When the generation of solutions was complete, they applied critical judgment to them and agreed on the wording and relevance of each solution. When they were finished, their agreed upon solution list was as follows:

- We need to create a chore chart together.
- Everyone needs to have chore assignments, but they need to be age appropriate.
- We need to have a chore review meeting weekly at first and bi-weekly later on to monitor our progress.
- We should speak kindly, respectfully, and constructively to each other when we check in with each other about the chores.
- We should have cleaning and chore sessions when we all clean and do chores at the same time (e.g. nine to eleven a.m. on Saturdays).
- We should reward ourselves with a treat together when we finish (e.g. have ice cream).
- As necessary, we should also clean and do chores separately on our own schedules when it's convenient for us.
- Each person should make his or her own bed each morning.
- Each person should bus and rinse his or her own dishes after meals and snacks and put the dishes into the dishwasher.

- Each person should put his or her own dirty clothes in the laundry baskets.
- Some chores should be done on a weekly rotating basis by individuals or pairs/trios such as dusting, vacuuming, cleaning bathrooms, cleaning bedrooms, cleaning the family room, cleaning the living room, emptying waste baskets, taking out trash and garbage, changing bedding, doing laundry, and cooking.
- When a family member doesn't follow through on his or her assigned chores (this includes doing a quality job), that person is grounded from doing fun things (including the family reward treats) until the chores are done.

The family then proceeded to Step 6.

Step 6: Identifying & Agreeing on Implementation Steps

The members began by suspending critical judgment and brainstorming the question, *"What are the implementation steps for our agreed upon solutions that will address the issue and align with the agreed upon facts, spiritual principles, and values?"* When the brainstorming was complete, they applied critical judgment and agreed on the wording and relevance of each implementation step. When they were finished, their agreed upon implementation step list was as follows:

- Based on their knowledge of the chores, the parents will create a chore chart for review, discussion, possible revision, and approval by the whole family at a family review meeting. Parents will complete the chore chart by noon Sunday. The family review meeting will be held Sunday at three p.m.
- The chore chart will include both the individual chores that each family member must do each day (e.g. each person makes his or her own bed and puts dirty clothes in the laundry baskets) and the weekly rotating tasks that will be undertaken by individuals or pairs and trios.
- The weekly rotating chores need to be sized approximately alike so that there is justice and fairness, but age appropriateness of chores also needs to be considered.
- Weekly rotating chores will be made age appropriate by joining a younger family member with an older family member on a team so that the younger person has help and a way to learn how to do the task.

- We will brainstorm a list of economical yet fun reward treats to celebrate our successes. Parents will lead this listing process at the family review meeting on Sunday. The first reward treat will be on the Sunday of the weekend following the first week under the new program and on each Sunday thereafter.
- Have both a family hour each week for chore time when everyone will be doing chores at the same time and the freedom to do individual chores whenever there is time. The family hour chore time will be each Saturday morning from nine to ten a.m.
- Have a weekly chore review meeting on Sundays at three p.m. where we discuss how things are going, what's working, what isn't, what plan revisions we need to make, and whether any groundings are in order (decide later on when to switch to bi-weekly chore review meetings). The meetings will last only as long as they need to. The parents will be conveners of the meetings, and the first one will be on the Sunday of the weekend following the first week on the new program.
- The way we talk with each other about these issues (respectfully, compassionately, and constructively) is just as important as the fact that the tasks get done. Infractions on the way we talk with each other can be brought up at the weekly chore review meetings and can be the basis for getting grounded (subject to the majority decision of the group).
- If a person has a problem getting chores done because of other obligations, he or she is free to negotiate with other family members to switch chores, create IOUs, etc. Nevertheless, if things don't get done, it is always the person who has the assignment on the chore chart who is grounded and loses privileges.

As a result of the Lopez family's Compassionate Consultation process, they not only arrived at solutions to their problem, but also established a reliable procedure for them to use in coming together to address important issues in the future.

Using Compassionate Consultation at Transition Stages of Family Life

In the previous chapter, reference was made to the authors' use of Compassionate Consultation to create a 7-Year Concrete Vision of the Future for their relationship. The detailed steps and results of this process using the 4-Step V x D x F Model are included in Appendix III in the free PDF. Despite the power and value of a couple or family holding a joint concrete vision over a span of years, focused Compassionate Consultation sessions will often be needed to address unanticipated roadblocks on the way to the vision. One such example follows.

While the example involves just the authors as a couple, it has been placed in this family-focused chapter because it represents a transition stage of family life when children have been launched as young adults, and parents are trying to reshape their relationships with themselves, each other, and their adult children.

Transition Stage of Life Consultation—The Example of Jean & Bill

Within a few months after Jean and Bill created the 7-Year Concrete Vision of the Future for their relationship, Bill found himself stalled on the writing of the book and on several other elements of the concrete vision. Because the demands of his business were keeping him locked in his old patterns instead of creating new patterns in line with the Concrete Vision, he asked Jean to help him address this issue.

Bill and Jean decided to use the sticky wall version of the 6-Step Identify/Agree (I/A) Model which was referred to in Chapter 10 (see Appendix II in the free PDF for detailed steps of the sticky wall model, *and see Appendix IV of the free PDF for a more detailed description of the steps Jean and Bill used below*). The choice of this model was based simply on their desire to use four by four Post-It® notes rather than any feeling that the subject was highly controversial. In addition, because there were only two participants, each of the Step 2-5 sub-step phases of the model were reduced from four to two sub-steps (A and B) as shown in Figure 15.4 (i.e., Steps 2A and 2B take the place of the four sub-steps—Steps 2A, 2B, 2C, and 2D— used in the complete sticky wall model version shown in Appendix II, which is best suited for use with larger groups). The overview description of their procedure and findings follows.

The 6-Step Identify/Agree (I/A) Consultation Model—Sticky Wall Version (abridged for a 2-person procedure):

○	1.	Convening by praying for divine guidance
○	2A.	Identifying the issue—*individual member*
⊕	2B.	Agreeing on the issue—*whole group*
○	3A.	Identifying the facts—*individual member*
⊕	3B.	Agreeing on the facts—*whole group*
○	4A.	Identifying the spiritual principles involved—*individual member*
⊕	4B.	Agreeing on the spiritual principles involved—*whole group*
○	5A.	Identifying solutions—*individual member*
⊕	5B.	Agreeing on solutions—*whole group*
○	6A.	Identifying implementation steps—*individual member*
⊕	6B.	Agreeing on implementation steps—*whole group*

KEY

○ Suspend critical judgment (A-steps)

⊕ Apply critical judgment (B-steps)

Figure 15.4

Step 1: Convening by Praying for Divine Guidance

Jean and Bill began by reviewing the 12 Behavioral Standards and 7 Prime Requisites. Then they sat down together and each said a prayer for assistance and divine guidance.

Step 2A: Identifying the Issue—individual member (Suspend Critical Judgment)

Because Jean wanted to fully understand the issue presented by Bill, she asked him to tell her about the issue and made notes as he talked. Then they both suspended critical judgment, worked alone for about five minutes, and wrote down possible issue statements on their Post-It® note sheets (with each statement idea on a separate sheet). They then turned to Step 2B.

Step 2B: Agreeing on the Issue—whole group (Apply Critical Judgment)

Jean and Bill took turns sharing their Post-It® sheets with each other, and the possible issue statements were as follows (with the parenthetical J initial indicating it was from Jean and the B initial indicating it was from Bill).

How to:

- make time for Bill to spend on the book (B)
- free Bill from the demands of the business during certain spans of time so that he can work on the book (J)
- create more life balance for Bill (B)
- make time for Bill to spend with Jean (J)

Jean and Bill then applied critical judgment to the four issue statements and agreed on the following issue statement: *How to free Bill from the demands of the business so that he has more life balance, time to spend with Jean, and time to write the book.*

Jean and Bill now turned to Step 3.

Steps 3A & 3B: Identifying & Agreeing on the Facts

Now Jean and Bill suspended their critical judgment and worked alone to brainstorm the facts in relation to their agreed upon issue statement. When they had finished, they shared their fact ideas with each other, organized the facts into affinity groups, and then reached agreement on the master facts for each affinity group. When finished, their agreed upon master facts were as follows:

- Bill wants to spend at least one day a week (eight hours) writing the book.
- Bill needs to change his imbalanced and unhealthy work schedule into one where he has evenings and weekends free.
- Because our income needs have decreased, Bill can make the needed changes and see what impact it has on his business's annual revenue.
- Jean and Bill want to spend more quality time with each other on weekends (they can't during the week).

- There is evidence that Bill needs two days in the office doing administrative and support work for every three days with clients and that clients will delay projects in line with his availability.

Having reached agreement on the facts, Jean and Bill turned to Step 4.

Steps 4A & 4B: Identifying & Agreeing on the Spiritual Principles/Values Involved

Now Jean and Bill suspended their critical judgment and worked alone to brainstorm spiritual principles and values they wanted to live by which related to the issue and facts they had agreed upon. When they finished, they shared their spiritual principles and values ideas with each other, organized the spiritual principles and values ideas into affinity groups, and then reached agreement on the master spiritual principles and values for each affinity group. When finished, their agreed upon master spiritual principles and values were as follows:

- Unity of the family is foundational.
- Work done in the spirit of service is worship.
- Knowledge and talent we have developed in our professions should be shared for the advancement of society.
- Because the body is our vehicle for giving service in this world, we need to care for it and maintain it.
- In addition to our service in our professional field, we want to serve in ways that will help build our faith community.
- We should mindfully manage the paradox of striving for excellence and being moderate in all things.

Now, they were ready to turn to Step 5.

Steps 5A & 5B: Identifying & Agreeing on the Solutions

Jean and Bill now suspended their critical judgment and worked alone to brainstorm solutions to the issue that aligned with the facts and spiritual principles they had agreed upon. When they had finished, they shared their solution ideas with each other, organized the solution ideas into affinity groups, and then reached agreement on the master solutions for each affinity group. When finished, their agreed upon master solutions were as follows:

- Starting September first, see clients and client organizations on Tuesday, Wednesday, and Thursday and reserve Mondays and Fridays for background administration, support work, and book writing (half-day on Friday).
- Create an inventory of desirable activity ideas as a couple and as a family and then have at least two quality-time activities between Bill & Jean each weekend and at least one family gathering each weekend.
- Bill writes for a minimum of a half day each Friday and a half day on the weekend.
- Bill maintains his body by working out at least twice during the week and once during each weekend and serves his faith community at least once per week.
- Create an inventory of activities that would rejuvenate Bill's mind and soul and then do at least one each weekend and at least one evening activity sometime during the work week.

The Option of Omitting Step 6 When Step 5 Has Accomplished the Objective

With the completion of all the components of Step 5, Bill believed that the master solutions were at a level of clarity, specificity, and granularity from which he could implement them by simply transferring the master solutions into his day-planner. Whenever participants in the process feel that the solutions are in an actionable condition at the end of Step 5, Step 6 (Identifying and Agreeing on Implementation Steps) can be omitted.

Making Course-Correcting, Consultative Decisions En Route to the Vision

The Compassionate Consultation process created a great deal of relief for Bill. Not only did it allow him to get unstuck, but it strengthened his ability to move forward more freely and mindfully toward the Vision of the Future for his relationship with Jean. In addition, he had the satisfaction of knowing that Jean understood his struggles and was participating in and supporting his forward movement. Jean realized that Bill's frustrations dovetailed with some of her own and that the solutions addressed some of her issues as well.

The Transformative Effects of the Spiritual Principles & Values Step for Families

Step 4, Identifying & Agreeing on Spiritual Principles & Values, changes the hearts of Consulting members, releases us from narrow or tightly held perspectives, and facilitates our going over walls to personal and collective growth. This occurs because Step 4 reframes the issue being addressed from a seemingly mundane context to one of spiritual significance. As a result, our perspectives are also reframed so that we can see what is important in terms of the big picture of our lives—both individually and collectively. This step also establishes parameters for the sphere in which the solutions we seek reside. When this process is experienced regularly in a family, it changes how the members approach problems in all areas of their lives. This can be illustrated with a brief example.

The Chen Family Uses Spiritual Principles & Values to Resolve a Dispute

Sharon and Jake Chen and their two children needed some new furniture for their family room. Preliminarily, Sharon had picked out modular furniture because the room was small, and modular furniture would make it seem larger and less crowded. Jake, on the other hand, wanted two comfortable recliners. They could have continued to disagree, but they decided instead to have Compassionate Consultation with their children on the issue. During the fact-finding in Step 3 of the 6-Step Model, some of the facts that were agreed upon included the following:

- Jake's back has been bothering him, and he has pain when he sits on anything other than his desk chair which has good support.
- Jake has been doing daily back exercises, which help, but if he wants to sit for any length of time, he needs a chair that offers the right support.
- Sharon feels that the appearance of this particular room is very important to her because it can be seen from every other room.
- A chair that would suit Jake's needs could be put in some other room.
- The room in question is where the family spends the most time together.
- Jake wants his chair in the room where the family gathers most often.

When Sharon, Jake, and their children came to the spiritual principle and value-finding in Step 4, three of the spiritual principles and values that were agreed upon were the following:

- Unity, togetherness, and harmony of the family are essential for happiness.
- The design and arrangement of our living spaces affects our energy and sense of well-being.
- We need to be sensitive, respectful, and compassionate to our fellow family members.

Based on these facts and spiritual principles and values, when the family did solution-finding in Step 5, Sharon originally said that the value of family time with Jake present was more important to her than the value of room design, so she was willing to sacrifice the value of room design and décor affecting people's energy and sense of well-being. But Jake and the children suggested that both values were important, and neither should be sacrificed. As a result, one of the key solutions the family agreed upon was doing research to find a company that manufactured modular furniture specifically designed for people with back problems. Their research was successful, and while this solution was more expensive than the other alternatives, it provided a lasting solution that wisely addressed all of the relevant values and spiritual principles that were important to the family. After reaching this decision, the family members knew they had grown both individually and collectively in their problem solving and decision-making abilities.

The Family as Crucible for Understanding the Primacy of Spiritual Principles & Values

The positive impact on children of establishing the practice in the family of making decisions based on spiritual principles and values cannot be overestimated. In a world where we see plentiful evidence of adults and institutions making decisions based on expediency and self-interest, having parents model within the family the practice of resolving problems by subjecting their personal whims and desires to the overriding wisdom of spiritual principles and values establishes a healthy and reliable habit that contributes mightily to their children's abilities to carry forward an ever-advancing civilization and navigate spiritually and socially successful lives.

The Family as Crucible for Learning Effective Communication Skills

Having effective communication skills expedites having effective Compassionate Consultation skills, and parents can expedite the development of both skill sets in their children when they proactively teach, and then model, effective communication skills. Following is a basic review of some concepts that can enhance effective communication.

A. Apply compassion to truly understand another person. Use compassion to dilate your own heart and open your mind to the other person's perspective by using the following sub-steps:

- Listen with an open heart (not just half-heartedly) and mind so that you can repeat back the thoughts of the other person. If you are not able to do this, ask the speaker to repeat the thought (i.e., "I'm not sure I got that. Could you please repeat what you said?").
- Reflect the thought BACK to the speaker—not necessarily parroting back the words, but expressing the thought as you understood it. Do not continue until the speaker has validated that you have heard correctly. Some examples of what you might say are:
- "What I hear you saying is _____. Is that right?"
- "So, you think that _____. Is that accurate?"
- "You are experiencing _____. Do I understand you correctly?"
- "Is this what you are saying: _____?"
- "Let me see if I have this: _____. Am I understanding you?"
- Validate the feelings that go with the thought. Check it out by asking:
- "If that is what you think, you must feel _____. Is that right?"
- "It looks like you're feeling _____. Is that accurate?"
- "It sounds like you're feeling _____, but it doesn't look like that's how you're feeling. What is going on?"
- "I can't tell what you're feeling. Help me out here."

B. Express your thoughts and feelings in a way that has a good chance of being heard and understood by the other person. Present your thoughts and feelings in a manner designed to avoid destructive conflict and increase the likelihood of the other person hearing and understanding you. The following two suggestions can help.

- **Use "I" messages** to communicate your feelings. "You" messages cause most people to respond as if they are being attacked; they then defend themselves and/or attack back rather than truly hearing your message. "I" messages are a statement of your feelings—they are about you and not about the other person. For example, "I am very uncomfortable when the house gets this messy" (an "I" message) is more likely to be heard and get a positive response than "You are so messy" (a "you" message). When you are experiencing a big feeling, the problem is yours; so, you need to state clearly what you are experiencing, such as the "I" comment, "I feel angry when no one picks up their soda cans in the family room. It feels as if no one cares enough about me to do what I request," states what this person is experiencing rather than criticizing others. The goal is to create a safe, respectful environment in which each person can express his or her thoughts, feelings, needs, and wants.

- **Do not label another person's character**—instead, refer to specific behaviors. It is counter-productive and often abusive to label a person's character, such as "You are an ungrateful, lazy person." Obviously, this kind of indictment is received as an attack. A person cannot act on this because it is a criticism of the person's character; it will only cause hurt feelings, with a possible result being anger and a counter-attack. It is not abusive, and it is useful to refer to specific behaviors, such as "I think you were being lazy and ungrateful when you didn't help clean up after the party you had here." This can be acted upon in a particular, constructive way—for example, the person may apologize or ask if he or she can do something now to make up for it.

Practicing these basic techniques can improve interpersonal communication and Compassionate Consultation dramatically.

Using Compassionate Consultation to Stay Connected to Adolescent Children

Communication is often strained and can break down between parents and a teenage daughter or son. A remedy is to use Compassionate Consultation to get the parties moving collaboratively with the common goal of determining what is in the best long-term interest of the young person. This constructive, emotionally connected pattern is important for all children, but especially for teenagers. Research has shown that teenagers who do not get into serious trouble are usually those who feel emotionally connected to their parents. "Emotionally connected" means the teenagers feel the parents are interested in them, listen to them, and want to spend time with them.

The Example of Shari and Michelle

Shari is a single mother with a fifteen-year-old daughter, Michelle. Shari was anxious and upset because Michelle was spending a lot of time in her bedroom with the door shut and was not communicating with her as much as she used to. Shari wondered whether Michelle was depressed or angry because of her parents' divorce two years earlier. Although Shari had tried to get Michelle to open up to her by asking her questions that demonstrated Shari's interested in her, the questioning seemed to make Michelle even more closed and resentful toward her mother.

Shari was particularly distressed because she and Michelle were in conflict at a time when Michelle was at a vulnerable age in a problematic, unsafe world. Shari found herself fruitlessly trying the same things repeatedly with a gradually increasing voice volume. She realized that she needed to do something different because what she had been doing was not working. Consequently, Shari proposed to Michelle that they use Compassionate Consultation to address the issues between them, and Michelle agreed.

The Compassionate Consultation Example of Shari & Michelle—Legal Pad Version of the 6-Step I/A Consultation Model

Shari and Michelle used the 6-Step Identify/Agree (I/A) Model, and they recorded their thoughts on a legal pad (rather than a flipchart) that both could see on the table in front of them. They each also had a small scratch pad in front of them to use when brainstorming ideas with judgment suspended. They went through the following steps.

1. Convening by Praying for Divine Guidance

Shari and Michelle sat down together and each recited a prayer for divine guidance and assistance. Then they used the Consultation Climate Safety Scale to make sure both felt the climate was at a level of seven or better. Finally, they reviewed the 12 Behavioral Standards and 7 Prime Requisites. Then they moved on to Step 2.

2. Identifying & Agreeing on the Issue

Shari and Michelle suspended critical judgment and each brainstormed alone. They wrote down their ideas about the issue they wanted to address on their scratch pads with each idea beginning with the words, "How to…" When they had finished brainstorming alone, they each shared their list of "How to…" phrases with the other and recorded them on the legal pad. Shari's ideas included the following.

How to…

- have a stronger emotional connection with Michelle.
- be a bigger part of Michelle's life.
- know what Michelle is really struggling with rather than worrying about non-existent problems.
- be able to help Michelle at a difficult stage of life.

Michelle's ideas included how to…

- have Mom stop bugging me (constantly questioning me, acting resentful and worried about me).
- feel that Mom is supportive rather than that she is assuming something must be wrong.
- feel that Mom has confidence in me rather than thinking I'll screw up.

Shari and Michelle then applied critical judgment; they discussed the seven phrases and agreed on the distilled issue statement as follows: *How to have Shari and Michelle understand each other better, feel more emotionally connected, and have Shari be supportive of Michelle rather than critical and worried.*

3. Identifying & Agreeing on the Facts

Michelle and Shari then suspended critical judgment and brainstormed together on the legal pad about the facts that were relevant to the agreed upon issue. When the generation of facts was complete, they applied critical judgment to the facts and agreed on the wording and relevance of each fact. When they were finished, their agreed-upon fact list was as follows:

- Shari feels hurt when Michelle shuts her out.
- Shari is worried when she doesn't know what Michelle is thinking or doing; she is concerned that Michelle might be depressed, or she may have gotten into trouble.
- Michelle feels intruded upon when Shari peppers her with questions.
- Michelle is resentful because her mother won't give her the space she needs.
- Michelle doesn't want advice unless she asks for it.
- Michelle prefers making decisions through logic and by analyzing data.
- Shari prefers making decisions based on feelings and the impacts on people.
- Michelle is in the habit of figuring out how much time she needs for homework, school activities, and solitude/reflection time; this doesn't leave much discretionary time.
- Shari is in the habit of worrying that Michelle might be depressed and unhappy (since she doesn't talk to Shari as much); she spends a lot of time trying to connect emotionally with Michelle.
- Shari seldom thinks about how much time Michelle needs for homework, school activities, and solitude.
- Shari and Michelle both want to have a better relationship (to be more emotionally connected).
- Michelle needs time alone daily for reflection and working things through if she is to feel balanced.
- Shari is more comfortable working things through interactively.

4. Identifying & Agreeing on the Spiritual Principles & Values

Next, Michelle and Shari suspended critical judgment and brainstormed together on the legal pad about the spiritual principles and values that were relevant to the agreed-upon issue and facts. When the generation of spiritual principles and values was complete, they applied critical judgment to them and agreed on the wording and relevance of each spiritual principle and value. When they were finished, their agreed-upon spiritual principle and value list was as follows:

- The differences/diversity between Shari and Michelle are to be treasured and appreciated and can be a cause of deeper understanding and strength between them.
- A strong relationship between mother and daughter can be a cause of healthy development in both parties.
- Having a strong emotional connection with parents can help teenagers avoid trouble and walk a path that is in their best long-term interest.
- Unity of the family is important for a sense of happiness and well-being.
- Parents and children should be respectful toward each other.

5. Identifying & Agreeing on the Solutions

At this point, Michelle and Shari suspended critical judgment and brainstormed together on the legal pad about the solutions that were relevant to the agreed-upon issue, facts, and spiritual principles and values. When the generation of solutions was complete, they applied critical judgment to them and agreed on the wording and relevance of each solution. When they were finished, their agreed-upon solution list was as follows:

- Michelle will determine how much time she needs after school to 1) be alone to reflect, 2) do homework, and 3) be involved in school activities. She will make sure there is at least some relationship time in each day for her and Shari.
- Michelle and Shari will touch base with each other briefly each day about activities, thoughts, and feelings. At that point, they will set another time to meet about whatever needs further discussion if there isn't time then.
- Shari won't "bug" Michelle (pepper her with questions) outside of the time they schedule to connect with each other.
- Shari will listen, reflect back Michelle's thoughts, and validate Michelle's feelings.

- Michelle will listen, reflect back Shari's thoughts, and validate Shari's feelings.
- Shari will try not to offer advice unless Michelle asks for it, or Shari gets Michelle's permission to give her some suggestions.
- Shari will use "I" messages rather than "you" messages, i.e., "I get very worried when you don't come home at the time you say you will. I need you to call and update me if there is a change in your schedule" (rather than "You are so inconsiderate when you don't let me know you'll be late").
- Shari will go out one time weekly or bi-weekly with a friend so that she has a support network beyond Michelle.
- Shari and Michelle will have a social outing together one time every three weeks in addition to their communicating/connecting times daily.

6. Identifying & Agreeing on Implementation Steps

Now Michelle and Shari suspended critical judgment and brainstormed together about the implementation steps that were relevant to the agreed-upon solutions, issue, facts, and spiritual principles and values. When the generation of implementation steps was complete, they applied critical judgment to them and agreed on the wording and relevance of each implementation step. When they were finished, their agreed-upon implementation step list was as follows:

- Michelle will develop her schedule by Saturday morning and share and discuss it with Shari.
- Michelle and Shari will go out to lunch Saturday to talk further about Michelle's schedule and agree on times they can build in for their daily communication.
- At the lunch they will also schedule regular back-up times for more in-depth discussions when they are needed (recognizing that flexibility may be needed for unexpected schedule changes).
- Shari will photocopy sheets on communication techniques (using "I" messages, listening, reflecting back, and validating feelings) and share them with Michelle by Friday evening.
- Michelle and Shari will practice these techniques with each other during their communication sessions starting with the lunch meeting on Saturday.

- When significant disagreements arise, Shari and Michelle will use the Compassionate Consultation process formally to resolve the issue and achieve unity of purpose together.

Compassionate Consultation & the Family

Bahá'u'lláh says:

> **The well-being of mankind, its peace and security, are unattainable unless and until its unity is firmly established.**[235]

This universal spiritual principle also applies to the most fundamental level of human society—the family. If a family has a method for "firmly establishing" unity, then that family can thrive—its "well-being... peace and security" are attainable. Compassionate Consultation provides this robust method.

Chapter 16

Making Transformative Decisions with Groups

Certainly, Consultation within the family qualifies as using Compassionate Consultation with groups; the models and practices illustrated in the last chapter are relevant to group contexts generally. This chapter focuses on three less commonplace examples of using Consultation with groups beyond the nuclear family—with the subsets of the *larger* human family in our communities, workplaces, institutions, and other organizations.

At the village, city, state, national, and international levels, more effective group deliberation and decision-making is needed than ever before because of the expanding diversity of the participants and the increasing complexity and universality of the issues, problems, and opportunities human beings are facing. Compassionate Consultation, the acquisition of the spiritual qualities required to successfully use it, and the consciousness of the oneness of humankind which needs to inform its practitioners are desperately needed if we are to address the challenges facing the human family in a way that increases understanding, unity, and the advancement of civilization.

'Abdu'l-Bahá provides us with a vision for the importance and potential power of group endeavor in this age when he says:

> O ye beloved of the Lord! This day is the day of union, the day of the ingathering of all mankind. 'Verily God loveth those who, as though they were a solid wall, do battle for His Cause in serried lines!' [1 Qur'an 61:4] Note that He saith 'in serried lines' -- meaning crowded and pressed together, one locked to the next, each sup-

porting his fellows. To do battle, as stated in the sacred verse, doth not, in this greatest of all dispensations, mean to go forth with sword and spear, with lance and piercing arrow—but rather weaponed with pure intent, with righteous motives, with counsels helpful and effective, with godly attributes, with deeds pleasing to the Almighty, with the qualities of heaven. It signifieth education for all mankind, guidance for all men, the spreading far and wide of the sweet savours of the spirit, the promulgation of God's proofs, the setting forth of arguments conclusive and divine, the doing of charitable deeds. Whensoever holy souls, drawing on the powers of heaven, shall arise with such qualities of the spirit, and march in unison, rank on rank, every one of those souls will be even as one thousand, and the surging waves of that mighty ocean will be even as the battalions of the Concourse on high.

What a blessing that will be—when all shall come together, even as once separate torrents, rivers and streams, running brooks and single drops, when collected together in one place will form a mighty sea. And to such a degree will the inherent unity of all prevail, that the traditions, rules, customs and distinctions in the fanciful life of these populations will be effaced and vanish away like isolated drops, once the great sea of oneness doth leap and surge and roll. I swear by the Ancient Beauty, that at such a time overwhelming grace will so encircle all, and the sea of grandeur will so overflow its shores, that the narrowest strip of water will grow wide as an endless sea, and every merest drop will be even as the shoreless deep.[236]

'Abdu'l-Bahá describes a largely untapped resource inherent in the human community—the power to achieve extraordinary things through reliance on divine assistance, spiritual thoughts and actions, and group action informed by unity and harmony; when "holy souls, drawing on the powers of heaven, shall arise with such qualities of the spirit, and march in unison... every one of those souls will be even as one thousand..." While these words certainly have many applications, they bring to mind Compassionate Consultation as a means of accessing divine guidance, harnessing and channeling the rich diversity of human capacity, and achieving deep understanding, unity, and unlimited results.

Since the international Bahá'í community is presently the only organized population in the world that has been experimenting with and honing its Consultation skills for several generations, the best examples of Compassionate Consultation in wider groups come from those composed entirely or largely of Bahá'ís. Accordingly, we will describe three examples in this chapter—two involving large groups of Bahá'í participants that push the envelope on what seems possible in group deliberation and one involving what we will call *hybrid* Consultation and consensus decision-making composed of members of a government agency and their collaborative partners.

A Remarkable Instance of Group Consultation to Deepen Understanding

The authors had the privilege of attending the 2006 United States National Bahá'í Convention, which was attended by over 150 highly diverse delegates from around the country. At this convention, we experienced a remarkable instance of Compassionate Consultation directed at deepening understanding. This experience was an illustration of the words of Bahá'u'lláh that "The maturity of the gift of understanding is made manifest through consultation."[237]

During one session, the delegates were using Consultation to deliberate on the issue of racial prejudice in the United States, especially between black and white Americans. While the Bahá'í community works diligently and continuously to root out racial prejudice, the attention of the convention focused on the significant distance we still needed to travel and on the pain and suffering still being experienced by black Americans in the larger society.

The session began with prayers for divine guidance and assistance. While this subject was not new for national conventions, the Consultation in this session was informed by a particularly high degree of compassion. It was largely white delegates who spoke compassionately on behalf of the suffering of black Americans, and black delegates reported their experiences in society with dilated hearts and without the least tone of indictment or blame. Many of the delegates quoted from the Bahá'í Writings about racial prejudice in the United States, which brought in the power of spiritual principles and values to inform the process. It was a very moving and mature discussion which engaged both minds and hearts. It exemplified 'Abdu'l-Bahá's vision of people coming together "...with pure intent, with righteous motives, with counsels helpful and effective, with godly attributes, with deeds pleasing to the Almighty, with the qualities of heaven."[238]

After about thirty minutes of Consultation, hearts had become so dilated and minds so illumined that some delegates began spontaneously rising to their feet and embracing their fellow delegates of a different race. This activity quickly swept throughout the auditorium to the point that the convention chairperson called for a pause in the Consultation so that the feelings of the delegates for each other could be expressed. The delegates, in all their multi-colored diversity, embraced each other with tears streaming down their cheeks while laughter and the murmur of soothing, loving phrases filled the air. It felt like the accumulated racial division, suffering, and guilt of an entire nation were being expiated in microcosm by these representatives from all over the country—in one unified outpouring of insight and compassion.

During this scene, a few black delegates with over-flowing hearts began singing an old spiritual dating back to the days of slavery, and as they sang, they formed a line, each one with a hand on the shoulder of the person in front, and started dancing rhythmically around the room. Other delegates fell silent, focused on them, and heard the words of their song:

> Done made my vow to the Lord and I never will turn back—
> Oh, I will go, I shall go, to see what the end will be.
> Amazing grace, how sweet the sound—
> To see what the end will be.
> I once was lost, but now I'm found—
> To see what the end will be.

Soon, other delegates spontaneously joined in. The line continued snaking through the auditorium, taking on new links in the human chain until every delegate in the room had joined the line and shared in the unified celebration of joy, insight, compassion, and healing. The song continued—now in a roar of voices:

> Done made my vow to the Lord and I never will turn back—
> Oh, I will go, I shall go, to see what the end will be.
> If you get to heaven before I do—
> To see what the end will be.
> Tell all my friends I'm a coming too—
> To see what the end will be.
> Done made my vow to the Lord and I never will turn back—
> Oh, I will go, I shall go, to see what the end will be.
> Sometimes I'm up and sometimes I'm down—
> To see what the end will be,
> But my souls been heavenly bound—
> To see what the end will be.
> Done made my vow to the Lord and I never will turn back—
> Oh, I will go, I shall go, to see what the end will be.

At the end of this experience, the delegates broke into cheers; they then formed small groups and pairs where embraces, tears of joy, and loving discussion continued.

This interlude of what one delegate called "spiritual pandemonium" lasted about thirty minutes. Finally, the convention chairperson called the delegates back to order, and after being seated the delegates spontaneously broke into thunderous applause in recognition of the extraordinary process of Compassionate Consultation they had just experienced. Indeed, in the words of 'Abdu'l-Bahá, we had seen first-hand "What a blessing that will be—when all shall come together, even as once separate torrents, rivers and streams, running brooks and single drops, when collected together in one place…"

We had seen "overwhelming grace… encircle all" and had seen ourselves "…form a mighty sea," "the inherent unity of all prevail" and "…the traditions, rules, customs, and distinctions in [our] fanciful life… effaced and vanish away like isolated drops" into "…the great sea of oneness…"[239] It was amazingly clear that the combination of Consultation with compassion has a transformative power to deepen understanding, forge unity, and alter lives beyond our wildest dreams, and that it represents a frontier we are just beginning to cross.

The Limitations to Consultation Imposed By Most Present Day Group Cultures

The Bahá'í Convention example (just described) and World Congress example (to be described later in this chapter) provide a partial vision of the transformational potential of Compassionate Consultation when used with larger groups. In contrast, most groups in present-day society remain deprived of the inherent power of Compassionate Consultation because of either their unawareness of it as a decision-making process, or their hesitancy to admit the validity and appropriateness of the spiritual dimension as a strategic resource in making decisions. Present day communities, workplaces, and other organizations are often bastions of what 'Abdu'l-Bahá calls "…the traditions, rules, customs and distinctions in the fanciful life of…"[240] their members. Differences of culture, gender, race, religion, nationality, status, power, privilege, wealth, and political affiliation can easily blind us to the unity of humankind and create an environment in which saying prayers for divine guidance and developing the spiritual attributes and detached behaviors required for Compassionate Consultation seem risky, naïve, or inappropriate to propose.

Adding Consultation Elements into Traditional Group Processes—a *Hybrid Process*

Nevertheless, the growing complexity and urgency of the issues being faced by increasingly more diverse groups calls out for a decision-making process that helps participants: root out the limited thinking and biases that are getting in the way of seeing the reality of situations under consideration; fully understand points of view different from their own; let go of prior attachments to any particular outcome; and gain a perspective in which spiritual principles are the guideposts to enlightened, unified decisions. Because Compassionate Consultation provides all of these benefits, it would behoove group leaders and members to increasingly make use of it and align their group cultures with its requisites and standards.

To assist traditional group environments in the transition to Compassionate Consultation, the authors often help groups improve their consensus decision-making skills while simultaneously adding certain components of Compassionate Consultation to the process. We call the resulting process *a hybrid between consensus and Consultation decision-making*. The Consultative components typically include introducing an abbreviated version of the 12 Behavioral Standards—especially honoring the inherent value of each member, treasuring diversity, striving to arrive at a unanimous decision, having unity in implementing decisions, and detaching one's ego from one's ideas. We also typically modify the wording for Step 4 in the 6-Step Model to read "Identifying & Agreeing on the

Relevant Values" (having eliminated reference to Spiritual Principles). In addition, a short period of centering, reflection, or meditation is usually substituted for the members praying together for divine guidance at the beginning. While necessary in many current organizational environments, these modifications to the true Compassionate Consultation process limit its power and potential.

As an illustration, the group application example below is a *hybrid* of consensus decision-making with some aspects of Compassionate Consultation added in. It especially illustrates how agreeing on human values and principles during the decision-making process can significantly reduce entrenched partisanship and conflicting interests, generate a collaborative spirit, and lead to more enlightened decisions.

A State Steering Committee Uses the 6-Step I/A Model (Sticky Wall Version)

Over the years, the authors have facilitated decision-making for several state health and nutrition steering committees focused on improving the nutritional quality of school meal programs for children and young people. The following example illustrates an early phase in this work, how a *hybrid version* of the 6-Step Identify/Agree (I/A) Model has be used in this context, and the nature of the decision-making content generated.

The forward-looking leaders of a division responsible for school food and nutrition programs within a state department of education were concerned about the epidemics of obesity and diabetes in the state's school-aged children and young people. Consequently, and for the first time, leaders of the division convened a twenty-five-person steering committee made up of representative school administrators, food and beverage suppliers/distributors from private industry, educators, school food service managers, health care professionals, and researchers from higher education institutions. The purpose of the steering committee members was to work together as stakeholders to reach collaborative decisions that would begin to improve the health and nutrition environments within the state's schools and reverse the obesity and diabetes trends.

The Steering Committee's Dilemma

The steering committee's challenge was that its members, representing most of the stakeholders in the state-wide school meal program, often found themselves working at cross-purposes with conflicting incentives. For example, food and beverage manufacturers and distributors were accustomed to meeting consumer demand based on what would sell, and they believed families rather than schools should make decisions about what is healthy and nutritious and what is not. Their orientation was to strongly favor free market principles. Educators, healthcare professionals, and researchers tended to strongly favor government intervention to encourage the healthy nutritional habits that the research dictated. School administrators and school food service managers found themselves caught in the middle—wanting to promote healthy and nutritious meals for students, but also feeling dependent on the revenues generated by the in-school sale of unhealthy snack foods and beverages to students, which largely sustained extra-curricular activities in an under-funded educational environment. What later proved to be a false dichotomy of conservative versus liberal ideologies threatened to tear the stakeholders apart at the very beginning. In the end, it was the honoring of certain Behavioral Standards, the separation of decision-making steps, and particularly the identification and agreement on values (Step 4 below) that laid the foundation for a wisely blended set of solutions and implementation steps.

Because of the potentially contentious nature of the issue and the relatively large group of people, the steering committee members decided to use the sticky-wall version of the hybrid 6-Step Identify/Agree (I/A) Model. Prayers for divine guidance were not used. Instead, the members of the steering committee spent twenty minutes prior to the deliberation process each time they met reviewing an abbreviated version of the 12 Behavioral Standards that had been edited for political correctness in that particular organizational environment. Step 4, which is normally called "Identifying & Agreeing on the Spiritual Principles," was called "Identifying & Agreeing on the Values."

After a series of meetings, when the twenty-five-person steering committee had reached consensus on all six steps, the finalized sticky-wall content read as shown below. The resulting data is presented without showing the sub-steps in Steps 2 through 6 that occurred as a result of first suspending and then applying critical judgment in both small groups and the large group. See Appendix II in the free PDF for a detailed description of these sub-steps.

Step 1: Review of the Key Behavioral Standards

Reviewed and discussed an abbreviated version of the 12 Behavioral Standards in place of praying for divine guidance.

Step 2: Identifying & Agreeing on the Issue

Issue: *How to take collective responsibility for creating a school environment that fosters good health.*

Step 3: Identifying & Agreeing on the Facts

- One's health and performance throughout life are directly impacted by nutrition.
- Childhood obesity is increasing at an epidemic rate.
- Childhood diabetes is increasing at an epidemic rate.
- Poor diet is a contributory factor to certain chronic diseases.
- Young people's food choices are influenced by advertising and marketing.
- Young people's food choices are influenced by family eating and nutritional patterns.
- Physical activity is another factor that impacts health.
- Reduced physical activity, decreased calcium consumption, and increased soft drink consumption contribute to osteoporosis in later life.
- Cultural patterns and lifestyle choices are leading some young people to become more sedentary.
- Curriculum changes are leading some young people to become more sedentary.
- In many places the school lunch period and physical education time are getting reduced.
- Limited funding leads schools to rely on vending machine revenues to fund many extra-curricular activities.
- Effective child nutrition programs are a function of many things, but adequate school funding is central among them.
- School food service program budgets are comprised of a combination of federal, state, and non-traditional funding resources.
- The dynamics of child nutrition programs are complicated and inadequately understood.

- Closed campuses prevent students from getting fast food lunches off campus.
- The majority of students consume imbalanced diets.
- The families of many students rely on the school meal program for the majority of their children's nutrition.
- Young people tend to feel immortal and may not take the importance of good nutrition seriously.
- Progress has been made by the food industry in improving the nutritional value of foods, but more progress needs to be made.

Step 4: Identifying & Agreeing on the Values

- Adults need to take responsibility for the well-being of children.
- Access to nutritional and safe food is a right of children.
- We believe that good nutrition contributes to effective learning.
- We believe that good nutrition contributes to good health.
- We believe that physical activity contributes to good health.
- We value education and its ability to help people make informed choices.
- We value freedom of choice.
- We value ethnic and cultural diversity.
- We value a healthy community and society.
- We value the role of families in overseeing the health of their children.
- We value the contribution of free enterprise to our communities.
- We value responsible financial management.

Step 5: Identifying & Agreeing on the Solutions

- Increase children's involvement and input in decision-making regarding choices in school food programs.
- Create a nutrition and physical activity promotional program that reaches the extended school community (including families).
- Create nutrition and physical activity educational materials for the extended school community (including families and other stakeholders).
- Develop public and private strategic partnerships to help fund and promote our physical activity and nutrition efforts.

- Develop and commit to child-centered standards for the advertising of beverages and foods in the school environment.
- Create nutritional standards that must be met for competitive foods and fundraiser foods used in and by the schools.
- Discover best practices regarding the optimum amount of time for the school lunch period and publish/broadcast the data.
- Discover best practices regarding the minimum optimum time for physical education/physical activity in the school day and publish/broadcast the data.
- Build a library of recipes and menus reflecting cultural diversity that also meet nutritional guidelines.

Step 6: Identifying & Agreeing on the Implementation Steps

Note: The following implementation steps and sub-steps were assigned to a variety of cross functional teams from a cross section of stakeholders for implementation:

1. Increase children's involvement and input in decision-making regarding choices in school food programs.
    a. Create and use a survey to assess students' preferences within nutrition parameters for types of foods, food substitutes, and service frequency.
    b. Develop a leadership cadre of students in each school who want to be spokespeople and role models for good nutrition and physical activity.
    c. Create in-school competitions in which students find/develop recipes and menus within nutrition parameters and get rewarded when they are used in school meals.
    d. As a follow-on to the previous step, have inter-school food and beverage tasting events with rewards for best submissions.
    e. Develop a way of monitoring and rewarding students who consistently make good nutrition and physical activity choices.
2. Create a nutrition and physical activity educational and promotional program that reaches the extended school community (including families and other stakeholders).
    a. Research and identify best practices in the field.

b. Develop draft education and promotional materials based on best practices.
c. Test market materials to assure desired outcomes.
d. Finalize education and promotional materials.
e. Disseminate materials to all stakeholders.
f. Use follow-up surveys to confirm effectiveness and drive program refinements and enhancements.

3. Develop public and private strategic partnerships to help fund and promote our physical activity and nutrition efforts.
    a. Identify and budget financial and non-financial resources needed.
    b. Identify candidate strategic partners.
    c. Develop a persuasive case and an effective presentation that enumerates the urgency and benefits of strategic partnering.
    d. Develop a support-seeking letter based on the persuasive case.
    e. Make in-person calls on prospective partners to make the persuasive case and establish strategic partnerships.

4. Develop and commit to child-centered standards for the advertising of beverages and foods in the school environment.
    a. Establish a marketing committee at each school site to create child-centered advertising and marketing guidelines for food and beverages that align with Nutrition Advisory Committee policy.
    b. Integrate, publish, and promote these standards to all outside vendors of food and beverages in advance of implementation.
    c. Implement the new standards at the district level when contracts with outside vendors are being renewed.

5. Create nutritional standards that must be met for competitive foods and fundraiser foods used in and by the schools.
    a. Develop and publish nutrition standards (e.g. protein, fiber, fat, calories, sugar, vitamins, and minerals) for beverages and foods offered for sale or fundraisers.
    b. Publish and promote a list of the food products from vendors and schools that meet the nutritional standards.

    c. In concert with Implementation Steps 1 and 2 above, promote acceptance of the products that meet the nutritional standards by holding taste tests and other events that help students experience healthy food choices.
6. Discover best practices regarding the optimum amount of time for the school lunch period and physical education/activity period and publish/broadcast the data.
    a. Conduct focus groups with students to identify their issues and concerns regarding the optimum school lunch period and physical education/activity period.
    b. Review existing research on optimum meal service and physical education/activity times.
    c. Survey school principals regarding their practices and learning about optimum meal times, physical education/activity times and related issues.
    d. Conduct observational studies of actual lunch periods and physical education/activity periods at various schools to determine what works best.
    e. Prepare a report on the data obtained and promote the best practices standards.
7. Build a library of recipes and menus reflecting cultural diversity that also meet nutritional guidelines.
    a. Identify existing resources for institutional recipes that span international cuisine and ethnic/racial categories.
    b. Filter findings to yield those recipes that meet nutritional guidelines.
    c. Identify ethnic/racial categories represented in our jurisdiction in relation to acceptable recipe cuisine categories found.
    d. Identify matches, gaps, and remaining recipe needs.
    e. Develop and test recipes from missing categories using local resources.
    f. Publish a library of recipes, menus, and foods cross-referenced by cuisine category and racial/ethnic group.
    g. Identify suggestions for implementation and dissemination methods.

Debriefing the State Steering Committee Application Example

Adding components of Compassionate Consultation to the preceding *hybrid* decision-making process facilitated the breakdown of entrenched, polarized points of view. Polarization generally results from participants taking positions that consider only the information that supports their point of view while ignoring or discrediting any information that does not. The Consultation steps—including the modified Step 4 where agreement was reached on the relevant values that informed the issue—and the honoring of selected Behavioral Standards (e.g., detaching one's ego from one's ideas, honoring the inherent value of each member, treasuring diversity, striving to arrive at a unanimous decision, and having unity in implementing decisions) helped enable participants to break free from personal frames of reference and see the issue in more universal and holistic terms. This enabled them to reach an integrated, balanced, and effective set of solutions to the issue.

For example, the agreement in Step 4 on the apparently incompatible values of "Adults need to take responsibility for the well-being of children" and "We value freedom of choice" helped steering committee members to reject false dichotomies and reach integrated rather than ideological solutions in Step 5 such as:

- Develop public and private strategic partnerships to help fund and promote our physical activity and nutrition efforts.
- Develop and commit to child-centered standards for the advertising of beverages and foods in the school environment.
- Create nutritional standards that must be met for competitive foods and fundraiser foods used in and by the schools.

At the time the steering committee was formed, such agreements were deemed possible but unlikely due to entrenched positions. Because of the elements of Compassionate Consultation that had been added to the consensus decision-making process, these breakthrough agreements became a reality and paved the way for further advances.

Spontaneous, Multi-Directional Consultation in a Continuous Change Environment

The third group application example is a pure rather than hybrid Compassionate Consultation example, and it was experienced by the authors when they attended the 1992 Bahá'í World Congress in New York City. Twenty-seven thousand Bahá'ís from all over the world came to observe the centenary of Bahá'u'lláh's passing in 1892 and to celebrate the emerging, united, spiritually-centered global civilization that His teachings have fostered.

This week-long event at the Jacob Javits Center entailed the equivalent of organizing a small city to support the needs of a community of people representing virtually every nation, race, ethnicity, and heritage on the planet and doing it with a volunteer labor force composed only of congress attendees. Because of the size of the gathering and limits of auditorium capacity, each day's session was held once in the morning and once in the afternoon, and each attendee was assigned to one of the two sessions. Those assigned to the morning session provided a volunteer worker pool for the afternoon, and those assigned to the afternoon session provided a pool for the morning.

The authors were charged with managing a component of the human resources function involving organizing, preparing, training, and deploying volunteer workers to the various other functions and venues of the congress such as registration, security, guiding, information desks, language translation, emergency healthcare, point-of-purchase book sales, ushering, public relations/media, childcare, volunteer recruitment, etc. There had been a lot of pre-congress planning and organizing by a sizeable cadre of people from around the world with the appropriate backgrounds and experience to manage and serve the attendees of the congress; but all of those involved realized that they had never attempted to organize, manage, and serve an organization of this scale, diversity, complexity, and transience—and do it with a volunteer labor force!

On the first morning of the congress, as the first set of 13,500 people prepared to flood into the morning session, we discovered that most of our plans had to be scuttled for a variety of unforeseen and uncontrollable reasons. For example, to assure a smooth congress launch, we had pre-scheduled and pre-oriented cadres of volunteer workers for the first day of the conference; however, 50 percent of those volunteers coming from far-flung locations could not show up for work due to travel delays they experienced, and volunteer workers who *had not* been pre-scheduled and pre-oriented were showing up for work.

What is more, all those involved in managing the various functions of the congress were connected by two-way radios, and the volunteer worker requests flowing in to us from various functions and venues of the congress were ramping up and changing constantly. We would get an urgent call for twenty-five guides, and by the time we had identified and oriented a group of twenty-five people to be deployed as guides, the original caller would call again saying that they had found ten people to work as guides, still needed fifteen guides, and now urgently needed thirty security workers. Five minutes later, the same caller would report that they needed fifty, not thirty, security workers. This was one caller, but we were receiving a dozen such calls simultaneously. By the end of the first hour we were sweating profusely! We were in a high-speed, continuous change environment that was forcing us to throw out our conventional ways of organizing, managing, and deploying human resources.

The amazing thing was that by the end of the third hour of the first morning, everything began working smoothly. We eventually concluded that there were three main reasons for this. First, Bahá'ís treasure human diversity and acknowledge the oneness of the human family, and this created a highly inclusive environment in which intense, equal, and reciprocal care and concern for every person's welfare was foundational. At every turn, people encountered kindness, courtesy, and empathy.

Second, the Bahá'ís recognize that service to others is a form of worship. This created a remarkable level of service quality between all attendees—whether in the role of attendee or volunteer worker. This passion for providing service not only resulted in initiative and leadership being widely distributed, but in compassion being widely distributed—everyone took proactive action to *alleviate* any distress in others around them.

And third, virtually everyone had at least a rudimentary grasp of the principles and process of Consultation. Many of the 7 Prime Requisites and 12 Behavioral Standards were either faintly or clearly evident in the great majority of deliberative interactions. This expedited individual and collective growth-seeking resulting in high-quality solutions to problems that were rapidly and unitedly implemented.

Because these three characteristics were in place, a culture quickly emerged in the congress environment which drew the best out of people. People's higher natures were called forth. And when those attempting to manage the congress functions by conventional means were forced to throw up their hands in frustration with the accelerating, continuous change environment, spontaneous, compassionate, multi-directional Consultation took its place.

As a result, we witnessed the emergence of new patterns in our area. Instead of having our waiting pool of volunteer workers separated into subgroups according to skill sets as planned, we shared the rapidly rising and changing needs we were trying to address with all of the volunteers in the room. Informal Consultation ensued with all those present, and there was unanimous agreement to have all waiting volunteer workers sit in one common space together. We would receive a call from the bookstore that twelve point-of–sale workers (four of them French speaking) were needed. We would immediately ask the entire volunteer group who felt capable of doing this work, and a sizable group would raise their hands. We would ask those who could speak French to stand up, count the first four from the standing group, and then the remaining eight from those seated with raised hands. As the group rose to deploy, we would ask them to use Consultation in order to adapt to the realities they found when they reached the bookstore. Just then, another call from the bookstore would come in requesting that two of the point-of-sale workers be able to speak Spanish. Two volunteers from the pool who spoke Spanish would jump to their feet, join the original group on the way to the bookstore, and we would ask any of them who were not needed once they arrived at the bookstore to please return for a different assignment.

When conflicting or overwhelming resource needs were radioed in, we would immediately share the dilemma with the waiting pool of volunteers, informal Consultation would ensue, a decision would be rapidly arrived at, and workers would be deployed accordingly. Sometimes, the volunteer pool would dwindle to ten or fifteen people, and a portion of the remaining volunteers would spontaneously hurry into the hallways and recruit additional volunteers. After Consulting among themselves, the waiting workers created signs with the words, "Volunteer Workers Needed," and some of them paced the congress hallways like pied pipers recruiting and channeling a steady flow of workers to our room. Additional Consultation among the pooled volunteers led to signs on the walls of our waiting room that said, "Waiting is also service." All of these developments occurred during the first morning of the congress.

Another pattern also developed. In the beginning, we had someone from our staff take each group of assigned volunteers from our centrally located, lower level office to the targeted work site in the Javits Center.

However, it wasn't working because things were so busy and constantly changing at each work site that we were having trouble locating the person at the work site who had called in the worker request and who could orient the workers to their tasks. Accordingly, and in Consultation with the volunteer workers and work site representatives, we established the policy that we would have the requested workers ready and waiting, and a person from the work site would come to our space and conduct the group of workers to the work site while simultaneously orienting them to what would be required of them. This worked well, and by early afternoon of the first day, all of the other functions and venues at the congress knew that they could give us ten to fifteen minutes' advance notice regarding their personnel needs, come down to pick up the volunteers, and conduct them to the work site.

By the second day of the congress, experienced volunteers waiting in the pool were sharing their learnings with new volunteers, some choosing to become specialized in certain on-going functions, while others were shifting to different and emerging areas of service. Workers would return to the volunteer waiting room from one work assignment, join the waiting pool of volunteers, cross-fertilize their learning, and new assignments and departures would occur. Increasingly, workers were also huddling at their work sites and in hallways to proactively Consult about and resolve problems to improve the services they were providing.

There was no sense of hierarchy—it felt like everyone was on the same level distinguished only by the different roles they were playing. The environment was so participative that the role of leadership had become facilitative rather than directive. Instead of managers being the sources of knowledge, knowledge sources during Consultation exchanges shifted around the room as those with the most relevant insights arising from their accumulating experience on the ground shared their thoughts. People were not vying for leadership, they were vying to serve. There was a remarkable flow and grace that informed the approach to very complex situations.

The deliberation patterns took the shape of fast-evolving, constantly changing, large and small group Consultation exchanges that involved spontaneously praying for guidance, assessing the facts, identifying spiritual principles, arriving at solutions, and fostering action—usually, but not always, in that order. There were a few formal Consultation sessions, but most of them were like the huddles of an American football team—taking action, huddling to assimilate and share what was learned, planning the next action, and taking action again. In our case, however, the quarterback was not dictating the actions; the team members were collaboratively designing them with the quarterback. It was possible to make mistakes, instantly confer to modify a decision based on new learning, and move in unity in a new direction without any complaints or recriminations. The good-natured patience, unity, flexibility, and passion for service shown by all participants were astonishing to us based on our years of experience in conventional organizations. It occurred to us that conventional organizations tend to be relatively homogeneous, which makes collaborative activity easier; but this organization of twenty-seven thousand people was as heterogeneous as the world itself—and yet we were witnessing unity in diversity and mature, spontaneous, multi-directional Consultation in a continuous change environment. It was a temporary city in which all the citizens were taking full responsibility for the collective welfare and advancement of the community.

At week's end, the congress had been a resounding success. No small part of that was the fact that the citizens of this temporary city had served with selfless devotion in numerous volunteer worker capacities while also contributing mightily to the Consultation that drove the continuously-improving congress processes. We had received a week-long glimpse of what is possible in a maximally diverse human community where certain spiritual attributes are embodied and certain universal values and decision-making practices are held in common. In the words of 'Abdu'l-Bahá, we had seen people "weaponed with pure intent, with righteous motives, with counsels helpful and effective, with godly attributes, with deeds pleasing to the Almighty, with the qualities of heaven," and recognized that human capacity, individually and collectively, is far greater than what is traditionally assumed. People from all corners of the earth had come together "as once separate torrents, rivers and streams, running brooks and single drops" to "form a mighty sea."[241] During the week, the social and spiritual maturity characterizing the congress culture provided a stark contrast for attendees between what is possible in spiritually-centered, Consultative human communities and what we usually settle for.

The Evolution from Hybrid to True Consultation Decision-Making in Groups

The difference between the first and third *true* Compassionate Consultation examples in this chapter and the second *hybrid* example lies in the whole-hearted commitment by participants in the first and third examples to the use of a divinely ordained decision-making process specifically prescribed by Bahá'u'lláh for the healing and optimization of human affairs in this day. Bahá'u'lláh reminds us that:

> **The Prophets of God should be regarded as physicians whose task is to foster the well-being of the world and its peoples, that, through the spirit of oneness, they may heal the sickness of a divided humanity....No man, however acute his perception, can ever hope to reach the heights which the wisdom and understanding of the Divine Physician have attained....The whole of mankind is in the grip of manifold ills. Strive, therefore, to save its life through the wholesome medicine which the almighty hand of the unerring Physician hath prepared.**[242]

The use of Consultation combined with compassion is one component of this "wholesome medicine" that we must apply in our deliberation and decision-making processes if we are to unlock the full potential of human beings individually and collectively. The application of this medicine can change the adversarial principles that inform deliberation in many of our social institutions—in the courts, politics, government, organizations, and international affairs—into collaborative, spiritually-based principles that foster wise, just, and unifying decisions. To apply this medicine means that we must wholeheartedly commit to a *spiritual* deliberation process—to using prayer and to honoring the 7 Prime Requisites and 12 Behavioral Standards of Compassionate Consultation. Put another way, transformative results are a function of the group's sincerity in asking for and relying upon divine guidance, the degree of compassion the members generate, and the vibrancy of the growth-seeking spirit manifested by the members in their Consultative interactions.

As members of societal groups at all levels learn to honor and manifest these qualities and practices with greater consecration, commitment, and skill, transformative decision-making results will increasingly become the norm in society at large. And the very act of working together in this spirit will contribute to the healing and advancement of the world.

'Abdu'l-Bahá says:

> If a few souls gather in a beloved meeting with the feelings of the Kingdom, with the divine attractions, with pure hearts and with absolute purity and holiness, to consort in spirit and fragrance, that gathering will have its effect upon all the world.[243]

Postscript

To receive the **free PDF** containing the four appendices to this book, which include more detailed examples and instructions on how to use the Compassionate Consultation models introduced in this book, please sign-up at **billandjeanharley.com/actionplan**

We encourage our readers to share their own growth-seeking and Compassionate Consultation stories, experiences, and needs with us at **Contact@HarleyCoaching.com**

About the Authors

Bill and Jean Harley are the principals of Harley Consulting & Coaching, a Minneapolis-based human and organization development firm providing coaching, counseling, consultation, education, and group facilitation services to release human and organizational potential in service to others. Jean is a Psychologist and Bill is an organization development consultant and a Certified Personal & Professional Coach. They work with individuals, couples, families, groups and communities to accelerate growth and facilitate unity of purpose. Bill and Jean have been married for 48 years and have two adult daughters and sons-in-law plus three grandchildren.

Bibliography

'Abdu'l-Bahá. *'Abdu'l-Bahá in London*. Chicago: Baha'i Publishing Society, 1921.
'Abdu'l-Bahá. *Divine Philosophy*. Approved by Bahá'í Committee on Publications. London: Isabel Chamberlain, 1911.
'Abdu'l-Bahá. *Foundations of World Unity*. Wilmette, Illinois: Bahá'í Publishing Trust, 1971.
'Abdu'l-Bahá. *Paris Talks.* London: The Bahá'í Publishing Trust, 1995.
'Abdu'l-Bahá, quoted in *Star of the West*, Vol. VIII, no. 4 (17May 1917).
'Abdu'l-Bahá, quoted in *Star of the West*, Vol. VIII, no. 9 (20 August 1917).
'Abdu'l-Bahá, quoted in *Star of the West*, Vol. VIII, no. 11 (27 September 1917).
'Abdu'l-Bahá. *The Promulgation of Universal Peace*. Wilmette, Illinois: Bahá'í Publishing Trust, 1982.
'Abdu'l-Bahá. *The Secret of Divine Civilization*. Wilmette, Illinois: Bahá'í Publishing Trust, 1975.
'Abdu'l-Bahá. *Selections from the Writings of 'Abdu'l-Bahá*. Haifa: Bahá'í World Centre, 1978.
'Abdu'l-Bahá. *Some Answered Questions*. Wilmette, Illinois: Bahá'í Publishing Trust, 1994.
'Abdu'l-Bahá. *Tablets of 'Abdu'l-Bahá Abbas, volume 3*. Chicago: Bahá'í Publishing Society, 1916.
'Abdu'l-Bahá. *The Will and Testament of 'Abdu'l-Bahá.* Wilmette, Illinois: Bahá'í Publishing Trust, 1971.
Augustine, and Rochelle, John E. *Sermons (51-94) on the New Testament.* (Part III, Vol 3, Sermon 88.5) Brooklyn, New York: 1991.
Baha'i Meetings. Wilmette, Illinois: Baha'i Publishing Trust, 1976.

Bahá'í Prayers. Wilmette, Illinois: Bahá'í Publishing Trust, 1991.

Baha'u'llah. *Gleanings from the Writings of Bahá'u'lláh.* Wilmette, Illinois: Baha'i Publishing Trust, 1969.

Bahá'u'lláh. *The Hidden Words.* Wilmette, Illinois: Baha'i Publishing Trust, 1970.

Bahá'u'lláh. *The Kitab-i-Aqdas.* Haifa: Bahá'í World Centre, 1992.

Bahá'u'lláh. *The Kitab-i-Iqan, The Book of Certitude.* Wilmette, Illinois: Bahá'í Publishing Trust, 1960.

Bahá'u'lláh. *The Seven Valleys and the Four Valleys.* Wilmette, Illinois: Baha'i Publishing Trust, 1952.

Baha'u'llah. *Tablets of Bahá'u'lláh revealed after the Kitab-i-Aqdas.* Wilmette, Illinois: Baha'i Publishing Trust, 1988.

Bradshaw, John. *Healing the Shame that Binds You.* Deerfield Beach: Health Communications, Inc., 1993.

The Compact Edition of the Oxford English Dictionary. New York: Oxford University Press, 1973.

The Compilation of Compilations. Australia: Bahá'í Publications, 1991.

Consultation: A Compilation. Extracts from the Writings and Utterances of Bahá'u'lláh, 'Abdu'l-Bahá, Shoghi Effendi, and The Universal House of Justice. Compiled by the Research Department of the Universal House of Justice. Wilmette, Illinois: Bahá'í Publishing Trust, 1980.

Esslemont, J. E. *Bahá'u'lláh and the New Era.* Wilmette, Illinois: Bahá'í Publishing Trust, 1987.

Gail, Marzieh. *Six Lessons on Islam.* Wilmette, Illinois: Bahá'í Publishing Trust, 1969.

Goldberg, Marilee C. *The Art of the Question: A Guide to Short-Term Question-Centered Therapy.* New York: John Wiley & Sons, Inc., 1998.

Gottman, John M. and Silver, Nan. *The Seven Principles for Making Marriage Work.* New York: Crown Publishers, Inc., 1999.

Hall, Jay. "Managing For Group Effectiveness", in *Models for Management: The Structure of Competence.* The Woodlands, Texas: Woodstead Press, 1992

Harley, Bill and Harley, Jean. *Now That I'm Here What Should I Be Doing—Discover Life's Purpose.* Minneapolis, Minnesota: Wisdom Editions, 2016.

Hendrix, Harville. *Keeping the Love You Find*. New York: Simon & Schuster Inc., 1993.
Jacobs, R. W. *Real-Time Strategic Change*. San Francisco: Berrett-Koehler, 1994.
Kabat-Zinn, Jon. *Wherever You Go, There You Are*. New York: Hyperion, 1994.
King James Bible. Gordonsville, Tennessee: Dugan Publishers, Inc., 1987.
Kolstoe, John. *Consultation: A Universal Lamp of Guidance*. Oxford: George Ronald, 1985.
Lights of Guidance. Ed. Helen Hornby. New Delhi: Baha'i Publishing Trust, 1983.
Mahmud-in-Zarqani, Mirza. *Mahmud's Diary*. Oxford: George Ronald, 1998.
Merriam-Webster's Collegiate Dictionary, Eleventh Edition. Springfield: Merriam-Webster, Incorporated, 2004.
Peace & Change, Vol. 28, No. 3, July 2003.
The Qur'an (J. M. Rodwell, M.A., tr.). New York: Everyman's Library, Dutton, 1971.
Rogers, Carl. *On Becoming a Person*. Boston: Houghton Mifflin Company, 1961.
Seventeenth Century Prose and Poetry. (Alexander M. Witherspoon and Frank J. Warmke, ed.). New York: Harcourt, Brace & World, Inc., 1963.
Shoghi Effendi. *Bahá'í Administration*. Wilmette, Illinois: Bahá'í Publishing Trust, 1968.
Shoghi Effendi. *Call to the Nations*. Haifa, Israel: Bahá'í World Centre, 1977.
Stosny, Steven. *Treating Attachment Abuse: A Compassionate Approach*. New York: Springer Publishing Company, Inc., 1995.
Taherzadeh, Adib. *The Revelation of Bahá'u'lláh: Volume Three*. Oxford: George Ronald, 1984.
Thompson, Juliet. *The Diary of Juliet Thompson*. Los Angeles: Kalimat Press, 1983.
The Universal House of Justice. *The Promise of World Peace*. Haifa: Bahá'í World Centre, 1985.
World Scripture, a Comparative Anthology of Sacred Texts. St. Paul: Paragon House, 1995.

Endnotes

1 Bill Harley & Jean Harley, *Now That I'm Here, What Should I Be Doing—Discover Life's Purpose*. Wisdom Editions, Minneapolis, 2016.

2 Bahá'u'lláh, "The Glory of God" (1817-1892), born Mirza Husayn-`Alí, is the Prophet-Founder of the Bahá'í Faith. Bahá'u'lláh's Writings, which envision the re-gathering of the human family that has been occurring in the 19th, 20th and 21st Centuries as the vanguard of an emerging, spiritually-centered global civilization, are contained in over one-hundred volumes penned during a forty-year period of exile, imprisonment, and persecution from 1853 to 1892.

3 'Abdu'l-Bahá, *Bahá'í Prayers*, p. 154.

4 Michael Karlberg, "The Paradox Of Protest In A Culture Of Contest", *Peace & Change*, Vol. 28, No. 3, July 2003, pp. 329-351.

5 John Kolstoe, *Consultation: A Universal Lamp of Guidance*, p. 9.

6 Bahá'u'lláh, *Tablets of Bahá'u'lláh revealed after the Kitab-i-Aqdas*, p. 126.

7 Bahá'u'lláh, quoted in *Consultation: A Compilation*, p. 3.

8 We refer to the following religions (with the divine Messengers and approximate founding dates in parentheses): Hinduism (Krishna—date unknown), Judaism (Moses—13th Century B.C.), Zoroastrianism (Zoroaster—7th-6th Century B.C.), Buddhism (Gautama Buddha—560 B.C.), Christianity (Jesus Christ—1 A.D.), Islam (Muhammad—622 A.D.), the Bábí Faith (The Báb—1844 A.D.), and the Bahá'í Faith (Bahá'u'lláh—1853 A.D.).

9 See Shoghi Effendi, *Call to the Nations*, pp. xi-xii.

10 Bahá'u'lláh, *Tablets of Bahá'u'lláh revealed after the Kitab-i-Aqdas*, p. 220.

11 'Abdu'l-Bahá, "Servant of Glory" (1844-1921), born Abbas Effendi,

is the eldest son of Bahá'u'lláh and, at His passing in 1892, was designated in Bahá'u'lláh's will and testament as the Center of Bahá'u'lláh's Covenant, the perfect exemplar of His teachings and the sole authorized interpreter of Bahá'u'lláh's Writings during the remainder of his lifetime (the period 1892-1921).

12 'Abdu'l-Bahá, *The Promulgation of Universal Peace*, pp. 72-73.

13 Shoghi Effendi (1897-1957) is the eldest grandson of 'Abdu'l-Bahá and the great grandson of Bahá'u'lláh. At the time of 'Abdu'l-Bahá's passing in 1921, Shoghi Effendi was designated in 'Abdu'l-Bahá's will and testament as the Guardian of the Bahá'í Faith and the sole authorized interpreter of the Bahá'í Writings during the remainder of his lifetime (the period 1921-1957).

14 May 18, 1948, letter written on behalf of Shoghi Effendi to a National Spiritual Assembly.

15 John Kolstoe, *Consultation: A Universal Lamp of Guidance*, p. 25.

16 'Abdu'l-Bahá, *Selections from the Writings of 'Abdu'l-Bahá*, p. 88.

17 For the reader encountering this incident in the lives of Christ's disciples for the first time, it is important to understand that in the context of progressive revelation, additional details from earlier Holy Books are sometimes given in subsequent ones. For example, stories from the *Bible* are repeated in the *Qur'án* with additional details that cannot be found in the Old or New Testaments. Similarly, stories from the *Bible* and the *Qur'án* are repeated in the Bahá'í Scriptures with additional details that cannot be found in the earlier texts. The repetition of stories from earlier Holy Books in new Revelations centuries later is one of the proofs of the authenticity of the earlier Holy Books.

18 'Abdu'l-Bahá, *The Promulgation of Universal Peace*, p. 73.

19 'Abdu'l-Bahá's ability to have knowledge of the events described here can be attributed to the fact that 'Abdu'l-Bahá was at Bahá'u'lláh's side during His entire 40-year ministry as a Manifestation of God—sharing all of His exiles and imprisonments; and to the fact that Bahá'u'lláh conferred infallibility on 'Abdu'l-Bahá. For a discussion of conferred infallibility, see Adib Taherzadeh, *The Revelation of Bahá'u'lláh*, Vol. 3, pp. 300-305.

20 'Abdu'l-Bahá, quoted in Shoghi Effendi, *Bahá'í Administration*, pp. 22.

21 'Abdu'l-Bahá, quoted in Shoghi Effendi, *Bahá'í Administration*, pp. 22.

22 'Abdu'l-Bahá, *The Promulgation of Universal Peace*, pp. 72-73.
23 'Abdu'l-Bahá, *The Promulgation of Universal Peace*, p. 15.
24 'Abdu'l-Bahá, quoted in Shoghi Effendi, *Bahá'í Administration*, pp. 22.
25 Matthew 22:37-38.
26 Bahá'u'lláh, *Tablets of Bahá'u'lláh revealed after the Kitab-i-Aqdas*, p. 168.
27 'Abdu'l-Bahá, *The Promulgation of Universal Peace*, p. 72.
28 Bahá'u'lláh, quoted in *Consultation: A Compilation*, p. 3.
29 Alan Scheffer is a Principal of Management Associates, Sioux City, Iowa, and co-author, along with Mark Scheffer and Nancy Braun, of the book, *Hanging the Mirror: The Discipline of Reflective Leadership*.
30 'Abdu'l-Bahá, *Foundations of World Unity*, p. 101.
31 John Bradshaw, *Healing the Shame That Binds You*, p. 78.
32 Bahá'u'lláh, *Gleanings from the Writings of Bahá'u'lláh*, p. 149.
33 Robert W. Jacobs, *Real-Time Strategic Change*, p. 122.
34 "Compassion." *The Compact Edition of the Oxford English Dictionary*. 1973.
35 "Compassion." *Merriam-Webster's Collegiate Dictionary*. 11th ed. 2004.
36 *Bhagavad Gita*, 6:34.
37 'Abdu'l-Bahá, *Selections from the Writings of 'Abdu'l-Bahá*, p. 88.
38 Augustine, and John E. Rochelle. *Sermons (51-94) on the New Testament,* Part III, Vol. 3, Sermon 88.5, p. 422.
39 Bahá'u'lláh, *The Hidden Words, #12,* from the Persian, p. 26.
40 3 Kings, 3:7-3:11.
41 Bahá'u'lláh, *The Hidden Words*, #1, from the Arabic, p. 3.
42 Carl Rogers, *On Becoming a Person,* pp. 37-38.
43 'Abdu'l-Bahá, *Promulgation of Universal Peace*, pp. 72-73.
44 'Abdu'l-Bahá, *Selections from the Writings of 'Abdu'l-Bahá*, pp. 27-28.
45 Bahá'u'lláh, *Tablets of Bahá'u'lláh revealed after the Kitab-i-Aqdas*, p. 35.
46 Researchers have said this quotation in all its variations was not said or written by Gandhi, but that at best it can be attributed to Arun Gandhi as a summary of what he learned from his grandfather.
47 Bahá'u'lláh, *The Hidden Words*, #3, from the Arabic, p. 4.

48 *Bhagavad Gita* 12:13.
49 *Nagarjuna*, Precious Garland 437.
50 *Mishnah*, Abot 1:12.
51 1 Corinthians 13.
52 *Hadith of Bukhari.*
53 Bahá'u'lláh, *The Hidden Words*, #5, from the Arabic, p. 4.
54 'Abdu'l-Bahá, *The Promulgation of Universal Peace*, p. 92.
55 Bahá'u'lláh, *The Hidden Words*, #13, from the Arabic, p. 6.
56 'Abdu'l-Bahá, *Selections from the Writings of 'Abdu'l-Bahá*, p. 24.
57 John 8:7.
58 John 8:9.
59 John 8:10-11.
60 Bahá'u'lláh, *Gleanings from the Writings of Bahá'u'lláh*, p. 314.
61 'Abdu'l-Bahá, *The Promulgation of Universal Peace*, p. 244.
62 *World Scripture: A Comparative Anthology of Sacred Texts*, p. 114. Mahabharata, Anusasana Parva 113.8.
63 Leviticus 19:18.
64 *World Scripture: A Comparative Anthology of Sacred Texts*, p. 114. Sutta Nipata 705.
65 Luke 6:31.
66 *World Scripture: A Comparative Anthology of Sacred Texts*, p. 114. Forty Hadith of an-Nawawi 13.
67 Bahá'u'lláh, *Tablets of Bahá'u'lláh revealed after the Kitab-i-Aqdas*, p. 71.
68 *World Scripture: A Comparative Anthology of Sacred Texts*, p. 656. Basavanna, Vacana 248.
69 Proverbs 5:18.
70 *World Scripture: A Comparative Anthology of Sacred Texts*, p. 655. Dhammapada 223.
71 Ephesians 4:26.
72 *The Qur'an* (Yusuf Ali, Translator), Surah 3:134.
73 *The Compilation of Compilations*, Volume 1, p. 460.
74 Jon Kabat-Zinn, *Wherever You Go, There You Are*, p. 50.
75 Steven Stosny, *Treating Attachment Abuse-A Compassionate Approach*, p. 120.
76 'Abdu'l-Bahá, *Selections from the Writings of 'Abdu'l-Bahá*, p. 87.
77 'Abdu'l-Bahá, *Selections from the Writings of 'Abdu'l-Bahá*, p. 87.

78 Management Associates is an organization development consulting firm located in Sioux City, IA. The principals of the firm are Alan Scheffer, Marie Scheffer, and Nancy Braun.

79 'Abdu'l-Bahá, *The Promulgation of Universal Peace*, p. 72.

80 Bahá'u'lláh, *Tablets of Bahá'u'lláh revealed after the Kitab-i-Aqdas*, p. 34.

81 Bahá'u'lláh, *Tablets of Bahá'u'lláh revealed after the Kitab-i-Aqdas*, p. 168.

82 In *Gleanings from the Writings of Bahá'u'lláh*, section lxxiv, Bahá'u'lláh says, "Every single letter proceeding out of the mouth of God is indeed a mother letter, and every word uttered by Him Who is the Well Spring of Divine Revelation is a mother word, and His Tablet a Mother Tablet. Well is it with them that apprehend this truth."

83 'Abdu'l-Bahá, *Selections from the Writings of 'Abdu'l-Bahá*, p. 87.

84 The Universal House of Justice is the international and highest governing body of the Bahá'í Faith. It was endowed by Baha'u'llah with the authority to legislate on all matters not specifically laid down in the Baha'i scriptures. In this way, the Universal House of Justice keeps the Baha'i community unified and responsive to the needs and conditions of an evolving world.

85 The Universal House of Justice, quoted in *Lights of Guidance*, p. 47.

86 'Abdu'l-Bahá, *Selections from the Writings of 'Abdu'l-Bahá*, p. 87.

87 'Abdu'l-Bahá, *The Promulgation of Universal Peace*, p. 92.

88 'Abdu'l-Bahá, *Selections from the Writings of 'Abdu'l-Bahá*, p. 87.

89 'Abdu'l-Bahá, *The Promulgation of Universal Peace*, p. 191.

90 'Abdu'l-Bahá, *The Promulgation of Universal Peace*, p. 4.

91 'Abdu'l-Bahá, quoted in *Star of the West*, vol. 8, no. 9 (20 August 1917), p. 114.

92 'Abdu'l-Bahá, quoted in *Consultation: A Compilation*, p. 9.

93 'Abdu'l-Bahá, *The Promulgation of Universal Peace*, pp. 72-73.

94 'Abdu'l-Bahá, *Selections from the Writings of 'Abdu'l-Bahá*, p. 88.

95 Bahá'u'lláh, *The Hidden Words*, #5, from the Arabic, p. 4.

96 'Abdu'l-Bahá, quoted in *Star of the West*, Vol. VIII, No. 4 (17 May 1917), p. 41.

97 'Abdu'l-Bahá, quoted in *Star of the West*, Vol. VIII, No. 9 (20 August 1917), p. 114.

98 Bahá'u'lláh, *Gleanings from the Writings of Bahá'u'lláh*, p. 288.

99 Shoghi Effendi, *Bahá'í Administration*, p. 79.

100 Bahá'u'lláh, quoted in *Bahá'í Meetings: The Nineteen Day Feast*, p. 17.

101 'Abdu'l-Bahá, *The Will and Testament of 'Abdu'l-Bahá*, pp. 13-14.

102 'Abdu'l-Bahá, quoted in *Consultation: A Compilation*, p. 8.

103 See, for example, Jay Hall, "Managing for Group Effectiveness", in *Models for Management: The Structure of Competence*, pp. 326-7.

104 'Abdu'l-Bahá, quoted in *Consultation: A Compilation*, pp. 8-9.

105 'Abdu'l-Bahá, quoted in *Consultation: A Compilation*, p. 8.

106 'Abdu'l-Bahá, *Foundations of World Unity*, p. 103.

107 'Abdu'l-Bahá, *The Promulgation of Universal Peace*, p. 195.

108 'Abdu'l-Bahá, quoted in Juliet Thompson, *The Diary of Juliet Thompson*, pp. 303-304.

109 'Abdu'l-Bahá, quoted in *Consultation: A Compilation*, p. 7.

110 'Abdu'l-Bahá, quoted in Shoghi Effendi, *Bahá'í Administration*, pp. 21-22.

111 Bahá'u'lláh, *Tablets of Bahá'u'lláh revealed after the Kitab-i-Aqdas*, p. 138.

112 Shoghi Effendi, *Bahá'í Administration*, p. 80.

113 Bahá'u'lláh, *The Kitab-i-Aqdas*, Questions & Answers, p. 136.

114 Shoghi Effendi, quoted in *Lights of Guidance*, p. 47.

115 'Abdu'l-Bahá, *The Promulgation of Universal Peace*, p. 72.

116 Shoghi Effendi, quoted in *Consultation: A Compilation*, p. 16.

117 'Abdu'l-Bahá, quoted in *Consultation: A Compilation*, p. 6.

118 'Abdu'l-Bahá, quoted in *Consultation: A Compilation*, p. 7.

119 "Culture." *Merriam-Webster's Collegiate Dictionary*. 11th ed. 2004.

120 Shoghi Effendi, quoted in *Consultation: A Compilation*, p. 16.

121 'Abdu'l-Bahá, quoted in *Bahá'í Administration*, pp. 22-23.

122 'Abdu'l-Bahá, quoted in *Consultation: A Compilation*, p. 7.

123 'Abdu'l-Bahá, quoted in *Consultation: A Compilation*, p. 8.

124 'Abdu'l-Bahá, quoted in *Consultation: A Compilation*, p. 7.

125 'Abdu'l-Bahá, quoted in *Bahá'í Administration*, p. 21.

126 'Abdu'l-Bahá, *Paris Talks*, p. 136.

127 'Abdu'l-Bahá, *The Secret of Divine Civilization*, p. 64.

128 'Abdu'l-Bahá, quoted in *Bahá'í Administration*, p. 21.

129 Ibid.

130 'Abdu'l-Bahá, quoted in *Consultation: A Compilation*, p. 10.

131 Ibid.
132 'Abdu'l-Bahá, quoted in *Bahá'í Administration*, p. 21.
133 Bahá'u'lláh, quoted in *Consultation: A Compilation*, p. 3.
134 'Abdu'l-Bahá, quoted in *Bahá'í Administration*, pp. 22-23.
135 'Abdu'l-Bahá, quoted in *Consultation: A Compilation*, p. 10.
136 'Abdu'l-Bahá, quoted in *Consultation: A Compilation*, p. 8.
137 Bahá'u'lláh, quoted in *Consultation: A Compilation*, p. 3.
138 'Abdu'l-Bahá, quoted in *Consultation: A Compilation*, p. 7.
139 Bahá'u'lláh, *The Kitab-i-Aqdas*, pp. 63-64.
140 'Abdu'l-Bahá, quoted in *Bahá'í Administration*, p. 22.
141 Shoghi Effendi, *Bahá'í Administration*, pp. 63-64.
142 'Abdu'l-Bahá, quoted in *Bahá'í Administration*, p. 22.
143 Bahá'u'lláh, *Gleanings from the Writings of Bahá'u'lláh*, p. 289.
144 'Abdu'l-Bahá, quoted in *Bahá'í Administration*, p. 21.
145 Bahá'u'lláh, *Tablets of Bahá'u'lláh revealed after the Kitab-i-Aqdas*, p. 173.
146 Mary Hanford Smith, *Star of the West*, vol. VIII, No. 11 (27 September 1917), p. 139.
147 Bahá'u'lláh, *The Hidden Words*, #68, from The Arabic, p. 20.
148 'Abdu'l-Bahá, quoted in *Consultation: A Compilation*, p. 8.
149 'Abdu'l-Bahá, *The Promulgation of Universal Peace*, pp. 72-73.
150 Bahá'u'lláh, *The Hidden Words*, #42, from the Arabic, p. 13.
151 'Abdu'l-Bahá, *Selections from the Writings of 'Abdu'l-Bahá*, p. 88.
152 'Abdu'l-Bahá, *Selections from the Writings of 'Abdu'l-Bahá*, p. 87.
153 Genesis 1:26.
154 John 14:20.
155 *Qur'an* 15:29.
156 Bahá'u'lláh, *The Hidden Words*, #13, from the Arabic, pp. 6-7.
157 Bahá'u'lláh, *The Kitab-i-Aqdas*, Questions and Answers, No. 106, p. 139.
158 'Abdu'l-Bahá, *Foundations of World Unity*, p. 31.
159 *Mahabharata*.
160 Romans 7:15-23.
161 *Avesta*, Yasna 30: 3-5.
162 'Abdu'l-Bahá, *Some Answered Questions*, p. 118.
163 'Abdu'l-Bahá, *Foundations of World Unity*, p. 110.
164 'Abdu'l-Bahá, *Some Answered Questions*, p. 119.

165 'Abdu'l-Bahá, *Some Answered Questions*, p. 118.

166 'Abdu'l-Bahá, *Some Answered Questions*, pp. 119-120.

167 'Abdu'l-Bahá, *Foundations of World Unity*, p. 110.

168 Shoghi Effendi, quoted in a letter from the Universal House of Justice to the National Spiritual Assembly of the Bahá'ís of the United States dated 11 September 1995.

169 'Abdu'l-Bahá, *Foundations of World Unity*, p. 110.

170 Bahá'u'lláh, *Gleanings from the Writings of Bahá'u'lláh*, p. 259.

171 'Abdu'l-Bahá, *Foundations of World Unity*, p. 110.

172 'Abdu'l-Bahá, *Paris Talks*, pp. 17-18.

173 'Abdu'l-Bahá, *Foundations of World Unity*, p. 76.

174 'Abdu'l-Bahá, *Divine Philosophy*, p. 134.

175 'Abdu'l-Bahá, *Some Answered Questions*, pp. 124-125.

176 Bahá'u'lláh, *The Hidden Words*, #19, from the Persian, p. 28.

177 Bahá'u'lláh, *Gleanings from the Writings of Bahá'u'lláh*, p. 323.

178 'Abdu'l-Bahá, *Foundations of World Unity*, p. 110.

179 Bahá'u'lláh, *Gleanings from the Writings of Bahá'u'lláh*, pp. 326-327.

180 Bahá'u'lláh, *Gleanings from the Writings of Bahá'u'lláh*, p. 249.

181 John Kolstoe, *Consultation: A Universal Lamp of Guidance*, p. 25.

182 'Abdu'l-Bahá, quoted in *Consultation: A Compilation*, pp. 10-11.

183 'Abdu'l-Bahá, *Selections from the Writings of 'Abdu'l-Bahá*, p. 110.

184 Leviticus 19:18.

185 'Abdu'l-Bahá, *Paris Talks*, p. 88.

186 The Universal House of Justice, *The Promise of World Peace*, p. 13.

187 Marzieh Gail, *Six Lessons on Islam*, p. 21.

188 'Abdu'l-Bahá, quoted in *Consultation: A Compilation*, p. 6.

189 'Abdu'l-Bahá, quoted in *Consultation: A Compilation*, p. 8.

190 Bahá'u'lláh, *Tablets Of Bahá'u'lláh revealed after the Kitab-i-Aqdas*, p. 72.

191 'Abdu'l-Bahá, *Paris Talks*, p. 174.

192 'Abdu'l-Bahá, quoted in *Consultation: A Compilation*, p. 9.

193 'Abdu'l-Bahá, quoted in *Consultation: A Compilation*, pp. 8-9.

194 Some aspects of this model have been adapted from the Institute of Cultural Affairs' Technology of Participation.

195 Bahá'u'lláh, *Tablets of Bahá'u'lláh revealed after the Kitab-i-Aqdas*, p. 35.

196 Ibid.

197 'Abdu'l-Bahá, quoted in *Consultation: A Compilation*, pp. 8-9.

198 One of the gifts to humanity from the Revelation of Bahá'u'lláh's Forerunner, The Báb, "The Gate" (1819-1850), born 'Alí Muhammad, is the Badí Calendar, which Bahá'u'lláh later confirmed and incorporated into His Own dispensation. This calendar is composed of 19 months of 19 days each, and each month is named after one of the attributes of God with the fifteenth month being named, Questions. The months in order are as follows: Splendor, Glory, Beauty, Grandeur, Light, Mercy, Words, Perfection, Names, Might, Will, Knowledge, Power, Speech, Questions, Honor, Sovereignty, Dominion, and Loftiness.

199 Marilee C. Goldberg, *The Art of the Question: A Guide to Short-Term Question-Centered Therapy*, p. 15.

200 Bahá'u'lláh, *Gleanings from the Writings of Bahá'u'lláh*, p. 215.

201 'Abdu'l-Bahá, *Paris Talks*, p. 174.

202 Bahá'u'lláh, *The Hidden Words*, #2, from The Persian, p. 22.

203 From the Hadith. Quoted in Bahá'u'lláh, *The Kitab-i-Iqan (The Book of Certitude)*, p. 46.

204 Bahá'u'lláh, *The Seven Valleys and the Four Valleys*, p. 53.

205 'Abdu'l-Bahá, *The Promulgation of Universal Peace*, p. 147.

206 'Abdu'l-Bahá, *Some Answered Questions*, p. 283.

207 Bahá'u'lláh, *Gleanings from the Writings of Bahá'u'lláh*, p. 213.

208 Groups of birds demonstrate flocking behavior when they are in flight—usually when foraging or migrating. The flocking patterns of starlings are generally considered to be the most beautiful and complex. Related patterns are demonstrated by schools of fish in shoaling behavior and by land animals in herd behavior and are studied in the science of synchrony. Video examples of bird flocking patterns can be seen by doing a web search using the phrase, "bird flocking." Then select "Starlings."

209 Bahá'u'lláh, *Tablets of Bahá'u'lláh revealed after the Kitab-i-Aqdas*, p. 138.

210 'Abdu'l-Bahá, quoted in Mirza Mahmud-i-Zarqani, *Mahmud's Diary*, translated by Mohi Sobhani, p. 425.

211 'Abdu'l-Bahá, *Paris Talks*, p. 178.

212 'Abdu'l-Bahá, *Selections from the Writings of 'Abdu'l-Bahá*, p. 256.

213 Shoghi Effendi, *Bahá'í Administration*, p. 66.

214 'Abdu'l-Bahá, quoted in J.E. Esslemont, *Bahá'u'lláh and the New Era*, p. 88.

215 'Abdu'l-Bahá, *Paris Talks*, p. 174.

216 Bahá'u'lláh, *Tablets Of Bahá'u'lláh revealed after the Kitab-i-Aqdas*, p. 35.

217 Bahá'u'lláh, *Tablets Of Bahá'u'lláh revealed after the Kitab-i-Aqdas*, p. 268.

218 Ibid.

219 'Abdu'l-Bahá, *Divine Philosophy*, p. 134.

220 Bahá'u'lláh, *Tablets Of Bahá'u'lláh revealed after the Kitab-i-Aqdas*, p. 35.

221 Bahá'u'lláh, quoted in *Consultation: A Compilation*, p. 3, from a previously untranslated Tablet.

222 'Abdu'l-Bahá, quoted in *Consultation: A Compilation*, pp. 8-9.

223 Bahá'u'lláh, quoted in *Bahá'í Prayers*, p. 105.

224 Bahá'u'lláh, quoted in *Consultation: A Compilation*, p. 3, from a previously untranslated Tablet.

225 Harville Hendrix, *Keeping The Love You Find*, p. 165.

226 Harville Hendrix, *Keeping The Love You Find*, p. 162.

227 John M. Gottman, *Seven Principles for Making Marriage Work*, p. 130.

228 John M. Gottman, *Seven Principles for Making Marriage Work*, pp. 27-34.

229 John Donne, "Meditation XVII", quoted in *Seventeenth Century Prose and Poetry*, p. 68.

230 'Abdu'l-Bahá, *Selections from the Writings of 'Abdu'l-Bahá*, p. 122.

231 Bahá'u'lláh, *Tablets of Bahá'u'lláh revealed after the Kitab-i-Aqdas*, p. 126.

232 Bahá'u'lláh, *Tablets of Bahá'u'lláh revealed after the Kitab-i-Aqdas*, p. 168.

233 'Abdu'l-Bahá, *'Abdu'l-Bahá in London*, p. 48.

234 'Abdu'l-Bahá, *The Promulgation of Universal Peace*, pp. 144-145.

235 Bahá'u'lláh, *Gleanings from the Writings of Bahá'u'lláh*, p. 286.

236 'Abdu'l-Bahá, *Selections from the Writings of 'Abdu'l-Bahá*, pp. 260-261.

237 Bahá'u'lláh, quoted in *Consultation: A Compilation*, p. 3.
238 'Abdu'l-Bahá, *Selections from the Writings of 'Abdu'l-Bahá*, pp. 260-261.
239 Ibid.
240 Ibid.
241 Ibid.
242 Bahá'u'lláh, *Gleanings from the Writings of Bahá'u'lláh*, pp. 80-81.
243 'Abdu'l-Bahá, *Tablets of 'Abdu'l-Bahá*, p. 508.

www.ingramcontent.com/pod-product-compliance
Lightning Source LLC
Chambersburg PA
CBHW030218170426
43201CB00006B/125